634

*Publications of the Committee on
Taxation, Resources and Economic Development*

12

*Proceedings of a Symposium Sponsored by the
Committee on Taxation, Resources and
Economic Development (TRED)
at the Lincoln Institute of Land Policy,
Cambridge, Massachusetts, 1980*

Other TRED Publications

State and Local Finance:

The Pressures
of the 1980s

Edited by

George F. Break

Published for the Committee on Taxation,
Resources and Economic Development by
THE UNIVERSITY OF WISCONSIN PRESS

Published 1983
The University of Wisconsin Press
114 North Murray Street
Madison, Wisconsin 53715
The University of Wisconsin Press, Ltd.
1 Gower Street
London WC1E 6HA, England

First printing
Printed in the United States of America

For LC CIP information see the colophon
ISBN 0-299-09340-9

Publication of this book was made possible in part by support from the
Schalkenbach and the Lincoln foundations.

Contributors

Richard M. Bird
Professor of Political Economy, University of Toronto

George F. Break
Professor of Economics, University of California, Berkeley

Frederick C. Doolittle
Public Affairs Analyst, Woodrow Wilson School of Public
and International Affairs, Princeton University

Arthur D. Lynn, Jr.
Professor of Social and Behavioral Sciences, The Ohio State University

Charles E. McLure, Jr.
Senior Fellow, Hoover Institution, Stanford University

Richard A. Musgrave
Professor Emeritus of Economics, Harvard University, and Adjunct Professor,
University of California, Santa Cruz

Richard P. Nathan
Professor of Public and International Affairs, Woodrow Wilson School of Public
and International Affairs, Princeton University

Attiat F. Ott
Professor of Economics, Clark University

Enid Slack
Ontario Economic Council, Toronto, Ontario

Jon Sonstelie
Professor of Economics, University of California, Santa Barbara

Wayne R. Thirsk
Professor of Economics, University of Waterloo

R. Charles Vars, Jr.
Professor of Economics, Oregon State University

Contents

List of Tables and Figures

Tables

Figures

State and Local Finance:
The Pressures of the 1980s

Introduction

As the 1970s drew to a close, disturbing signs began to appear that the easy-to-finance, high-growth years for the state and local governmental sector were over. These signs were far from unambiguous, but it seemed likely that a new and more difficult era for policymakers was about to dawn. Meeting at the beginning of the new decade, the nineteenth annual conference of the Committee on Taxation, Resources and Economic Development (TRED) focused on what the participants perceived to be some of the most important fiscal issues that state and local governments would face in the coming years.

The rapid growth of the state-local sector during the postwar years is readily documented. In 1947 its output of goods and services was 5.5 percent of Gross National Product (GNP), as was the federal government's share of total output. By 1975 state and local purchases of goods and services had expanded to 14.1 percent of GNP, compared to the federal government's 8 percent share. In real terms, that represented an average annual growth rate of over 5 percent, notably higher than the 3.5 percent rate of increase for GNP. After 1975, however, state and local governmental output grew less rapidly than the total economy. By 1981 its share of GNP was down to 12.3 percent, whereas the federal government's share had held steadily at close to 8 percent. Even so, the 1980s began with a much larger state-local sector than did the 1950s.

Hindsight makes it easy to document not only the turning points in the growth of the public sector during the 1970s but also the simultaneously mounting signs of trouble ahead for state-local finance. These portents include the slowly developing economic dislocations and costs resulting from drastically higher energy prices, recurring periods of weak economic performance with their high rates of inflation and unemployment and low rates of productivity growth, and the psychological distress accompanying the changed expectations about future living standards brought about by these developments. The most dramatic fiscal event of the period was undoubtedly the passage of Proposition 13 in California in June of 1978. Though not the first of its kind, this proposition was by far the most visible, and it encouraged the subsequent appearance of similar measures in other states. The result was sharply increased awareness of the political risks attached to any tax increase proposal.

How strong and how sustained this tax revolt movement will be, however, is still unknown. During the first three years of its existence, Proposition 13 was mainly a means of distributing large state surpluses to local property taxpayers. Hard choices involving either reductions in the quality and quantity of government services or increases in alternative sources of revenue had to be made, but at first they were relatively infrequent in occurrence and small in impact. By mid-1981, however, the easy adjustments were over, and a true test of the staying power of the tax revolt in California was about to begin.

A second major fiscal development also occurred in 1978, though it went unnoticed for some time. In that year federal grants-in-aid reached their postwar peaks both in purchasing power and in relation to state-local revenue from own sources (31.7 percent), total federal government outlays (17.4 percent), and Gross National Product (3.7 percent). In nominal dollars federal aid did increase from $77.9 billion in fiscal 1978 to $94.8 billion in 1981, but in 1972 dollars this represented a 5 percent decline (from $50.3 to $47.8 billion). Budget proposals of the Reagan Administration contemplated a sharp acceleration of this decline. It is no wonder that state and local officials, squeezed between stronger voter resistance to tax increases on the one hand and the prospect of greatly reduced federal aid on the other, faced the future with trepidation.

In this new pressure-laden fiscal environment, at least five major themes appear likely to dominate state and local governmental policy making during the rest of the 1980s. All five are addressed in varying degrees in the present volume.

The first, and most important, is a general need to find ways of providing more and better public services with less tax money. This is not an easy or pleasant task, and certainly not one that the high-growth years prepared politicians or bureaucrats to deal with. Yet if reluctant and dis-illusioned taxpayers are to be induced to loosen up on the purse strings, some hard evidence of better public sector performance seems essential. Recent technological advances and improvements in the quality of economic benefit-cost analysis both promise valuable help to harried government officials. The opportunities are there, but there are also many pitfalls to be circumvented on the way. The nature of some of these difficulties, as well as ways of dealing with them, are discussed in the chapters by Frederick Doolittle. Richard Nathan, and Charles Vars. Readers interested in urban economic development, the evaluation of broad-gauged, multipurpose federal grants, land use planning, and natural resources management will find these chapters to be helpful guides over a difficult landscape.

A second major theme of the 1980s will surely be the reform of state and local governmental revenue systems. That bad taxes drive out good expenditures may not be as firmly established in public finance as is Gresham's famous law in money and banking, but certainly there is no need to document the many interpersonal inequities and economic inefficiencies generated by poorly designed revenue systems. Revenue reform is an important policy objective, and one that has many interrelated dimensions. One that is especially important in this country is tax harmonization. Defining that process as "the search for fiscal arrangements which will preserve expenditure diversity in a federal system with the least amount of fiscally induced distortion in the allocation of the economy's resources." Wayne Thirsk discusses a number of alternative ways of achieving federal fiscal harmony and then uses that theoretical framework to evaluate Canada's accomplishments since the passage of the British North America Act in 1867. That process is interesting in its own right, particularly for its strong suggestion of repetitive phases, involving fiscal chaos at the nadir, gradual fiscal reform on the upswing, followed by a steady disintegration into another period of fiscal chaos. For U.S. readers there are valuable lessons to be learned from Canadian experience and practice. General revenue sharing is more important there and is based on a type of allocation formula long advocated for this country by the Advisory Commission of Intergovernmental Relations (1982). Opportunities in Canada to "opt out" of federal conditional grant programs in return for additional unrestricted aid may appeal to advocates of greater decentralization of political power here. Some of the revenue risks attached to a policy of tax separation for different levels of government, however, are vividly illustrated by reactions to the Canadian federal government's abandonment of the estate and gift field in 1972. The provinces did pick up those taxes in the short run but then gradually abandoned them until only Quebec remained in the field. Tax separation, it appears, was mainly a means of tax extinction.

One of Thirsk's avenues to fiscal harmonization involves greater use of benefit financing on the part of subnational governments, particularly those at the local level. Richard Bird and Enid Slack analyze the role that user charges should play in urban finance, and, after considering the role they do play in Canada, conclude that "many users of urban public services are at present being significantly subsidized by general taxpayers, for no apparent economic or social reason." Hard-pressed local finance officers, of whom there are many both in Canada and here, will find much to think about in the Bird-Slack chapter, but as the authors note, they will need considerable political courage if they are to follow this avenue to fiscal harmonization.

Another important dimension of local tax reform concerns the nature of the role that property and land taxes should play. The two chapters on this topic provide an interesting contrast in both substance and style. The one by Arthur Lynn brings a full lifetime of professional and practical experience with local government finance to bear on a topic that only experts, such as Lynn, should attempt—namely, the different directions that property tax changes might take during the 1980s. The other, by Richard Musgrave, brings a powerful and subtle intellect to bear on the internal logic and economic implications of a difficult, but fundamental ethical doctrine—namely the dual theory of entitlement. Comparing the contributions made to that doctrine by John Locke, Henry George, and Robert Nozick, Musgrave elucidates and evaluates their accomplishments and, in the process, sheds light on the strong, continuing appeal of land taxation to the general public. There are no answers to the everyday problems of local officials in either of these chapters, but there is much food for thought.

At the state level one of the most difficult subjects for reform is the corporation income tax. This enigmatic levy is a tempting but dangerous source of revenue to politicians, an inequitable and inefficient part of the nation's tax system to economists, and a frustrating but rewarding part of their jobs to administrators and lawyers. Many lives would be simplified if state corporation income taxes were simply to disappear from the fiscal scene. Since they are not likely to do so any time soon, they provide an important field for study and reform. Unfortunately, few economists, with the notable exception of Charles McLure, have been attracted to that area. In his first chapter McLure focuses on the many problems for smooth intergovernmental relations created by the existence of state corporate profits taxes. Determining the proper tax base for each state is mainly a matter either of allocating the unallocatable or separating the inseparable. Nonarbitrary solutions do not exist, but some are more arbitrary than others, and there is much to be said for picking one of them, making its application uniform throughout the country, and turning one's attention to other matters.

A third major theme in state and local finance in the 1980s, as it has been in every preceding decade, will be intergovernmental fiscal relations. Several of the chapters already noted deal with different aspects of that basic topic. Another aspect, shoved into prominence by the oil price increases of the 1970s, is the state and local taxation of natural resources. In his second chapter in this volume McLure challenges the traditional economic doctrine that state or local taxation of economic rents, in this case from the ownership of natural resources, creates no geographic misallocations of resources. His analysis demonstrates that misallocation is in fact quite likely to result. Careful policy making at all levels of government will be required in the future if disruptive and damaging fiscal and economic effects are to be avoided.

The fourth major theme, the operation and financing of public schools, is guaranteed a place on our list by its fiscal and economic importance alone. Moreover, disillusion with the quality of school services may be an important factor underlying contemporary tax revolts, and many observers feel that the time has come for a fundamental review of this whole area of government activity. It is in that spirit that Jon Sonstelie addresses the subject. He analyzes some of the important aspects of the two basic ways in which governments can finance schools —by supplying their services free of charge in the public sector, or by subsidizing purchases of those services in the private sector. Can these two modes coexist peaceably and productively? Or will proponents of education vouchers and tuition tax credits carry the day and emasculate the public school system? Or, on the other hand, will the public schools beat off the challenge and retain their position as the strong majority choice? All these questions have acquired enhanced urgency in recent years. Sonstelie's chapter is an important contribution to that fundamental debate.

The fifth theme considered at the conference, the effects of persistent inflation on state and local governments, is one that came into prominence in the 1970s and is likely to maintain its significance even if the most optimistic expectations concerning inflation in the 1980s are realized. This, too, is a multidimensional theme, and for her chapter Attiat Ott picked one of the less frequently discussed aspects. Balance sheet accounting for governments is still in an underdeveloped stage, and one of the challenges of the 1980s is for state and local officials to assess and make use of its potential contributions to better policy making. Ott's important work on balance sheet behavior in an inflationary economy will both stimulate and strengthen progress in that fiscal area.

As a group these chapters pit some of the best minds in the public finance field against a number of the most important and perplexing problems facing state and local governments today. They promise no easy solutions, but they offer a wealth of thoughtful counsel regarding issues that not only will not go away but will demand compassionate understanding on the part of the public as hard choices have to be made.

Reference

Advisory Commission on Intergovernmental Relations. 1982. *Tax Capacity of the Fifty States: Methodology and Estimates*. Information Report M-134 (March 1982).

I. THE FISCAL ENVIRONMENT

1 *Attiat F. Ott*

The Effect of Inflation
on the Balance Sheet
of the State-Local Sector

In a period of rising inflation expectation, most economic units are likely to feel "cheated" when the rise in the inflation rate exceeds the anticipated rate. In such a period of reassessment of one's financial statement, in view of past and anticipated rates of inflation, may be warranted, so that appropriate action may be taken to achieve the "desired" position.

If one were to view the state-local sector as a rational economic unit, then one can hypothesize that the sector as a whole or as individual entities has a desired net worth target which may be set at the beginning of the year. Since net worth is equal to the difference between assets and liabilities revalued between the beginning and the end of the year, a surplus or a deficit budget may be called for to close the gap between the desired and the actual net worth target. That is, if net worth position were to fall short of the desired one, budget saving (surplus) would have to be planned; a budget deficit or a balanced budget otherwise.

In a world of stable prices, the state-local sector saving may be written as equal to the difference between desired net worth and actual net worth.

$$S = W_t^* - W_{t-1} \tag{1}$$

where S = saving,
    W_t^* = target net worth, and
    W_{t-1} = net worth at the beginning of year t.

Net worth, W_{t-1}, may be written as the difference between assets (A_{t-1}) and liabilities (L_{t-1}).

$$W_{t-1} = A_{t-1} - L_{t-1} \tag{2}$$

If prices were not stable, however, Equation 1 would have to be modified to reflect the change in the values of assets and liabilities during these years. That is,

$$S = W_t^* - \{a\, A_{t-1}\, (1 + \Pi) + b\, A_{t-1}\, (1 + \Pi)^{-1} - L_t\, (1 + \Pi)^{-1}\} \tag{3}$$

where $a,\ b$ are distribution parameters for tangible and financial assets, and Π is the inflation rate.

Inflation affects the balance sheet and thus the net worth position of the state-local sector in the following ways: *First,* it erodes the real value of the sector's financial assets although it increases the value of its tangible assets. *Second,* to the extent that it is not anticipated and/or claims are not indexed, inflation reduces the real burden of the sector's liabilities.

If inflation reduces the real burden more than it erodes the value of their assets, state-local governments net worth may not be reduced. In effect it may be enhanced. Budget implications that follow are quite desirable—smaller deficits or larger surpluses than anticipated would be realized.

Alternatively, if rising inflation rates were to reduce the real value of assets much more than erode their liabilities, the state and local sector may be faced with an unfavorable position both on current as well as capital accounts.

To account fully for the effect of inflation on the balance sheet of the state and local sector is not only a much larger task than I can hope to carry out in this chapter, but also is hampered by the lack of up-to-date data on the price of physical assets, particularly land. For these reasons, my aim is quite modest. In this chapter I shall concentrate on estimating the effect of inflation on only a few components of the balance sheet.

The first part of the chapter presents a framework within which inflation effects on the sector may be analyzed. This is followed by a look at some specific items in the balance sheet that seem to be particularly sensitive to the rate of inflation. The final section of the paper advances some qualitative judgment as to the effect of inflation on the sector during the past decade.

Cataloging the Inflation Effect: A Framework

There are two ways in which one might catalog the effects of inflation on the state-local sector. By concentrating on budget parameters—expenditures, taxes and borrowing—one can analyze the effect of inflation on the "resource-absorbing" activities of the sector. Alternatively one may be interested in determining how inflation affects the financial position of the sector vis-a-vis other sectors of the economy.

Although these two approaches are not mutually exclusive—that is, one cannot separate real budget activities from their financial implications—it may be helpful to do just that in discussing the effect of inflation on the sector's resource use as distinct from its effect on the sector's balance sheet.

The State-Local Sector Accounts

The overall activity of the state-local sector may be analyzed in terms of two accounts. The government sector's income and expenditures account and the sector's wealth account or its balance sheet.

The income and expenditures account includes data on receipts, expenditures, and saving. This total may be divided into two components: (a) the general government account, and (b) the trust fund account.

Table 1.1 gives the receipts, expenditures, and the surplus on the general government account for the state-local sector in the years 1969–1979. Table 1.2 gives the sector's trust fund account for the same period.

Inflation effects may be analyzed in terms of their impact on the following activities:

resource absorption by the sector,
the sector's income,
the cost of doing business, and
claims on the sector.

With the aid of data presented in Tables 1.1 through 1.6, the effect of inflation on resource use, income generated, and cost of doing business can be determined. The remaining item will be discussed with reference to data shown in Tables 1.7 and 1.8.

To assess the impact of inflation on the sector resource-absorbing activities, a rearrangement of data presented in Table 1.1 is called for. First, total expenditures on the general government account have been

Table 1.1. State and Local Government, General Government Account, 1969–1979 (dollar amounts in billions)

	1969	1970	1971	1972	1973	1974	1975	1976	1977	1978	1979
Total receipts, NIA	*112.4*	*126.7*	*143.0*	*166.5*	*180.9*	*196.6*	*220.5*	*248.3*	*275.2*	*304.0*	*324.1*
Tax receipts	92.1	102.2	114.0	129.0	140.8	152.7	165.9	187.2	207.7	226.6	243.7
Personal tax and nontax	21.7	24.4	27.7	33.0	36.1	39.2	43.4	49.9	56.8	64.1	69.9
Corporate profits tax account	3.4	3.7	4.1	5.0	5.7	6.8	7.1	9.3	10.9	12.5	14.3
Indirect business tax	67.0	74.1	82.2	91.0	99.0	106.7	115.4	128.0	140.0	150.0	159.5
Federal grants-in-aid	20.3	24.4	29.0	37.5	40.1	43.9	54.6	61.1	67.5	77.3	80.4
Total expenditures, NIA	*117.4*	*131.5*	*146.8*	*160.9*	*176.8*	*199.4*	*226.7*	*246.1*	*268.0*	*300.0*	*325.9*
Purchases of goods & services	111.2	123.3	136.6	151.0	167.3	191.6	215.4	231.6	251.8	283.0	309.8
Transfer payments	6.7	9.8	11.7	12.6	13.2	12.3	14.5	15.9	17.0	18.4	19.6
Net interest paid	3.0	2.2	2.4	1.7	.5	−.1	1.3	3.4	4.2	4.0	3.4
Subsidies less surplus of gov't. enterprise	−3.5	−3.8	−4.1	−4.2	−4.3	−4.4	−4.5	−4.8	−5.0	−5.5	−6.8
Less: wage accruals less disbursement	0	0	.2	−.2	0	0	0	0	0	.2	−.1
Surplus or deficit (±) general gov't. account	−5.0	−4.8	−3.8	5.6	4.1	−2.8	−6.2	2.2	7.3	4.0	−1.0

Source: U.S. Department of Commerce, Bureau of Economic Analysis, *Survey of Current Business* (several issues: July 72, 74, 76, 80).
Note: Totals may not add up because of rounding.

14

Table 1.2. Social Insurance Funds Receipts and Expenditures, 1969–1979 (dollar amounts in billions)

	1969	1970	1971	1972	1973	1974	1975	1976	1977	1978	1979
Receipts	*9.6*	*10.9*	*12.4*	*14.6*	*16.3*	*18.5*	*22.5*	*27.1*	*32.8*	*38.2*	*43.2*
Contributions for social insurance	7.3	8.3	9.2	10.8	12.1	13.7	16.4	19.7	23.6	27.1	30.5
Investment income	2.3	2.7	3.2	3.8	4.2	4.8	6.1	7.4	9.2	11.1	12.7
Expenditures	*3.9*	*4.4*	*5.1*	*6.6*	*7.4*	*8.3*	*10.0*	*11.5*	*13.2*	*14.9*	*16.6*
Benefits	3.8	4.3	5.0	6.3	7.1	8.0	9.6	11.1	12.8	14.4	16.1
Administrative costs	.1	.1	.1	.3	.3	.3	.4	.4	.4	.5	.5
Surplus or deficit (±)	*5.7*	*6.5*	*7.3*	*8.1*	*8.9*	*10.1*	*12.5*	*15.7*	*19.6*	*23.2*	*26.6*

Source: U.S. Department of Commerce, Bureau of Economic Analysis, *Survey of Current Business* (several issues: July 72, 74, 76, 80).
Note: Totals may not add up because of rounding.

15

Table 1.3. State and Local Resource-Absorbing Expenditures in 1972 Dollars and in Relation to S & L Real Income, 1969–1979 (dollar amounts in billions)

	1969	1970	1971	1972	1973	1974	1975	1976	1977	1978	1979
Resource-absorbing Expenditures,											
Total	134.9	139.5	145.5	151.0	158.6	150.8	144.9	150.1	156.6	158.1	171.4
Consumer-type purchases[a]	99.1	105.7	112.3	119.4	127.0	113.7	114.4	122.2	130.8	130.4	NA
Investment-type purchases[b]	35.8	33.8	33.2	31.4	31.6	37.1	30.5	27.9	25.8	27.7	NA
Total income[c]	139.5	144.6	152.0	166.6	169.5	172.4	176.4	183.9	188.5	193.5	191.6
Own sources (excluding trust fund accounts)	114.3	116.9	121.2	129.1	131.6	133.9	132.7	138.6	142.3	144.3	144.1
From federal gov't.	25.2	27.2	30.8	37.5	37.9	38.5	43.7	45.3	46.2	49.2	47.5
Resource-to-income ratio	.96	.96	.95	.90	.93	.87	.82	.82	.83	.82	.89

Source: Same as Table 1.1.
Note: Totals may not add up because of rounding.
[a] Deflated by government consumption deflator.
[b] Deflated by deflator for structures and equipment.
[c] Deflated by state and local GNP deflator.

16

classified by type of expenditure and deflated through the use of the appropriate price index. Secondly, state and local government incomes were divided into "own" and "other" sources, then deflated by the implicit price deflator of GNP originating in the state-local sector. Expenditures or receipts that represented transfers between the public and private sectors (such as transfer payments and interest payments) were excluded because they did not give rise to resource transfer between the two sectors.

In looking at Table 1.3, several observations can be made:

1. The state and local sector resource-absorbing activities increased only slightly during the decade of the 1970s. Although the total has remained constant over this period, a marked shift has taken place in the mix of purchases. Real consumption-type outlays have increased by about 27 percent, whereas outlays for capital formation fell from their peak level of $36 billion in 1969 to $27.7 billion in 1978.

2. Inflation seems to generate "tax dividends" for the state-local sector. Revenues from own sources, adjusted for inflation, have increased by 26 percent during the 1969–1979 period. Federal grants-in-aid also increased, although their rate of growth seems to have been halted over the last three years.

3. The resources-to-income ratio has declined from its highest level of 1.07, reached in 1972, to around .82 percent by the mid-1970s.

The above findings seem to suggest that the state and local sector has fared well (at least not badly) during the inflation era of the 1970s. They also lend credence to the assertion that the financial position of the sector as a whole is far better than that of the federal government, and a great deal better than the sector's position during the 1950s or 1960s.

Based on the findings one is also inclined to argue that the claim often directed at the federal government as the originator of inflation cannot be levied against the state-local sector. The sector as a whole may have had a "dampening effect" on inflation through its continuing and increasing surplus position.

Cost of Doing Business

Granted that inflation erodes the general purchasing power of a dollar of earning, it may be worth noting that such an effect was not uniform for all types of spending. There are at least three types of state-local spending that seem to have been affected at various degrees by inflation. These are

1. compensation of employees,

Table 1.4. State and Local Government Purchases by Type in Constant Dollars, 1969–1978

	1969	1970	1971	1972	1973	1974	1975	1976	1977	1978
	in constant 1972 dollars (billions)									
Government purchases, Total	*134.9*	*139.5*	*145.5*	*151.0*	*155.9*	*161.1*	*166.1*	*166.9*	*167.9*	*174.6*
Compensation of employees	76.8	80.1	83.5	87.3	90.6	93.1	96.0	97.3	98.4	100.8
Nondurable goods	7.4	8.6	9.9	10.6	10.6	11.2	12.8	13.7	14.9	16.0
Services	15.6	17.8	19.7	21.7	23.1	24.9	27.1	28.0	28.9	30.4
Durable goods	4.1	4.4	4.7	5.0	5.4	5.8	5.4	5.3	5.3	5.2
Structures (excluding construction force account compensation)	31.0	28.7	27.7	26.4	26.2	26.1	24.8	22.5	20.4	22.1
	implicit price deflators (1972 = 100)									
State and local purchase deflator	.81	.88	.94	100	109	118	130	139	150	162
Compensation of employees	.80	.87	.94	100	107	114	125	135	146	157
Nondurable goods	.87	.92	.97	100	109	127	140	149	158	170
Services	.85	.91	.95	100	106	120	133	144	158	172
Durable goods	.88	.91	.95	100	103	116	130	138	145	157
Structures	.80	.87	.99	100	108	129	140	143	152	170

Source: Same as Table 1.1.
Note: Totals may not add up because of rounding.

2. welfare and other transfer payments, and
3. The cost of borrowing, or present and future interest payments on the debt.

Because compensation of employees is by far the largest component of the state and local sector purchases (over 50 percent), how inflation affects this type of outlay is important not only to the sector financing but also to the welfare of its employees. As Table 1.4 shows, the constant dollar cost per unit of purchases was lowest for employees' services; it is highest for nondurable goods purchases and for services.

The success of the sector in keeping employees' salary adjustments below the general inflation rate (the state and local purchase deflator was constantly above that of the compensation of employees) explains in part the stability of resource-absorption expenditures noted earlier as well as the improvement in their overall financial position.

The effect of inflation on transfer payments is not insignificant, even though this type of outlay represents a small fraction of total spending. In Table 1.5, growth rates of transfer payments in nominal and real terms are compared with other types of outlays during the period of 1960–1979. With the exception of investment-type outlays, other types of spending have all increased.

Another cost of doing business is the sector's cost of obtaining borrowed funds. Data on state-local borrowing and interest payments reported in the National Income and Product Accounts (NIPA) and the Flow of Funds account are not appropriate for determining such a cost, since they tend to overstate the sector's expenditures or underestimate its saving and net worth. To the extent that unanticipated inflation rates reduce the real value of both the sector debt burden and interest payments, inflation tends to enhance the sector's net financial position.

To account for the true debt burden and the cost of borrowing, two adjustments should be made. First, interest payments should be adjusted

Table 1.5. Growth Rates of State and Local Spending by Major Category, 1969–1978

	Nominal Rate	Real Rate
Total purchases	2.6	1.3
Compensation of employees	2.5	1.3
Structure	1.5	−.3
Durables	2.3	1.3
Nondurables	4.2	2.2
Services	3.9	1.9
Transfer payments	2.8	1.5

Source: Calculated from data reported in Table 1.4.

Table 1.6. The Effect of Inflation on Interest Payments, Saving, and Debt Burden of the State-Local Sector, 1969–1977

	Ratio of Adjusted to Actual Interest Payments	Ratio of Adjusted to Unadjusted Debt Burden	Ratio of Adjusted Saving to NIPA Saving	Inflation Rate (consumer prices)
1969	.64	.78	1.4	4.5
1970	.62	.72	2.2	6.6
1971	.58	.79	1.8	5.9
1972	.66	.84	1.2	4.3
1973	.62	.85	1.2	3.3
1974	.42	.76	1.7	6.2
1975	.33	.69	2.3	11.0
1976	.45	.73	1.3	9.1
1977	.51	.81	1.3	5.8

Source: Columns 1–3 are author estimates; column 4 is from the Council of Economic Advisers, *Economic Report of the President,* January 1980 (Washington, D.C.: U.S. Government Printing Office).

to remove the inflation premium, and, second, the accrued gain on outstanding bonds should be excluded in computing the real debt burden.

An attempt to adjust interest payments and the debt burden for inflation was carried out in an earlier paper (Ott 1980). Although the calculations are very tentative, it may be worthwhile to report some of the findings. Table 1.6 shows the ratio of inflation-adjusted interest payments to actual payments and the ratio of adjusted to unadjusted debt burden for the period 1969–1977. Also shown is the ratio of the state-local sector adjusted saving to NIPA saving.

As can be seen from Table 1.6, both real interest payments and debt burden have declined with rising inflation rates. The sector's saving, after adjusting for the effect of inflation on interest payments, is shown to be much larger than that reported in NIPA, particularly during periods of high inflation rates.

Although the real cost of past borrowing for state-local government may have been reduced during an inflationary period, future borrowing costs may be increased if such costs are compared to those paid by other borrowers. In a recent article, Birati and Cukierman (1979) listed the conditions under which high inflation rates increase the cost of borrowing for the state and local sector as compared to the cost for corporate borrowers. Assuming that there are only two types of borrowers, corporate borrowers and state and local governments, then a rise in the infla-

Table 1.7. State and Local Retirement Fund Selected Indicators, Fiscal Years 1957–1978 (dollar amounts in billions)

	Receipt	Payments	Ratio of Payments to Receipts	Book Value of Assets	Earnings	Average Rate of Return	Market Interest Rate (3–5 years U.S. bonds)
1957	$ 2.4	$ .9	37%	$ 12.8	$ .4	3.0%	3.6%
1967	6.6	2.7	41	39.3	1.6	4.0	5.1
1970	9.8	3.6	37	54.9	2.5	4.6	7.3
1972	12.6	4.9	39	68.7	3.4	4.9	5.9
1975	18.9	7.5	40	98.1	5.3	5.4	7.5
1977	25.3	9.5	38	123.5	7.7	6.2	6.9
1978	28.0	10.8	39	142.6	8.7	6.1	8.2

Source: U.S. Department of Commerce, Bureau of the Census, Statistical Abstract of the United States, several issues.

Table 1.8. Estimated Value of Mature Trust Fund, Unfunded Balance, and Required Net Annual Payments to Trust Funds at Selected Interest Rates (dollar amounts in billions)

System	Interest Rate		
	4%	5%	6%
Retirement at age 65;			
15 years growth in payroll			
at a constant rate of 11.2%			
Mature Trust Fund (MTF)	1,163.3	1,052.8	954.6
Unfunded balance (UB)[a]	965.1	795.1	622.0
Annual payments (A_n)[b]	20.4	14.5	9.7
Retirement at age 60;			
15 years growth in payroll			
at a constant rate of 11.2%			
Mature Trust Fund (MTF)	1,716.3	1,551.3	1,407.2
Unfunded balance (UB)[a]	1,518.1	1.294.6	1,075.6
Annual payments (A_n)[b]	32.2	23.6	16.8

Source: Aronson (1975, Tables 43, 44, and 45)

[a] Unfunded balance is equal to the mature trust fund less the future value (in year 2000) of fund assets as of 1971.

[b] Annual payments needed to amortize the unfunded balances over 27 years.

Assets, Liabilities, and Net Worth

To assess the impact of inflation on the wealth position of the state-local sector, a complete system of accounts incorporating tangible as well as intangible assets and liabilities is needed. Although such a system of accounts has been constructed, revaluing the balance sheet to reflect rising prices is not feasible at this time due to lack of price information, particularly regarding tangible assets. Given such a constraint, an attempt is made here to ascertain as far as possible, the direction of effect which inflation may exert on the net worth position of the state-local sector.

Since the balance sheet shows the position of the state-local sector at the end of a period, resulting from its saving, investment, borrowing, and lending activities, the sector's net worth reflects both the net change in these activities as well as the change in their valuation.

Rewriting the sector net worth to reflect revaluation, we have:

$$W = (aA_{t-1}(1 + \Pi) + bA_{t-1}(1 + \Pi)^{-1} - L_{t-1}(1 + \Pi)^{-1} \qquad (8)$$

where aA_{t-1} = tangible assets,
$\quad bA_{t-1}$ = intangibles,
$\quad L_{t-1}$ = liabilities, and
$\quad \Pi$ = the inflation rate.

Inflation effects may be ascertained by comparing the revalued assets with those of liabilities. In other words, last period net worth, W_{t-1}, may be revalued by revaluating the components of the balance sheet.

With respect to assets, tangible assets will be revalued upward as the rate of inflation increases. Accrued capital gain on tangible assets increases, other things being equal, the net worth position of the sector. These gains, however, must be balanced against capital losses on other forms of assets, especially those in the form of cash and fixed financial assets, to obtain the overall asset position of the sector.

The sector liabilities must also be revalued to reflect the change in the rate of inflation. Since inflation reduces the real burden of fixed debt instruments, a rising inflation rate reinforces the gains secured on tangible assets.

In short, for a given value of liabilities, an increase in the inflation rate will add to or subtract from the net worth of the sector through its impact on the asset side of the balance sheet.[1]

Differentiating equation 8 with respect to Π, we get,

$$\frac{dW}{d\Pi} = \frac{aA_{t-1}\,(1\,+\,\Pi)^2\,-\,bA_{t-1}\,rL_{t-1}}{(1\,+\,\Pi)^2}$$

or

$$dW = (aA_{t-1}) + \frac{Lt}{(1\,+\,\Pi)^2}\,-\,\frac{bA_{t-1}}{(1\,+\,\Pi)^2}\;d\Pi \qquad (9)$$

Thus, for any value of liabilities, the net worth position of the sector will rise if $a > b$, that is, if the ratio of tangibles to total assets exceeds that of intangibles.

Assume that the sector has a target net worth position in period t equal to W_t^*. Suppose further that W_t^* is some multiple of the sector income, that is,

$$W_t^* = ky_{t-1} \qquad (10)$$

Since savings close the gap between the sector's desired and actual net worth position, higher inflation rates would reduce the sector's need for accumulating budget surpluses to meet the target.

1. Evaluating assets by a general price index is an oversimplification for exposition purposes only. Tangible assets have to be revalued using price data for every age in every period. With respect to financial assets, revaluation requires that the stock of debt be revalued in terms of the market value rather than book value while cash holdings be discounted by the inflation rate.

Table 1.9. Balance Sheet of State and Local Governments (general government), Year Ends (dollar amounts in billions)

	1969	1970	1971	1972	1973	1974	1975	1976	1977	1978
Total assets	527.8	586.3	644.9	717.1	835.3	966.7	1,039.8	1,079.7	1,132.7	1,196.1
Tangible assets	463.2	514.4	566.8	621.9	724.6	846.3	918.5	944.7	972.7	1,011.0
Structures	358.6	404.1	446.0	489.6	577.8	681.3	733.0	743.1	751.7	773.8
Land	80.7	84.1	92.3	101.4	111.2	122.1	134.0	146.0	¢59.1	168.7
Equipment	23.2	25.5	27.7	30.0	34.6	41.6	48.0	53.8	59.8	66.1
Inventories	0.6	0.7	0.8	0.9	1.0	1.3	1.5	1.8	2.1	2.4
Intangible assets	64.6	71.9	78.1	95.2	110.7	120.4	123.3	135.0	160.0	185.1
Demand deposit currency	15.3	12.5	13.5	15.2	14.9	14.2	14.4	13.8	15.2	14.1
Time deposit	13.2	23.2	30.4	37.2	44.4	50.1	48.1	50.2	57.2	65.3
U.S. gov't. securities	26.7	25.5	22.3	29.0	34.8	35.8	36.8	41.1	54.6	67.1
State & local obligations	2.2	2.4	2.1	1.8	2.1	2.6	4.1	6.5	6.4	7.4
Mortgages	3.7	4.6	5.6	7.0	8.7	11.2	12.8	14.1	14.7	15.7
Miscellaneous	3.5	3.7	4.2	5.0	5.8	6.5	7.1	9.3	11.9	15.5
Liabilities	143.8	155.7	174.0	189.0	202.1	220.1	233.2	249.1	270.5	295.0
Credit market instruments	137.8	149.2	166.9	181.4	193.7	209.9	221.0	236.2	256.6	280.1
State & local obligations	133.1	144.4	161.7	175.9	188.8	204.3	215.2	228.4	248.6	273.7
U.S. gov't. loans	4.7	4.8	5.2	5.5	4.9	5.6	5.8	7.8	8.0	6.4
Trade debt	5.9	6.5	7.1	7.6	8.4	10.2	12.2	12.9	13.9	14.9
Net worth	384.1	430.6	470.9	528.1	633.2	746.6	806.6	830.6	862.2	901.1

Source: Columns 1969–1974 are from Ott and Yoo (1980, p. 226). Columns 1976–1978 are author estimates based on data from the Bureau of Economic Analysis and Flow of Funds Accounts.

Note: Total may not add up because of rounding.

Inspection of the balance sheet of the state-local sector over the past decade (Table 1.9) shows that the sector has a much higher ratio of tangible to nontangible assets and a much larger value of tangible assets to liabilities. Moreover, the sector net worth position in relation to income, which declined during the 1960s and early 1970s shows a steady improvement with the rise in ther rate of inflation (Table 1.10).

A word of caution may, however, be in order. Although a revalued balance sheet of the state-local sector would show the sector to be in a "comfortable" financial position, such a finding may be somewhat misleading. Unlike households or firms, the appreciation in the value of the sector's tangible assets (although enlarging their net worth position) can be used to offset neither their current nor future liabilities. Furthermore the balance sheet does not include in its total liabilities, claims on the sector. The unfunded liabilities of the retirement funds are not recognized in balance sheet accounts. If such liabilities were to be included, the overall position of the sector may not be as comfortable or prosperous as the data seem to suggest.

Conclusion

In this chapter an attempt has been made to determine the effect of inflation on the state-local sector by cataloging its effect on the use of resources, the cost of doing business, as well as the overall wealth position of the sector.

As a group, the state-local governments did not fare badly during the

Table 1.10. Assets-Liabilities Composition of State-Local Government Balance Sheet, 1969–1978

	Ratio of Tangible to Total Assets	Ratio of Liability to Total Assets	Ratio of Liability to Financial Assets	Ratio of Net Worth to Income
1969	.88	.27	2.22	3.42
1970	.88	.27	2.16	3.39
1971	.88	.27	2.23	3.18
1972	.87	.26	1.98	3.17
1973	.87	.24	1.82	32.50
1974	.88	.23	1.82	3.79
1975	.88	.22	1.93	3.66
1976	.87	.22	1.84	3.35
1977	.87	.23	1.19	3.13
1978	.85	.24	1.59	3.00

Source: From Table 1.1 and Table 1.9.

current inflationary era. Neither their resource-absorbing activities nor revenues seem to have declined during the past decade. Although their unit cost has increased, state and local outlays did not seem to have suffered by the increase. Real spending, except for capital formation, did not decline. The state-local sector has increased somewhat moderately, relative to GNP, during the period.

From the data presented in this chapter, several favorable "fall-outs" of inflation are noticeable. These are the effect of inflation on the interest earnings of the trust fund and thus on the present value of the trust fund's unfunded balance; the real burden of the state-local debt and interest payments; and the impact upon sector tangible assets. Taken together or separately the outcome is favorable. If the wealth position of the state-local sector has not been significantly improved, at least it has not deteriorated because of inflation.

Because of the tentative and aggregative natures of the data, one should be extremely cautious in applying these findings to individual government units, however. Moreover, because the balance sheet of the state-local sector does not take into account future claims on the sector (the unfunded liability of the trust fund), the net worth position of the sector tends to be overstated at any rising rate of inflation.

References

Aronson, J. Richard. 1975. "Projections of State and Local Trust Fund Financing." In *State-Local Finances in the Last Half of the 1970's,* ed. David J. Ott, pp. 63–90. Washington, D.C.: American Enterprise Institute.

Birati, Assa, and Alex Cukierman. 1979. "The Redistributive Effects of Inflation and of the Introduction of a Real Tax System in the U.S. Bond Market." *Journal of Public Economics* 12: 125–39.

Otto, Attiat F. 1980. "The Effect of Inflation on the Financial Position of the State-Local Sector." *National Tax Journal* 33, 3: 291–305.

Ott, Attiat F., and Jang H. Yoo. 1980. "The Measurement of Government Saving." In *The Government and Capital Formation,* ed. George M. von Furstenberg. Cambridge, Mass.: Ballinger Publishing Co.

2 *Charles E. McLure, Jr.*

State Corporate Income Taxes

I. Introduction

Recent years have seen a substantial increase in interest in state corporate income taxes, at least among taxpayers, their lawyers, and state tax administrators, many of the last of whom have been engaged in innova-

The author is a Senior Fellow at the Hoover Institution at Stanford University. At the time this chapter was prepared, he was Vice President of the National Bureau of Economic Research. He wishes to acknowledge the insights gained from seminars at Harvard University, the University of Toronto, and the NBER, and to thank Eugene Corrigan, Harvey Galper, Walter Hellerstein, George Mundstock, and various others for their comments on earlier drafts of this and related papers on which it draws (including McLure 1981, without implicating anyone in the chapter's conclusions. The opinions expressed here are solely the author's and not those of the Hoover Institution or the National Bureau of Economic Research.

Since this paper was written, the Supreme Court has handed down decisions in *ASARCO v. Idaho State Tax Commission, F. W. Woolworth v. Taxation and Revenue Department of the State of New Mexico,* and *Container Corporation of America v. Franchise Tax Board* and *Chicago Bridge and Iron v. Caterpillar Tractor.* In addition, the author organized a major conference on state corporate income taxes held at the Hoover Institution in November 1982. Time has not allowed this chapter to be revised extensively to discuss these four court cases or literature on state corporate income taxes that has appeared since the 1980 TRED conference. Of the papers presented at the Hoover conference, those of special relevance to this chapter are those by Carlson and Galper, Jerome Hellerstein, Walter Hellerstein, McLure, Miller, Musgrave, and Sheffrin and Fulcher.

tive and provocative approaches to state corporate taxation. This increase in interest is commonly dated from the 1959 Supreme Court decision in *Northwestern States Portland Cement Company v. Minnesota,* which led to a major congressional study, the Willis Report (U.S. Congress, 1964). But interest has reached a crescendo during the past several years, as novel statutory provisions and administrative interpretations, combined with new fiscal institutions and more aggressive administration, have broadened the reach of state income taxes. This state activity has been answered by litigation testing the constitutionality of both the new institutions and the tax statutes and their interpretations. The failure of taxpayers to prevail in recent cases appears to be encouraging states to adopt even bolder measures to obtain additional revenues from corporations, particularly in the petroleum sector.

Business concern, strong throughout the period since *Northwestern States,* has been expressed in attempts to have limits placed on the latitude states have in imposing and interpreting their corporate income taxes, as well as in litigation. These efforts have taken the form of legislation introduced in both the U.S. Congress and the legislature of California, the most innovative of the states. Of even more note, the U.S. Treasury has entered the fray on the side of taxpayers by including in the original draft of the recently concluded tax treaty with the United Kingdom a limitation on the application of so-called worldwide unitary combination, the approach used by California that so annoys many businessmen, including those in foreign countries.[1]

This chapter outlines the issues at stake in this debate, describes recent institutional, judicial, and legislative activity in the area, and discusses the desirable attributes of a federal bill that would limit state corporate income taxation. It begins in section II with a short discussion of the basic issues. Section III then briefly describes developments over the past two decades. Section IV (a) contrasts source and residence-based taxes and notes several alternative interpretations of the source principle and (b) briefly discusses the concept of a unitary business. It is crucial to have a clear understanding of these concepts in thinking about the proper course of public policy in this area. Finally, the concluding section builds on that conceptual discussion to outline what might ideally be contained in a federal law intended to promote uniformity in this area. It will be seen that certain of the desirable attributes of state corporate taxes are fairly obvious, even if there is not general agreement about them. But two other attributes—the proper definition of a unitary business and the

---

1. In addition the State Department submitted an *amicus* brief in *Japan Line, Ltd. v. City of Los Angeles* on behalf of the taxpayer which is generally considered to be the key to the decision.

proper treatment of arguably foreign-source income, especially the propriety of using worldwide unitary combination—are, unfortunately, not clear.

II. The Issues[2]

Uniformity in state income taxation has the obvious advantage of reducing costs of compliance and administration, of forcing all states to treat a given firm identically, and of requiring all firms to report the same facts to every state. Moreover, uniformity has the potential to reduce the international friction currently being created by the disparities in the ways various states tax income.

The first issue that must be faced in seeking uniformity involves the rule used to determine whether or not a given corporation has *taxable nexus* in a particular state. When the Supreme Court ruled in *Northwestern States Portland Cement* that Minnesota could levy its corporate tax on the net income of an Iowa corporation whose only activities in Minnesota were exclusively in interstate commerce, the U.S. Congress responded by passing P.L. 86–272, which prohibited imposition of an income tax on a firm whose only activity in the taxing state was soliciting orders or using an independent contractor to make sales of tangible personal property within the state.[3] To date this is the only federal legislation dealing with taxable nexus under state corporate income taxes or, indeed, with any aspect of uniformity of state corporate income taxes. Taxable nexus has, however, played an important role in many court cases, particularly including several recent cases to be discussed in greater detail in section III below. The Supreme Court has ruled that before a state can impose its tax on a given corporation, there must be a "minimal connection" between the corporation's activities and the taxing state.

In the mid-1960s, when the Willis Report was issued, there was an amazing amount of diversity in the *definition of taxable income* used by various states (see U.S. Congress [1964]). This situation is much improved: a majority of states now use the federal definition of taxable income as a starting point.[4] At this point the primary, substantive interstate differences in the way taxable income is defined involve dividends and income that is arguably from foreign sources. But compliance and

2. These issues, including the advantages of uniformity, are discussed at somewhat greater length in McLure (1981).

3. Because P.L. 86–272 applies only to income derived from sales of tangible personal property, much of commercial activity is not affected by it.

4. This situation has deteriorated as a result of changes in the federal corporate income tax passed in 1981. States have been unwilling to go along with all these changes, since doing so would involve substantial loss of revenue.

administration are still needlessly complicated by adjustments to the federal tax base that vary from state to state.

Even uniform nexus rules and a common definition of taxable income would not be sufficient to assure uniformity of taxation across states. There are three ways in which a given income flow can be divided among the states: formula apportionment, specific allocation, and separate accounting. Unless states agree on which of these to employ in given situations and how to implement each, uniformity will not prevail.

The most important means of dividing income among the states is *formula apportionment.* Under it, a state taxes a fraction of the total apportionable income of a corporation equal to a weighted average of one or more measures of the firm's economic activities in the state. In the most common formula a simple average is taken of the state's shares in total sales, payrolls, and property of the corporation. Some states, however, do not weight the three factors equally, and some use only one or two of the factors in their formulas. Failure to adopt a common formula clearly opens the door for inconsistencies that can easily lead to aggregate overtaxation or undertaxation of a given income flow.

Even if all states were to use the same formula, important issues could still remain in exactly how to define and measure the factors (sales, payroll, and property) and allocate them among states.[5] For example, sales are ordinarily attributed to the state of destination, but some states attribute them to the state of origin. Business spokesmen tend to argue that under the destination approach sales destined for states lacking taxable nexus should remain in the denominator of the sales factor, but appear in the numerator of no state. State tax administrators, for their part, argue rightly that this approach leads to "nowhere income" and argue that in such cases the state of origin of sales to states lacking taxable nexus should be allowed to include the sales in its apportionment formula. More sensible than either the business position or this "throwback" provision is "throw-out," under which sales to states lacking taxable nexus would simply be eliminated from both numerator and denominator. It is hardly used at all.

Some states argue that, when affiliated firms are engaged in a *"unitary" business,* failure to recognize this allows legal fiction to prevail over economic fact. They therefore require (or permit) groups of affiliated firms deemed to be engaged in a unitary business to file *combined reports.* Such a report lumps together the income of the corporate affiliates after netting out transactions, especially dividends, between members of the group. An apportionment fraction based on the sales, pay-

5. Musgrave (forthcoming) discusses the theoretical foundations for choices of apportionment formulas.

roll, and property of the entire group is then used to determine the fraction of the group's aggregate income that can be taxed by the state.

A few states, most notably California, extend formula apportionment to the international operations of affiliated groups of firms. They do this by applying the unitary concept and combination to foreign as well as domestic members of groups of affiliated firms. State success in using the unitary approach, especially to tax income that can be argued to originate abroad, seems to be encouraging other states to consider adopting this approach.[6]

It is not surprising that many corporations have objected to so-called *worldwide unitary combination,* since it can distort economic incentives, create burdensome administrative problems, run counter to confidentiality statutes in other countries, and result in state taxation of income that under federal law would be tax-free until repatriated, if it were taxed at all. (Income of foreign parents and other foreign affiliates of domestic subsidiaries would not, of course, be taxed by the U.S. government.) In this they have been joined by the governments of several foreign countries, particularly so far as combination involves foreign parents of American subsidiaries, and by the U.S. Treasury Department.[7]

Income from intangibles, such as interest, dividends, and capital gains on securities, as well as income attributable to real and personal property, such as rents, royalties, and capital gains on physical assets, has traditionally been attributed by many states to specific locations. *Specific allocation* has generally attributed the first group of income flows to the state of commercial domicile of the corporate recipient and the second to the state in which the property is located. There has recently been a trend away from this practice of specific allocation toward *full apportionment,* that is, toward including all income in the total to be apportioned by formula.[8] Duplicative taxation can obviously occur if states do not agree whether to use allocation or apportionment to tax a given income flow.

Under *separate accounting,* activities occurring in a given state are treated as though conducted by a legally distinct firm. Though many states treat affiliated firms as separate entities for tax purposes, this

6. The cases involved, *Mobil* and *Exxon,* are discussed in section III. As noted in section III, state success has not involved a legitimate application of worldwide unitary combination, which has not yet been tested in the Supreme Court, but is before it in the *Container* and *Chicago Bridge and Iron* cases. Whether states will adopt reasonable approaches to the taxation of unitary businesses remains to be seen.

7. For an extensive discussion of conflicts in state and federal interests in the state taxation of multinational business, see Carlson and Galper (forthcoming).

8. This trend has, however, been arrested by the decisions in *ASARCO* and *Woolworth* that dividends can be taxed to a nondomiciliary recipient only if the recipient and payer are engaged in a unitary business.

approach is rarely used to determine the interstate division of income of one corporation; rather, formula apportionment is the predominant method used to divide operating income of a firm deemed to be engaged in a unitary business among the states. Indeed, as noted above, even legally distinct firms are sometimes required to file combined reports. This is in marked contrast to the common practice in the analogous situation at the federal level, where separate accounting is the procedure normally employed to determine the nation in which the income of a multinational corporation (in particular, a member of a group of affiliated firms) originates. Many states do, however, follow federal practice to the extent of using separate accounting to determine the amount of income originating within the United States before employing formula apportionment to arrive at their share of that American-source income. That is, these states do not practice worldwide unitary combination.

III. Recent Activity

Following the decision in *Northwestern States Portland Cement,* owners of many small and medium-sized businesses became concerned that they might be subject to income taxes, and the administrative burdens the taxes would entail, in states in which they did only minimal amounts of business. As a result, P.L. 86–272 was passed. Fearing that this was only the first volley in a larger battle to restrict state taxation of corporate income, a group of tax administrators, primarily from midwestern and western states, began in 1966 to work toward the formation of what eventually became the Multistate Tax Commission in 1969. As stated in its various annual reports, the purpose of the MTC is

. . . to bring even further uniformity and compatibility to the tax laws of the various states of this nation and their political subdivisions insofar as those laws affect multistate business, to give both business and the states a single place to which to take their tax problems, to study and make recommendations on a continuing basis with respect to all taxes affecting multistate business, to promote the adoption of statutes and rules establishing uniformity, and to assist in protecting the fiscal and political integrity of the states from federal confiscation.

The MTC has pursued these goals formally by (a) incorporating the Uniform Division of Income for Tax Purposes Act (UDITPA) in the Multistate Tax Compact,[9] (b) issuing regulations interpreting that

9. For a state to become a regular member of the MTC, its legislature must vote to adhere to the Multistate Tax Compact. A state can become an associate member, with no vote in the Commission, by action of its governor.

uniform act, and (c) initiating a program of joint audits under which states can cooperate in having the MTC audit a particular firm on behalf of more than one state. In addition, the MTC attempts to persuade both members and nonmember states to adopt such controversial approaches as full apportionment of dividends and the unitary method.

The UDITPA is a model law originally drafted in 1957 by the National Conference of Commissioners of Uniform State Laws. It was an attempt to codify much of common practice. If widely adopted, it would have provided the basis for substantial uniformity of state income taxes. But by 1963 only three states had actually adopted the act, two with substantial modifications. Over thirty states have now adopted the UDITPA, in part because of its inclusion in the Multistate Tax Compact. But without generally accepted regulations, a law such as the UDITPA is potentially subject to diverse interpretations that could undermine the impression of uniformity given by formal adherence to the uniform act. In 1971 the MTC issued preliminary UDITPA regulations, which were subsequently put in their final form in 1973.

These regulations aroused considerable business opposition. Though they recognize the formal distinction between business (apportionable) and nonbusiness (allocable) income originally contained in the UDITPA, these regulations would, in effect, result in apportionment of most income that would have been subject to specific allocation under the original interpretation of UDITPA. Particularly important was the implied change in the treatment of intercorporate dividends, which are apportioned by formula under the MTC regulations. Under UDITPA as originally written, such dividends would be allocated specifically to the state of commercial domicile. But New York, the state of commercial domicile of the vast majority of corporate America, levies almost no tax on such dividends! It will be argued below that this result is not as bad as it may appear at first blush.

The early history of the MTC was one of relative harmony with at least part of the business community. Tax administrators met with businessmen in what was called the "Ad Hoc Committee," to attempt to hammer out a model bill providing uniform state taxation that would be acceptable to both groups. This effort eventually came to naught, in part because of business unhappiness with the UDITPA regulations, and much of the past decade has been marked by considerable animosity between the MTC and representatives of the business community. During the 1970s, in *U.S. Steel et al. v. Multistate Tax Commission et al.*, a group of Fortune 500 companies even attempted unsuccessfully to have the MTC and its joint audit program declared unconstitutional.

Business spokesmen have continued to attempt to gain passage of federal legislation that would limit the latitude of the states to tax corporate income. Some of the early bills were quite ambitious. They dealt with taxable nexus, an optional three-factor formula, throw-back, consolidated returns[10] and combined reports, the definition of a unitary business, the taxation of dividends, and the treatment of foreign-source income. More recent legislative initiatives have been more modest. S. 983, introduced by Senator Mathias in the 96th Congress, would limit state latitude in defining taxable income in three important ways. Domestic portfolio dividends could be taxed only by the recipient corporation's state of commercial domicile, dividends received from firms in which the recipient owns more than a 50 percent interest could not be taxed by any state, and foreign-source income as defined by federal statute could not be taxed by any state. The bill would also provide a uniform three-factor formula. States would be forced to allow commonly owned corporations to file combined reports, but corporations with substantially all their income from foreign sources would not be combined.

A more limited approach (introduced most recently as H.R. 1893 and S. 655 in the 97th Congress) would effectively outlaw worldwide unitary combination by prohibiting states from taking into account the income of foreign affiliates until such income is subject to federal income tax. The taxation of foreign-source dividends would also be limited to the percentage of such dividends effectively taxed by the federal government, after allowance for the foreign tax credit.[11] Legislation that would outlaw application of worldwide unitary combination to foreign parents and their foreign affiliates has also been introduced in California, and related provisions are now law in Illinois.

This approach appears to have had its genesis in a rather unusual episode in which the U.S. Treasury enrolled against the states applying worldwide unitary combination on the side of multinational corporations and a foreign government. During the negotiation of the current

10. In a consolidated return, firms characterized by a high degree of common ownership, all of which are subject to the jurisdiction of the taxing state, file only one return. By comparison, a combined report is employed to determine the portion of the total income of a group of affiliated firms that should be apportioned to the in-state activities of one or more firms within the group having taxable nexus within the state. In what follows, reference is made only to the much more important issue of combination.

11. For a more detailed description of this bill, introduced as H.R. 5076 and S. 1688 in the 96th Congress, including an example illustrating the proposed limitation of the state taxation of foreign-source dividends, see U.S. Congress (1980). It can be objected that state taxation should not be limited to the part of income taxed by the federal government, since, by assumption, the U.S. is yielding priority in taxation to the host country. But it can also be argued that under the source approach underlying state income taxes foreign-source income should not be taxed at all. See also section IV.

double-taxation treaty with the United Kingdom, the U.S. government agreed to a provision that would have prohibited combination of British parents and their foreign subsidiaries for purposes of calculating the state tax liability of their American subsidiaries. This provision—and the attempt to gain its passage through treaty negotiations, rather than legislation—was roundly criticized by the states and was eventually eliminated before the treaty was ratified. But to mollify those in British commerce and industry who had demanded the provision, it was agreed that analogous legislation would be introduced and that Congressional hearings would be held on it. Belgium has recently also requested an end to worldwide combination in the opening rounds of its treaty negotiations with the United States.

Several court cases decided recently may give added impetus to the efforts of those who would limit state prerogatives in this field through federal legislation. Enough of the flavor of those cases is given here to set the stage for the discussion in sections IV and V.[12]

Just how one should interpret the interstate commerce clause as applied to state corporate income taxes is far from clear.[13] The Supreme Court seems, however, to have settled on an interpretation that, among other things, outlaws *duplicative taxation* of the same income flow by two or more states.[14] Yet, in *Moorman Manufacturing Company v. Bair,* the Supreme Court rejected what would appear to have been a *prima facie* case that Iowa's use of a one-factor (sales) formula in conjunction with the use by Illinois of the conventional three-factor formula would subject income to duplicative taxation. It ruled that Moorman had failed

12. For a more complete discussion of these cases, especially *Mobil,* see Dexter (1981), *Harvard Law Review* (1980), Hellerstein (1980), McLure (1981) and Peters (1980a and 1980b).

13. Equally important is the question of how the interstate commerce clause should be interpreted so far as limitations on the taxation of natural resources are concerned. The recent decision in *Commonwealth Edison et al. v. Montana et al.,* which questioned the constitutionality of the 30 percent severance tax levied on coal by Montana, suggests that states have wide latitude in this area, so long as they do not engage in patently discriminatory taxes based on the destination of the resources. See Hellerstein (1983).

14. It is interesting to note how a test with such a flavor of due process became a commerce clause standard. The original idea of the commerce clause was to prevent discrimination against interstate business. The only clear-cut test of discrimination against interstate business the Supreme Court has ever been comfortable with is whether an interstate business is required to pay more taxes than a single-state business. This led them to the concept of duplicative taxation, which also has a due process flavor.

A similar interpretation applies to the foreign commerce clause, although in *Japan Line, Ltd. v. City of Los Angeles* the Court has indicated that there are circumstances in which the foreign commerce clause will impose more stringent requirements on state taxation than does the interstate commerce clause.

to establish by "clear and cogent evidence" that the two states actually engaged in duplicative taxation. Moreover, the Court rejected a plea based on due process that Iowa was taxing income that originated in Illinois. In so doing, it gave a clear suggestion that under certain circumstances separate accounting might be used to demonstrate where income originated.

Those who relied on the suggestion in *Moorman* that separate accounting might serve to undermine state taxation based on formula apportionment were disappointed by the *Mobil* and *Exxon* cases decided in 1980. In *Mobil Oil Corporation v. Commissioner of Taxes* the appellant excluded from apportionable income dividends it claimed it had been paid from foreign-source income by foreign firms and domestic corporations operating abroad. It did so despite the fact that under Vermont statute, which followed the federal model, 15 percent of dividends from domestic nonaffiliates and all dividends from foreign firms would be taxable.

The Supreme Court ruled that Mobil carried on a unitary business with the firms from which it received the dividends in question and that there was therefore nothing about those dividends that would justify their exclusion from Mobil's apportionable income.[15] It dismissed the argument that the dividends were from foreign sources by ruling that this argument relied on separate accounting to determine the geographic source of the income. Noting that "the linchpin of apportionability in the field of state income taxation is the unitary business principle," the Court reiterated earlier decisions that separate accounting could not be used to impeach the results of formula apportionment of the income of a unitary business. Finally, in rejecting a Commerce clause argument that dividends could not be apportioned by formula because they are traditionally taxed under specific allocation, the Court gave the hint that it might favor the former approach over the latter, at least for unitary dividends.

In ruling that Mobil engaged in a unitary business with the firms from which it received dividends, the Court seems to have expanded the definition of a unitary business. It did this not so much when it spoke in terms of "profits derived from a *functionally integrated enterprise* [emphasis added]," as when it set a test of whether or not "income was earned in the course of *activities unrelated* [emphasis added] to the sale of petroleum products." (The definition of a unitary business is considered

15. Because of ambiguities in the language of the decision and the lack of rationality of the conclusion reached, there is actually an important question of whether the Court ruled (a) that Mobil was involved in a unitary business with the firms paying dividends or (b) that the dividends constituted part of the income of Mobil's unitary business. See Dexter (1981).

further in section IV.) Beyond that, in ruling that unitary dividends could be included in apportionable income, without the benefit of combination, it produced a result that has been considered by several observers, including Justice Stevens in his dissenting opinion, to be unfair. These charges will be considered further in section V.

A final blow to the use of separate accounting to determine the geographic source of income occurred in *Exxon Corp. v. Wisconsin Department of Revenue.* In it Exxon argued that it should be allowed to use separate accounting to determine the extent to which its profits should be attributed to its three operating departments: exploration and production, refining, and marketing. Since it consistently had losses in marketing, the only activity it conducted in Wisconsin, it argued that it owed that state no corporate tax revenue.

The Supreme Court ruled that Exxon conducted a unitary business that encompassed the three operating departments. Quoting from its decision in *Mobil* that "the linchpin of apportionability . . . is the unitary business principle," the court ruled that Wisconsin was within its rights in applying formula apportionment to the entire income of Exxon and that the company could not use separate accounting to question the results of formula apportionment. Even if one disagreed with the Court's sanction of formula apportionment, at the expense of separate accounting, in a case such as this, the same kind of gross injustice found in *Mobil* is absent in this decision.

Neither the *Mobil* case nor the *Exxon* case involved worldwide combination. But advocates of that approach could clearly take substantial comfort from both cases. (The court explicitly approved the use of formula apportionment where a unitary business exists. The relationships between *Mobil* and other firms paying dividends to it were much more tenuous than those within many multinational corporate groups where unitary combination might be at issue. Finally, the Court rejected any claim that states cannot tax foreign-source income as identified by separate accounting.) Legislation has therefore been introduced in several states that would apply worldwide unitary combination, either generally or only to the petroleum industry, quite independently of whether it is applied in other sectors.[16] These efforts, especially those to enact blatantly discriminatory taxes, as well as the result in *Mobil, Exxon,* and various other cases still pending at lower levels in the judicial process, give urgency as well as some credibility to those who favor federal legis-

16. Note, however, that Virginia has recently gone in the other direction, enacting what is, in substance, the proposed federal limitation on the taxation of foreign source income contained in H.R. 1893 and S. 655.

lation limiting state power to tax corporate income.[17] Following a brief discussion of two important principles, the concluding section discusses some of the contours such legislation should and should not take.

IV. Two Economic and Legal Principles

Corporate taxpayers have often felt themselves to be taxed unjustly by a given state or to be whipsawed between the inconsistent provisions of the tax laws of several states. In many notable instances their complaints have reached the U.S. Supreme Court. Such complains are generally based on alleged violations of due process, the interstate commerce clause, and occasionally the foreign commerce clause.[18] Due process claims frequently revolve around whether states have taxed "extraterritorial values," or income originating outside the state; this issue, especially recently, has involved the definition of a unitary business. It may therefore be useful, before turning to consideration of the ideal characteristics of federal legislation in this area, to have brief discussions of source and residence bases for taxation, including alternative interpretations of the source of corporate income and of the unitary concept. It will be seen that the legal principles that seem to have guided deliberation on the source of income in the state tax area are quite different from what an economist might expect, especially based on analogy with the international context. The search for a satisfactory definition of a unitary business is quite perplexing. Unfortunately, the Court's interpretation in the landmark *Mobil* case may have done more to obscure the issue than to clarify it.

Source versus residence. One familiar with standard literature on international tax conventions would probably identify state corporate income taxes as being based on a source principle. This can be understood by considering the usual international division of tax base and revenues. The first stage is to determine the division of income among *source* (host)

17. While the Supreme Court has often felt compelled to decide whether the permissible limits of state taxing powers in this area have been exceeded in particular instances, it has persistently refused to go further and say generally what federal limits on state tax policy *should* be. It has left that task to the Congress, and indeed has frequently urged that body to use its constitutional power to control interstate and foreign commerce by passing such laws as it deems necessary.

Since these words in the text were written, the Supreme Court has decided *ASARCO* and *Woolworth*. At least for the moment, the shoe seems to be on the other foot.

18. For an exhaustive discussion of federal limitations on state taxation, see W. Hellerstein (1982). Hellerstein (1983) deals with the related but narrower issue of limitations on taxation of natural resources.

countries, commonly by using separate accounting. Host countries apply their taxes to the income identified as having arisen within their borders.

Capital-exporting countries also commonly tax all the income of corporations chartered under their jurisdiction. This *residence*-based taxation is modified in two important ways to prevent it from clashing with the source-based taxes of host countries.[19] First, because the members of corporate groups are generally treated as separate entities, only income that is paid to parents by foreign subsidiaries is taxed by the country of residence of the former. As long as income is retained by the subsidiary, it is taxed only by the host country. (In comparison, income earned by foreign branches is taxed by the home country as it is earned, whether it is distributed or not.) Second, the United States and many other capital-exporting countries allow foreign tax credits for taxes paid to host countries, including taxes of subsidiaries deemed to have been paid on income giving rise to dividends.

This *mixed source–residence* principle stands in marked contrast to the way state corporate income taxes are imposed. These taxes are clearly based primarily on source, not on residence. First, all three approaches to the division of income described above can be interpreted as being aimed at determining where income originates. Specific allocation to the state of commercial domicile and the taxation of foreign-source dividends may appear to stand out as residence-based aberrations. But both are commonly justified on source grounds, no matter how strained the reasoning. States do not attempt, at least explicitly, to tax income of firms over which they have jurisdiction that is not deemed to be earned within their borders. Indeed, in the domestic context, in which the highly integrated operations of firms (or groups of affiliated firms) extend across state lines and the choice of state of "residence" is largely a matter of convenience, historical accident, or tax planning, it would make very little sense to base state taxation on a residence approach. (This is one reason taxation by the state of commercial domicile and taxation of foreign-source dividends have so little to recommend them.) Beyond that, under combination, all income of firms deemed to be engaged in a unitary business is apportioned by formula, regardless of whether it is distributed to parents or retained by the subsidiary. Finally, state taxation of corporations is not qualified by any allowance for "foreign" tax credits for taxes paid to other states; indeed, it is hard to see how this could be done in the absence of a residence-based tax against which taxes paid to source states could be credited.

19. Nations that employ the "territorial" principle exempt foreign-source income from tax. They generally also use separate accounting to determine the nation of source.

From the above description it might appear that the division of income between states of source is analogous to the first (source-based) stage in the international division of tax base and revenues and that the second (residence-based) stage is simply omitted. While the analogy would be apt, it can be misleading. As noted above, separate accounting is not commonly used to divide the income of unitary businesses among the states. Indeed, the Supreme Court has repeatedly ruled that a determination of the geographic source of income based on separate accounting cannot generally be used to impeach the results of formula apportionment.[20] All the Court requires for formula apportionment to satisfy due process is that the tax base attributed to the state be "rationally related" to economic activities in the state. This suggests that in the Court's view the purpose of rules for interstate division of tax base is not to determine the source of income. Thus while it is true that state corporate income taxes can be said to be levied at source rather than at residence, the term "source" carries a legal connotation in this instance quite different from both that in the international context and what one might expect from an economic point of view. Whether federal legislation should follow the judicial precedent or the economist's model in the attribution rules it specifies, lies at the heart of the debate over the choice between formula apportionment under the unitary approach and separate accounting. Technical difficulties and economic effects of the two alternative interpretations are, of course, crucial to this decision.

Unitary concept. There may be instances in which some economists would argue that separate accounting, reasonably applied, would give a more accurate division of income among states in which it originates than does formula apportionment. A good example of this is the recently decided *Exxon* case. The decision in that case may result in the attribution of more of Exxon's operating income to Wisconsin than actually originated there. And yet, from an economic point of view, the unitary rationale on which that case was decided is not without appeal.[21]

20. In *Mobil,* the Court said, "[a]pportionability often has been challenged by the contention that income earned in one State may not be taxed in another if the source of the income may be ascertained by separate geographical accounting. The Court has rejected that contention so long as the intra-state and extra-state activities formed part of a single unitary business. . . . Although separate geographical accounting may be useful for internal auditing, for purposes of state taxation it is not constitutionally required."

21. William Dexter, general counsel for the MTC, points out the following example. Suppose an oil company operating in two states drills only producing wells in one and dry holes in the other. An advocate of separate accounting might argue that all the income of the firm originated in one state and that the firm had only losses in the other state. But under the unitary approach, activities in the two states would be merged and both states would tax a share of the net profits of the entire firm. Which is the proper interpretation of the source of income is far from clear. We can extend the example by supposing that we

As can be appreciated from the above discussion of the unitary approach and its importance in dictating whether or not combination is appropriate, the nation's courts have frequently been asked to rule on whether or not a given business was unitary. Indeed, the unitary principle did not originate in corporate tax statutes. Rather, its use in the corporate income tax field began as an administrative approach used by tax administrators in California and has since been given solid judicial sanction and interpretation.[22]

As this concept has evolved in the state corporate income tax area, several largely subjective tests have been developed to determine whether a unitary business exists. One is the *three unities* of ownership, operation (as evidenced by central purchasing, advertising, accounting, and management), and use (in centralized executive force and general operations). A further test is whether "business done within the state is *dependent upon or contributes to* the operation of the business without the state." More recently, in the *Mobil* case, the Supreme Court placed the burden of proof on the taxpayer to show that income is earned in activities *unrelated* to its main line of business.

V. Standards for Legislation

In many respects the ideal contours of federal legislation intended to provide uniformity in state corporate income taxes are not really very controversial. In other instances, thought the proper contours may be no less clear to disinterested observers, parties with substantial stakes in the outcome may find recommendations controversial or unacceptable. The treatment of dividends is the most important example of such a case. Finally, there are important questions on which even scholars with no direct interest in the outcome may have difficulty determining to their own satisfaction what public policy should be. Unfortunately, two of the

were talking not about states but about a multitude of very small jurisdictions. In the limit each might be only large enough to contain one well. As the size of the jurisdictions becomes smaller and smaller, it becomes increasingly difficult to argue with conviction that only the lucky ones should have tax revenues (and presumably need only a low tax rate), while the unlucky ones should have no tax base, as would be the case under geographic separate accounting. Of course, in the *Exxon* case, *functional* separate accounting was employed unsuccessfully to argue that production, the firm's profitable function, did not occur in Wisconsin, but the point remains valid.

22. The unitary concept is commonly traced to cases involving implementation of property taxes on railroads and express companies, where it was held that limiting the tax base of one jurisdiction to assets physically located therein did not adequately reflect the contribution of the jurisdiction to the "going concern" value of a firm engaged in a unitary business in several states. For a discussion of the unitary concept and its historical origins, see Dexter (1978).

most important issues, the definition of a unitary business and the proper treatment of arguably foreign-source income, fall in this category.

There is little disagreement that formula apportionment should remain the primary means of dividing income from domestic sources among the states. (The treatment of arguably foreign-source income is discussed below.) Separate geographic accounting generally has little appeal in the domestic context, and specific allocation has little to recommend it. As has long been recognized, separate accounting is vulnerable to manipulation of the transfer prices employed for transactions within a firm or group of affiliated firms. It does not really seem feasible or advisable to attempt to implement for such transactions in the domestic context the kind of arm's length pricing rules contained in section 482 of the Internal Revenue Code for international transactions. In any event, there seems to be very little reason to attempt to undo a century of judicial preference for formula apportionment through federal legislation.[23]

Though supported by historical precedent and embodied in UDITPA, specific allocation is clearly not an attractive alternative to formula apportionment for the attribution of income. This is true whether specific allocation is thought of as being founded on residence or on source principles. Clearly a residence basis for state taxation of corporate income makes no sense. Nor can an impressive case be based on source principles.

It seems unlikely that most corporations really have significant amounts of income that should truly be characterized as "nonbusiness." And even if they did, there is no obvious state of source to which most of such income should be allocated. This is particularly true for income from intangibles. The state of legal domicile has long since been discredited, and the state of commercial domicile has little more in its favor. That formula apportionment is to be preferred to specific allocation does not, however, necessarily imply that full apportionment should be the prevailing practice, as urged by the MTC. This is explained further in the discussion below of the taxation of dividends.

Preference for formula apportionment as the predominant means of dividing income among the states does, however, have important deriva-

23. Source-based taxation has undesirable incentive effects, whether implemented via formula apportionment or separate accounting. These are not discussed further here; see, however, McLure (1980). But a somewhat different case for formula apportionment arises from recognition that, in a world in which natural resources are distributed unevenly across the nation, separate accounting may produce unacceptable disparities in the fiscal capacity of states. Great disparities can, in turn, lead to economically inefficient overallocation of capital and labor to resource-rich states and to wasteful public expenditures. This argument is developed in greater detail in McLure (Chapter 7, this volume). Formula apportionment has the advantage of spreading revenues from natural wealth more evenly across the nation and ameliorating these undesirable effects of fiscal disparities.

tive implications. Rules of taxable nexus appear to be largely unnecessary if formula apportionment is applied in a reasonable way. Presumably a state should have taxable nexus over any corporation that carries on in that state any of the activities that enter into the apportionment formula. That a state has taxable nexus over firms maintaining employees and property in a state is not really very controversial. The real issue involves sales made into a state in the absence of either payroll or property. Here the proper rule seems obvious. If the sales factor is based on destination and a firm makes sales detined to the state, it has taxable nexus in the state. In other words, the issue of taxable nexus should simply be replaced by consistant application of the rationale underlying formula apportionment.

This approach, while logical, should, of course, be tempered by recognition that in some instances firms make only a minimal sales in some states in which they have no payroll and property. In such instances they should be protected from an undue administrative burden through a *de minimis* rule that would excuse them from taxation if sales fell below some threshold level.[24] Sales affected by such a rule should, it seems, simply be eliminated from both the numerator and denominator of the sales factor (thrown out), rather than being included in all denominators but no numerator (the likely business position) or being included in the numerator of the state of origin (thrown back).

The unitary concept is an integral part of formula apportionment. This is clearly the case where single firms operating only domestically are concerned. As has long been recognized, the use of geographic separate accounting to divide the income of a unitary business operated as a single legal entity among states can easily lead to unacceptable results. (Note, however, that failure to divide the various activities of a given firm into one or more unitary businesses can also produce distortions.) But the same reasoning that leads to unitary apportionment in the case of single firms has as its logical conclusion the combination of affiliated firms engaged in a unitary business. Failure to apply combination can, as has commonly been noted, allow the manipulation of legal form to mask economic reality by either states or taxpayers.

Having said this, one must, however, ask how a unitary business is to be defined.[25] Only one of the three unities, ownership, is subject to objective quantification. The other two unities, operation and use, can

24. Stating the *de minimis* rule only in terms of sales recognizes the prevailing practice of according nexus to any state in which there is property or payroll. A more reasonable rule might be that at least one factor must exceed a threshold and that the revenue at stake must also exceed a specified minimum.

25. For extensive discussions of the proper definition of a unitary business, see J. Hellerstein (1982), McLure (forthcoming), and Miller (forthcoming).

be determined only subjectively. Similarly, the tests of contribution and dependency and of functional integration, while intuitively appealing, are not capable of objective determination. Much the same can be said about the test set in *Mobil,* under which a corporation must bear the burden of showing that income is earned in "activities unrelated" to the company's ordinary line of business. But the burden of proof seems to be much more difficult to sustain than that under the test of contribution and dependency. Moreover, one can question the value of following the precedent of *Mobil.* Any situation involving a possibility of manipulating the division of income among states probably involves a unitary business. For there to be a possibility of manipulation there must be common control and probably common business transactions. But minority ownership and transactions that do not present a possibility of moving income between states (as in *Mobil*) probably do not ordinarily indicate a unitary business.

The lack of objective criteria for the determination of whether or not a unitary business exists can lead to substantial uncertainty, which is often manifested in extended litigation. This had led at least one observer (Corrigan 1980) to propose that majority ownership be sufficient, but perhaps not necessary, for a determination that a unitary business exists. Though such an approach would be arbitrary and would sometimes lead to the combination of firms that even impartial observers might argue are not involved in a unitary business, there is much to be said for it. At least it avoids the present uncertainty, and it may not be much more arbitrary than the results often reached under the present ambiguous standards.

In the absence of the adoption of an objective standard, at least a uniform standard applied consistently across the nation would be desirable. It might even be desirable to vest in one institution authority for uniform determination of the propriety of combination for a given group of firms, based on whether or not a unitary business exists. That determination would, of course, be binding on all states. Whether that institution should be part of the executive branch of the federal government, an independent federal administrative agency, or a creature of the states, such as the Multistate Tax Commission, is unclear. In any event, such determinations would presumably be subject to judicial review in federal courts.

Given a uniform definition of income, apportionment formula, and determination of the propriety of combination, it would make no sense for the individual states to continue to act independently in levying their taxes. A centralized audit would protect both the states and corporations from each other, as well as reduce total costs of compliance and administration.

One of the most controversial aspects of the division of corporate income among states involves dividends. And yet much of the controversy, which has tended to involve whether dividends should be taxed under formula apportionment or be allocated specifically to the state of commercial domicile of the recipient corporation, seems largely to miss the point. Neither of these approaches is generally appropriate. Dividends flowing between two firms engaged in a unitary business should, of course, be eliminated through the combination of the reports of the two firms. Thus the issue of specific allocation versus formula apportionment should not even arise in this case. Acceptance of this position would seem not to be particularly controversial, provided combination of firms involved in a unitary business were uniformly the standard practice.

The proper treatment of portfolio dividends seems equally obvious. Income from which such dividends are paid, we can assume, has already been apportioned among the states and, to the extent appropriate, taxed by them in the hands of the paying corporation. There is very little reason that the dividends should also be taxed to the recipient corporation. Double taxation of income of this kind accentuates the distortions resulting from double taxation of dividend income at the corporate and individual shareholder level and should not be tolerated.[26] Intercorporate portfolio dividends should be exempt to the recipient.

The only potentially troublesome area remaining involves dividends flowing between affiliated firms deemed not to be engaged in a unitary business and therefore not eligible for combination. This problem could, of course, arise only in the absence of a simple ownership test of a unitary business. Here it seems that the proper approach is that suggested

26. This argument is related to the case for integration of the personal and corporate income taxes, but does not depend on it. For an extended discussion of that case, see McLure (1975). For a persuasive argument that limitation of the federal dividend received deduction to 85 percent of dividends makes no sense, see Schaffer (1979).

It should be noted that dividends differ from interest in that the paying corporation receives a deduction for interest payments but not for dividends. Since payments such as interest cannot be allocated among the states in which the recipient operates in any way that is defensible, it could be argued that a source-based tax would be better implemented by allowing no deduction for such payments and exempting them when received by corporations. Under that approach, all capital income originating in the corporate sector would be taxed by the state in which it originates. Present practice of allowing deductions for these expenses and taxing the income to recipients is more consistent with a residence approach than with source taxation. But meshing such an approach with the individual income tax would be difficult.

above for portfolio dividends. It may be objected that this approach would open the door for manipulation of the division of taxable income between various members of an affiliated group of firms. But manipulation of this kind, it seems, would occur only if it had been incorrectly determined that a unitary business did not exist. Reversal of that determination and combination of the firms in question would eliminate the problem.

The soluton proposed here for the treatment of dividends is quite different from that condoned by the Supreme Court in the *Mobil* case. The Court followed a totally inconsistent and patently unfair approach when it employed unitary reasoning to find that Mobil's dividends were paid by firms with which it was engaged in a unitary business, without also requiring combination.[27] Under the approach advocated here, dividends Mobil received from firms with which it operated a unitary business would have been netted out in combination.[28] Its other dividends would not have been taxed at all.

The conclusions stated earlier in this section are logically applicable to income that is arguably from foreign sources or is treated as being derived from foreign sources under federal tax law. That is, the same reasoning that leads to unitary combination in the domestic context clearly leads logically to worldwide unitary combination. So, for that matter, does the reasoning that suggests that portfolio dividends should be exempt in the hands of the recipient apply with no less force if those dividends are received from foreign corporations. If, however, federal legislation is to be adopted, it is worth considering whether this straightforward application of reasoning that is compelling in the domestic context should be extended to arguably foreign-source income.

One can argue that, whereas geographic separate accounting does not make sense for activities of a given corporation conducted in each of the

27. For more detailed expressions of this view, see *Harvard Law Review* (1980), Hellerstein (1980), and McLure (1981). Corrigan (1981) seems to agree with this opinion. For a different interpretation, see Dexter (1981).

28. There remains the basic issue of whether Mobil really was involved in a unitary business with the firms from which it received dividends. In the case of ARAMCO, there seems to be little doubt that it was. But combination is usually applied only in the case of majority ownership; Mobil's 10 percent ownership of ARAMCO fell well below that threshold. This suggests that a different standard for combination might be needed in the case of consortia, as Corrigan (1980) has noted.

The record in the *Mobil* case does not provide enough information about relations with the other firms from which it received dividends to allow a certain determination of whether the court erred in ruling that a unitary business existed. But even a casual examination of the list of firms from which Mobil received dividends suggests strongly that no unitary business existed, except under the extremely lax test set in *Mobil* that activities of the paying firm must be unrelated to the business of the recipient.

fifty states and the District of Columbia, it is both more feasible and more sensible in an international context. It is easier because multi-natonal groups of firms generally use distinct legal entities to operate in different countries, and those separate firms keep their own accounting records and report income based on separate accounting to national fiscal authorities, including those of the United States. Moreover, the contribution of various factors to overall profitability may differ more across countries than across states, rendering the results of formula apportionment particularly unsatisfactory in the former context. Finally, worldwide unitary apportionment creates international tension.[29]

This line of reasoning would suggest that worldwide combination should be prohibited and that the income to be apportioned among the states by formula should be that which is taxable under federal law. Even this approach might be said to go too far, since dividends received from abroad are taxable under federal law. As noted above, it can be argued that dividends flowing between firms not being combined should be excluded, regardless of their source. A quite different approach would be to argue that while exemption of nonunitary dividends is reasonable in the domestic context, there is no reason to extend this treatment to dividends paid by foreign firms.

Many states would, of course, find prohibition of worldwide unitary combination unacceptable, both because they object in principle to the use of separate accounting to determine the source of income of a unitary business and because they deny the feasibility of accurate determination of arm's length prices necessary for the implementation of separate accounting.[30] They are particularly concerned that U.S. firms will use offshore subsidiaries to manipulate the division of taxable income among nations to the detriment of the states.[31] A less extreme approach would be to prohibit combination only for foreign members of groups of affiliated firms headquartered abroad, as in the original U.S.-U.K.

29. These arguments have been made in the Container Corporation's brief to the Supreme Court.

30. State advocates of unitary combination frequently contend that the states lack the resources to implement separate accounting under rules such as those in section 482. This argument seems curious, given that states could employ the federal division of income between nations of source. Opponents of separate accounting also question the ability of even the federal fiscal authorities to administer the rules of section 482 satisfactorily. Even this argument is not totally persuasive, given the relative stake of the federal and state governments in the matter. It might be argued that the federal government should abandon separate accounting and adopt formula apportionment. Though this argument merits examination, it is not considered here. Prohibition of state use of worldwide unitary combination would, of course, make a federal switch to formula apportionment even more unlikely.

31. On this, see, for example, Dexter (undated).

treaty. This would avoid the major administrative difficulties of world-wide combination and meet most of the objections of our economic allies without opening the door to the manipulation by U.S. corporations that is feared by the unitary states and the MTC.[32]

References

Carlson, George N., and Harvey Galper. Forthcoming. "Water's Edge versus Worldwide Unitary Combination." Paper presented at a conference on State Corporate Income Taxation, Hoover Institution, November 10–12, 1982; forthcoming in a conference volume to be edited by Charles E. McLure, Jr. and published by the Hoover Institution Press, Stanford, California.

Corrigan, Eugene F. 1980. "Toward Uniformity in Interstate Taxation." *Tax Notes* 11, 11(September 15): 507–14.

Corrigan, Eugene F. 1981. "Mobil-izing Interstate Taxation." *Tax Notes* 13, 15 (October 12): 803–9.

Dexter, William D. 1978. "The Unitary Concept in State Income Taxation of Multistate-Multinational Businesses." *The Urban Lawyer* 10, 2(Spring): 181–212.

Dexter, William D. 1981. "Tax Apportionment of the Income of a Unitary Business: An Examination of *Mobil Oil Corp. vs. Commissioner of Taxes of Vermont.*" *Brigham Young University Law Review,* August: 107–32.

Dexter, William D. Undated. "An Analysis of and Comment on H.R. 1893 and S. 655 of the 97th Congress." Boulder, Colo.: Multistate Tax Commission. Xerox.

Harvard Law Review. 1980. "The Supreme Court, 1979 Term." *Harvard Law Review* 94, 1(November), esp. pp. 117–25.

Hellerstein, Jerome R. 1982. "Allocation and Apportionment of Dividends and the Delineation of the Unitary Business." *Tax Notes* 14, 4(January 25): 155–68.

Hellerstein, Jerome R. Forthcoming. "State Taxation Under the Commerce Clause: The History Revisited." Paper presented at a conference on State Corporate Income Taxation, Hoover Institution, November 10–12, 1982; forthcoming in a conference volume to be edited by Charles E. McLure, Jr. and published by the Hoover Institution Press, Stanford, California.

Hellerstein, Walter. 1980. "State Income Taxation of Multijurisdictional Corporations: Reflections on *Mobil, Exxon,* and H.R. 5076." *Michigan Law Review* 79, 1(November): 113–71.

Hellerstein, Walter. 1982. "Federal Limitations on State Taxation of Interstate Commerce." In *Courts and Free Markets: Perspectives on the United States and Europe,* Vol. 2, pp. 431–79. Oxford: Clarendon Press.

Hellerstein, Walter. 1983. "Legal Constraints on State Taxation of Natural Re-

---

32. It is noteworthy that the MTC is now recognizing the possibility that this distinction is not without merit: see Dexter (undated).

sources." In *Fiscal Federalism and the Taxation of Natural Resources,* ed. Charles E. McLure, Jr. and Peter Mieszkowski, pp. 135–66. Lexington, Mass.: Lexington Books.

Hellerstein, Walter. Forthcoming. "Dividing the State Corporate Income Tax Base: Developments in the Supreme Court and Congress." Paper presented at a conference on State Corporate Income Taxation, Hoover Institution, November 10–12, 1982; forthcoming in a conference volume to be edited by Charles E. McLure, Jr. and published by the Hoover Institution Press, Stanford, California.

McLure, Charles E., Jr. 1975. "Integration of the Personal and Corporate Income Taxes: The Missing Element in Recent Tax Reform Proposals." *Harvard Law Review* 88, 3(January): 532–82.

McLure, Charles E., Jr. 1980. "State Corporate Income Tax: Lamb in Wolves' Clothing." In *The Economics of Taxation,* ed. Henry J. Aaron and Michael J. Boskin, pp. 327–46. Washington, D.C.: Brookings Institution.

McLure, Charles E., Jr. 1981. "Toward Uniformity in Interstate Taxation: A Further Analysis." *Tax Notes* 13, 2(July 13): 51–63.

McLure, Charles E., Jr. Forthcoming. "Defining a Unitary Business: An Economist's View." Paper presented at a conference on State Corporate Income Taxation, Hoover Institution, November 10–12, 1982; forthcoming in a conference volume to be edited by Charles E. McLure, Jr. and published by the Hoover Institution Press, Stanford, California.

Miller, Benjamin F. Forthcoming. "Worldwide Unitary Combination: The California Practice." Paper presented at a conference on State Corporate Income Taxation, Hoover Institution, November 10–12, 1982; forthcoming in a conference volume to be edited by Charles E. McLure, Jr. and published by the Hoover Institution Press, Stanford, California.

Musgrave, Peggy B. Forthcoming. "Principles for Dividing the State Corporate Tax Base," paper presented at a conference on State Corporate Income Taxation, Hoover Institution, November 10–12, 1982; forthcoming in a conference volume to be edited by Charles E. McLure, Jr. and published by the Hoover Institution Press, Stanford, California.

Peters, James H. 1980a. "Supreme Court's *Mobil* Decision on Multistate Income Apportionment Raises New Questions." *Journal of Taxation* 53, 1(July): 36–40.

Peters, James H. 1980b. "Apportioning Multistate Income in Exxon: Analyzing the Decision; the Implications." *Journal of Taxation* 53, 4(October): 246–50.

Schaffer, Daniel C. 1979. "The Income Tax on Intercorporate Dividends." *Tax Lawyer* 33, 1(Fall): 161–82.

Sheffrin, Steven M., and Jack Fulcher. Forthcoming. "Alternative Divisions of the Tax Base: How Much Is at Stake?" Paper presented at a conference on State Corporate Income Taxation, Hoover Institution, November 10–12, 1982; forthcoming in a conference volume to be edited by Charles E. McLure, Jr. and published by the Hoover Institution Press, Stanford, California.

U.S. Congress. 1964. *State Taxation of Interstate Commerce.* Report prepared for the House Committee on the Judiciary by the Special Subcommittee on the State Taxation of Interstate Commerce. Washington, D.C.: U.S. Government Printing Office.

U.S. Congress. 1980. *Description of H.R. 5076: Relating to State Taxation of Foreign Source Corporate Income.* Report prepared for the House Committee on Ways and Means. Washington, D.C.: U.S. Government Printing Office.

3 *Wayne R. Thirsk*

Tax Harmonization in Canada

Canada is a country that has long enjoyed, at least until fairly recently, a relatively high degree of fiscal coordination both between the federal and provincial governments on the one hand and among the ten provinces on the other. There are some new and disturbing signs, however, that suggest a breakdown in the previous cooperative form of federalism may be imminent. If it occurs, it will be a direct consequence of the post-World War II devolution of fiscal powers from the federal government to the provinces. The main issue addressed in this chapter is whether the pervasive trend towards political decentralization in Canada must inevitably be accompanied by growing fiscal disharmony.

In order to provide some perspective on this issue, this chapter is divided into four sections. In the first section, a normative background is offered as a means of evaluating the essential features of the current fiscal system and alternative proposals for its reform. The next section describes the historical evolution of Canada's fiscal arrangements over the period 1867–1962. A third section outlines in some detail the set of fiscal arrangements which currently guides and determines intergovernmental fiscal relationships. In the final section, there is a discussion of the recent strains which have been imposed on the fabric of federalism and the kinds of measures which may be necessary to contain them.

I. Principles of Tax Selection in Open and Closed Economies

In an earlier paper (Thirsk 1980) addressed the matter of how tax principles appropriate for open economies are different from those appropriate for closed economies.[1] Here I will briefly summarize these arguments. Before doing so, however, it is important to have a clear definition of tax or fiscal harmonization, since the term has come to mean different things for different persons. For the purposes of this paper, harmonization is interpreted as the search for fiscal arrangements which will preserve expenditure diversity in a federal system with the least amount of fiscally induced distortion in the allocation of the economy's resources. The adoption of similar revenue systems on the part of subfederal levels of government and, among them, the elimination of nominal tax rate differentials are frequently proposed as suitable means for satisfying this efficiency criterion. Although the theory of tax harmonization is closely related to the well-established literature on the distorting effects of tax differentials, but on a geographic rather than sectoral basis, this approach to the harmonization problem is far too simple to be entirely satisfactory.

In the first place, it is the variation in effective rather than nominal tax rates which may have significant allocational consequences. The use of subsidy, grant, and tax credit instruments by subfederal governments can make a system of uniform nominal tax rates exhibit marked disparities in effective rates. Moreover, firms or individuals in different jurisdictions may possess unequal capacities for shifting their effective tax burdens, in which case the least distorting tax structure would call for a system of nonuniform rates that imposes the lowest rates in those jurisdictions where tax shifting is least likely to occur. Thus, in assessing the efficiency implications of alternative tax systems, some knowledge of the incidence of various taxes is required. Secondly, the decisions of firms and individuals regarding their locations are affected as much by the benefits they receive from government spending as by the tax burdens they face.

Another way of considering this point is to note that whatever may be done on the tax side in removing fiscal influences on the spatial distribution of economic activity can be undone on the expenditure side of government's budgets. Pressures to relocate are triggered by the perception of differences between benefits received and taxes paid, the so-called fiscal residuum, between one jurisdiction and another. It is for this reason that the concept of fiscal harmonization, taking into account how both spending and taxation influence resource allocation, is more funda-

1. This chapter differs from my earlier paper (Thirsk 1980) in that it emphasizes vertical coordination among different levels of government and traces the historical development of Canada's fiscal relationships.

mental than the notion of tax harmonization.[2] Saying this, however, in no way underestimates the enormous practical difficulties in obtaining reliable measurements of the benefits conferred on different economic units by government expenditure. Because of this difficulty, policy negotiations invariably tend to focus more narrowly on the effects of tax rate variations.

In attempting to clarify the concept of harmonization, I have purposely excluded some other formulations of it that are occasionally encountered. In order to avoid some confusion on this matter, I will mention them briefly. Instead of asking what kinds of changes in revenue systems and tax rates would improve economic welfare, one could ask what set of tax differentials would optimize economic welfare.[3] The latter frame of reference introduces vast complexities into the problem of harmonization, since it involves choosing the least distorting tax structure which makes allowance for the multitude of tax and nontax distortions that beset any economy. It is a simpler and much more manageable undertaking to inquire whether or not some prospective fiscal changes will enhance the level of economic welfare.

A somewhat related issue is that so much attention is paid to the possibly distorting effects of subfederal fiscal policies while so little concern is shown for the well-recognized distorting effects of federal fiscal policy. In Canada, for example, the Federal Department of Regional Economic Expansion offers subsidies enticing firms to relocate or to expand in areas of high unemployment and lagging economic growth, and the federal tax rate on corporations is lower for manufacturing than for nonmanufacturing activities, which favors those regions already well endowed with a manufacturing base. Similarly, the federal investment and employment tax credits have a regionally differentiated rate structure which makes effective corporate tax rates relatively lower in depressed areas. In addition, trade policies such as the level of Canadian tariffs provoke some loss of economic efficiency and are regionally nonneutral in their impact.

A country's tax and expenditure instruments may be harnessed to serve either federal or subfederal economic goals, and what appears as a harmonizing blend of fiscal measures under one set of goals will seem disharmonizing under the other. Although economists have no special expertise in selecting the appropriate objective function, there is a con-

2. Since resources are typically more mobile within countries than between them, fiscal harmonization is more relevant to the analysis of fiscal relationships in a single country, while tax harmonization, especially in the treatment of tradeable commodities, may be more applicable to international fiscal relationships.

3. Dosser (1967) refers to the latter formulation as the differentials approach and distinguish it from the equalization approach that is followed here.

stitutional presumption in a federal country that the policies of the federal government should not be thwarted by the actions of subfederal governments. If inefficient tax or trade policies are pursued by the federal government, it must be because they assist in meeting other objectives besides economic efficiency, such as national unity or income distribution. There is nothing inconsistent then in promoting efficiency-enhancing harmonization measures that take as "givens" the complex of nonneutral federal policies. To illustrate this reconciliation in a Canadian context, we can see that while Canada would be better off on efficiency grounds with no tariff, it would be worse off if the province of Alberta used its newly acquired, natural resource–based fiscal power to transfer tariff-protected industries to its jurisdiction.

There are a number of alternative routes by which a greater degree of harmonization might be achieved in a federal country. Requiring subfederal governments to impose common tax rates is one possibility, but it suffers from a number of flaws. Not the least of these is the restriction that would be imposed on the expenditure discretion of subfederal governments. Since the freedom to enjoy different expenditure levels is the raison d'être of a federal system, imposing this constraint on the tax system is likely to be unacceptable. Moreover, it overlooks the expenditure side of the budget as a potential distorting influence. The ideal federal solution would require that all subfederal expenditures be financed on a benefit basis and that the distribution function of the fisc be assigned exclusively to the federal government.[4] Tax differentials which would emerge in this type of setting would correspond to regional differences in taste patterns and would not provoke interregional migration of either capital or labor. There would be fiscal harmonization, since the fiscal residuum would be zero for each firm and household no matter where it resided. Only if subfederal government expenditures are redistributive will interjurisdictional tax differentials be distortive and give rise to a need for fiscal harmonization.

An alternative method of preserving fiscal harmony is to centralize taxation, thereby eliminating the problem of tax differentials, and to decentralize expenditure decisions through a system of revenue sharing between the federal and subfederal levels of government. In this manner, nonuniform expenditure efficiency would not have to be sacrificed to obtain more efficient federal financing. Nonetheless, this fiscal compromise has one glaring defect. By unlinking the tax and expenditure decisions, it may encourage an inefficient overexpansion of subfederal government spending. In Canada, perhaps the oldest game in fiscal

4. McLure (1971) discusses in greater detail this option and the major obstacles to its realization. He suggests that inadequate federal progressivity is the main barrier in its path.

politics is the continual attempt of subfederal politicians to shift the burden of financing to higher levels of government and to accept the credit for the expenditure benefits. Despite an awareness of how this game is played, federal-provincial transfers in recent years have constituted about one-quarter of provincial government revenues. The role played by unconditional transfers, mainly the federal revenue equalization program, in assisting fiscal harmonization in Canada is discussed later on.

A final possibility for improved harmonization is the judicious assignment of tax bases and taxing powers to subfederal governments. Provinces, and particularly municipalities, are most fruitfully viewed as small open economies whose exposure to product and factor market competition from outside their jurisdictions makes it extremely difficult for any one jurisdiction to permanently alter the structure of relative commodity and factor prices within their jurisdiction. Since the broad-based taxes available to these governments fall on some combination of income, consumption, or wealth, the crucial choice insofar as harmonization is concerned is whether the tax is imposed where the taxed object is enjoyed or, alternatively, where it originates or is produced. In the case of broad-based commodity taxes, the choice is between applying either the destination or the origin principles. The former imposes the tax at the point of consumption, the latter at the place of production. Because it automatically exempts exports and applies to imports, the destination principle can be applied in an open economy without disrupting the pattern of interjurisdictional trade flows and inducing the relocation of mobile resources. Origin-based commodity taxes by exempting imports and imposing a burden on exports exert much more pressure for factor relocation and, unless a common tax rate prevails in all jurisdictions, are therefore less suitable for adoption by subfederal governments.

A counterpart to this choice exists in determining the most appropriate methods of taxing incomes and wealth. Corresponding to the destination-tax treatment of products, the residence principle takes no account of where income is earned or wealth is held, but rather applies the tax according to where income is received or wealth holders are domiciled. The alternative source principle, like the origin principle in the case of commodities, taxes income in the location in which it is earned and wealth where it earns income. It is a tax on factor services rather than on factor owners and, as such, it influences factor owners' decisions about where to employ their services. The advantage of the residence principle over its rival is that taxes based on the residence of factor owners would not distort investment decisions if the tax rates levied on capital incomes were to vary across jurisdictions. The same is not true in the case of labor incomes, however, since ordinarily labor resides in the same area where its services are provided.

The distinction between residence and source principles as applied to open countries is closely related to the traditional contrast between the ability-to-pay and benefit criteria. On ability-to-pay grounds the residence principle is much more attractive than the source alternative, because it considers all of the means by which income is earned and makes a person's tax liability independent of whether the income stream is derived from either domestic or foreign sources. The source principle, on the other hand, is only concerned with where a person earns his income, not with how much he earns. However, if the taxing jurisdiction incurs budgetary expenses in supporting or maintaining the flow of income created within its territory, there is a benefit rationale for levying taxes on incomes at their sources.

Since producers, especially large corporations, do consume significant amounts of public services, there is a role for source-based benefit levies at the subfederal level. Beyond this, however, the adoption of the source principle by other than the federal level of governments will contribute to fiscal disharmony and interjurisdictional frictions. Unlike residence-based taxes, source taxes are capable of being exported to nonresidents in the form of either higher product prices for imported commodities if some degree of monopoly power exists, or lower factor prices if it does not. Of questionable ethical merit in any event, tax burden shifting of this kind will hinder the efficient allocation of resources and fail to satisfy the harmonization objective. Through its effect in reducing the costs borne by residents in providing public services for themselves, tax exporting will operate to draw resources from other jurisdictions where their productivity is higher.

Unfortunately, almost no empirical studies have been conducted in Canada to determine the degree and significance of interjurisdictional tax exporting. But to the extent that it occurs, as it undoubtedly does, it argues for the removal of source taxation powers from the control of subfederal governments. At the provincial level, this change would suggest the surrender of the corporate income tax field to the federal government. In addition to eliminating this avenue of tax exporting, federalizing the corporate income tax would stop provincial tax competition for new industries. At the municipal level, applying the same principle would result in revoking the nonresidential property tax which may be viewed as a local profits tax.[5] Finally, in the current federal-provincial squabble

5. For some evidence on the exportability of the nonresidential property tax, see Ballentine and Thirsk (1982).

over the sharing of natural resource rents, fiscal harmonization would be served by a much larger federal slice than is presently the case.[6]

The basic thrust of this last approach to harmonization is that tax differentials should be tolerated in a federal system if the distortions which they produce are kept to a minimum by forcing subfederal levels of government to rely on the residence and destination principles of taxation. According to this view, the problem of fiscal disharmony stems not so much from discrepancies in domestic tax structures as from irrationality in their design and in the choice of competing tax principles. It is from the perspective of this framework that the evaluation of the progress Canada has made towards tax harmonization is presented below. We begin with a historical review of the major developments in the next section.

II. The Evolution of Harmonization: From the Late 1860s to the Early 1960s

To appreciate the direction in which Canada's intergovernmental fiscal relations have evolved, it is necessary to start at the beginning of confederation in 1867 and consider the fiscal privileges and constraints that are embodied in Canada's constitution, the British North America Act. The relevant sections of that act are 91(2) and 91(3), which confer, respectively, exclusive legislative authority on the federal government in matters regarding the regulation of trade and commerce and "the raising of money by any mode or system of taxation," and section 92(2), which restricts the provinces to the imposition of "direct taxation within the province." Section 125, moreover, states that no lands or property belonging to Canada or any province shall be liable to taxation. At the time of confederation, customs duties and excise taxes were the major revenue sources. These were assigned exclusively to the federal government, which also assumed responsibility for the total outstanding provincial debts and all expenditures for national security and development. But this transfer of customs and excises left the provinces with less than one-fifth of their former revenues, and, although empowered to levy direct taxes, they failed to do so initially because of their unpopularity and the administrative difficulty of collecting them. To bridge the fiscal gap that was created between the expendture responsibilities of the provinces and their meager revenues from the public domain—licenses and fees—small annual federal subsidies were paid to the provinces.

6. In the petroleum industry it has been estimated that, of another dollar of net income earned by oil producers, $.10 would be received by the federal government in taxes compared to $.45 for the producing provinces.

The architects of confederation, however, made a serious miscalculation in assuming that the federal government had adopted all of the expanding functions of government while those of a static or declining nature had been reserved for the provinces. The failure to perceive that the provinces would experience a growing need for revenues if they were to carry out their functions meant that the initial fiscal arrangements were short-lived. Soon the federal government was forced to make a series of ad hoc adjustments and concessions in its subsidy payments to different provinces. Even these were inadequate to satisfy provincial expenditure demands, so by 1896 the provinces had stepped into all of the direct tax fields and were receiving about 10 percent of their revenue from corporation taxes, succession duties, and property and income taxes. In 1882 Quebec pioneered a new tax field with a tax on certain commercial corporations that depended on the amount of paid-up capital and the number of places of business. It was appealed to the Privy Council in London, who were obliged to interpret the direct taxation clause contained in the BNA Act. The council decided that the corporation tax met the criterion of a direct tax in that it was intended to be borne by those who paid it. Other provinces quickly followed the Quebec precedent.

In 1917, faced with the exigencies of wartime financial pressures, the federal government introduced its own direct taxes on individual and corporate incomes. Even the addition of these two instruments to the federal tax arsenal did not staunch the flow of federal deficits and the federal government responded by introducing a 1 percent turnover tax. It was replaced by a 6 percent manufacturers sales tax in 1924, which still exists today (at a higher rate) and is administered on a destination-principle basis.

The Great Depression revealed the fragility of the fiscal system in withstanding severe economic shocks. Provincial revenues declined drastically, welfare costs incurred by the provinces to support the army of unemployed reached staggering levels, and many municipalities defaulted on their debts. As the provinces scrambled to generate new revenue sources and turned to Ottawa for relief in the form of grants and loans, the federal government decided that a fresh review of the fiscal system was appropriate and appointed a royal commission, the Rowell-Sirois Commission, to investigate Canada's fiscal ills. (Report of the Royal Commission on Dominion-Provincial Relations, 1940). The commission found an extremely untidy and illogical form of fiscal federalism when it surveyed the chaotic conditions of the 1930s and probed the historical roots of the fiscal faults that were discovered. Many of the difficulties seemed to arise from what the commission saw as the difficulties of a divided jurisdiction. In the words of the commission (p. 241, Book I), "Costly government responsibilities which have become national in scope are being supported by regional and local revenues. Revenue sources which have become national in character are being employed by regional and local governments to the complete or partial exclusion of the central authority."

In its examination of the personal income tax, the commission concluded that rates varied to a remarkable degree in middle and upper income brackets and presented not only problems of serious horizontal inequities but also practical obstacles to freedom of movement. In Alberta and British Columbia for example, no deduction was permitted for federal income taxes paid, whereas in Ontario deductions were allowed and the provincial rate was pegged at one-half the federal rate. Discriminatory tax provisions were also common. British Columbia, for instance, exempted dividend income if it was received from corporations headquartered in that province. As a result of these and other features of the tax system, it was estimated that a person having taxable income of $100,000 in Alberta would face a tax rate of 26 percent compared to a rate of only 7.4 percent in Ontario. Divided jurisdiction also served to emasculate the ability of the federal government to enter into effective international taxation agreements, since the federal government could not compel provincial compliance on subjects within provincial jurisdiction.

In the case of corporate income taxes, the commission found that businesses conducting their affairs on a national level were double- and triple-taxed, that different forms of business were taxed at different rates in the same province, and the same kinds of business confronted different rates in different provinces. The corporate income tax was one of the major sources of interprovincial tax discrimination, although it was noted that interstate tax discrimination in the U.S. was probably more serious, and, in the view of the commission, was one of the tax devices provinces employed to extract transfers from "foreigners" in an arbitrary and inequitable manner. In the carefully chosen words of the commission (Book II, p. 271), "These provincial corporation taxes are peculiarly vexatious to those who pay them and particularly detrimental to the expansion of the national income."

A similar voice of concern was raised in the area of estate taxation. Provincial succession duties levied on a deceased resident often imposed a tax on movable property situated outside the province. The outcome was the double taxation of estates, because the provinces were unable to agree on whether the domicile of the decedent or the situs of his property was relevant in the taxation of estates. Provincial reciprocal agreements that were negotiated in order to avoid double taxation were repudiated soon after their negotiation. The hazard of double taxation was a distorting influence on the allocation of capital since investors were given a strong incentive to confine their investments to the provinces in which they were domiciled. In the commission's view, wealth accumulated in part out of the profits from nationwide enterprises should be taxed only at the national level.

Faced with this impressive absence of tax coordination, the commission felt strongly that to maintain the status quo would "intensify the evils of the existing competitive scramble for revenues" and "lead to increasing friction between governmental units, increasing double taxation, increasing arbitrary, discriminatory and confiscatory tax levies, increasing costs of tax compliance, increasing disparities in taxation burdens and government service levels between regions, and increasing disparities between burdens on and opportunities open to individuals" (The Royal Commission on Dominion-Provincial Relations, 1940, Book II, p. 134). As a means of preventing this outcome, the commission recommended that the provinces withdraw completely from the personal and corporate income tax and succession duty fields. In return, the federal government would assume the responsibility for existing provincial debts and the burden of unemployment relief and would provide annual adjustment assistance grants designed to enable each province to supply an adequate level of public services (at the average Canadian standard) without having to levy excessive (greater than average) tax rates. Moreover, a portion—10 percent—of the federal corporate income tax revenues was to be returned to the source provinces. With these funds it was hoped that the provinces would be compensated for their expenditures incurred in developing nonrenewable natural resources and would not resort to introducing retail sales taxes. The commission's resistance to provincial sales taxation was founded on the fear that it would be applied to weigh more heavily on externally produced than on locally made products and would thus induce the erection of miniature tariff walls throughout the country.

The philosophy of the Rowell-Sirois Commission is consistently evident on virtually every page of its report. Its carefully considered proposals for fiscal reform came in response to the fiscal chaos of the 1930s and vigorously asserted the principle, embodying what the commission construed as the spirit of the constitution, that there should be freedom of trade, investment, and movement, as well as freedom from discriminatory taxation. Provinces were to be left with limited powers of taxation, because widespread provincial tax autonomy had resulted in an abuse of those powers. Provinces had been observed using a battery of tax and nontax measures in the pursuit of provincial protectionist urges that violated the federal premise of a common or shared product and factor market. Licensing provisions, inspection and grading laws, preferential purchasing policies, and Liquor Control Board concessions to local products were cataloged as prominent examples of interferences with interprovincial trade flows. Withdrawal of the provinces from the major direct tax fields was seen as the only promising method of achieving reasonable tax rate uniformity and preventing the provinces from taxing objects which were in no sense provincial. However, the recommendations of the commission did not deprive the provinces of their direct tax participation. World War II did that.

The war had the effect of not only shelving the proposals of the commission but also the problems at which the proposals were directed. Recognizing the need for a federally directed war effort, the provinces temporarily ceded their occupation of the direct tax field in exchange for a system of tax rentals based on per capita federal payments to the provinces. This agreement was to be reviewed when hostilities ceased. Upon the restoration of peacetime conditions, the federal and provincial governments were unable to reach a satisfactory settlement until 1947, when an extension of the wartime tax rental system was accepted by most of the provinces. Ottawa clearly wanted to keep the provinces out of the direct tax areas against their will. Ontario and Quebec decided to remain outside this arrangement and imposed their own direct taxes, although Ontario later reconsidered and entered the agreement in 1952. Quebec was awarded an abatement in 1952 of the federal income taxes collected in that province. After much wrangling and dispute, it became obvious to both levels of government that no permanent solution would be acceptable, so the duration of all future agreements was restricted to a term of five years.

Although the system of tax rentals served to unify income tax bases and rates among provinces covered by the agreement, it had the distinct disadvantage of limiting provincial expenditure discretion and making Ottawa the unpopular provincial income tax collector. In 1957 tax sharing replaced the concept of tax rentals, and the implicit revenue equalization of the former arrangement was superseded by an explicit equalization scheme. For the privilege of collecting and imposing all of the income taxes, the federal government agreed to transfer to each province 10 percent of federal personal income taxes collected in it, 9 percent of the taxable corporate income earned in it, and one-half of the estate taxes paid in it. Equalization payments, similar in scope and design to the grants proposed by the Rowell-Sirois Commission, were instituted to bring tax yields in each province up to that of the two wealthiest provinces when a standard (Canadian average) rate was imposed. When this agreement lapsed in 1962, it ushered in a new set of tax collection agreements, which have remained essentially unaltered to the present day. The nature of these agreements is spelled out next.

III. Tax Collection and Other Agreements:
Tax Harmonization from 1962 to the Present

Prior to 1962 the provinces felt trapped in a fiscal straitjacket because they faced growing expenditure demands in the areas of health, education, and welfare and were denied the right to strike their own tax rates. Ottawa relented to these pressures for greater provincial tax autonomy by reducing its share of personal and corporate income taxes collected in each province and offering to collect any provincial taxes assessed if the province accepted the federal definition of the tax base in each case and maintained general conformity of its tax base with that of the federal government. Sixteen percent of the federal personal income taxes was abated to the provinces along with 9 percent of the taxable income of corporations earned in the province and 50 percent of federal estate taxes. Provinces were free to impose more or fewer taxes than the amounts surrendered by Ottawa.

Only Quebec wholly rejected this federal offer and decided to administer and collect its own revenue from a separate personal and corporate income tax system. Ontario accepted the federal offer for the collection of personal income taxes but stayed outside the agreement for the federal collection of corporate income tax revenues. In 1965 provinces were offered even greater latitude by being able to "opt-out" of federal conditional grant programs in exchange for a larger personal income tax abatement. Quebec immediately availed itself of this opportunity and received an extra abatement of 23 percent of federal personal income taxes when it withdrew from virtually all of the federal-provincial shared-cost programs.

Since provinces are required to choose a single personal income tax rate as a percentage of the basic federal tax collected in their jurisdiction, there is, outside of Quebec, a uniform degree of personal income tax progressivity across the provinces. The distribution of relative income tax burdens in each province rests on decisions made in Ottawa. Recently, however, there has been some relaxation of this federal monopoly on the distribution function. Since 1974 the federal government has permitted the provinces to apply either tax credits or surtaxes against provincial income tax. Nearly all provinces now utilize vanishing sales and property tax credits, which reduce tax burdens at the lower end of the income scale. Saskatchewan is currently unique in imposing a 10 percent surcharge on any amount of that province's tax in excess of $4,000. For these privileges the federal government charges the provinces a modest fee. Although marginal tax rates are beginning to diverge between provinces now, the largest tax differentials appear to exist between Quebec and the rest of the country. According to newspaper accounts, the significantly higher rates in Quebec have stimulated the migration of high income persons to other parts of the country and caused serious recruitment problems for firms in that province.

A further important feature of this system of piggy-backed personal income taxes is a revenue protection clause which prevents federal budgetary changes from reducing provincial tax revenues. Any provincial revenue loss in excess of 1 percent of basic federal tax due to a federal rule change coming after the start of a given tax year will be covered by a transfer from the federal government. After that, a province which wishes to recoup its revenue loss will have to raise its own tax rates.

Some appreciation of the provincial diversity in personal income tax rates can be obtained from a glance at Table 3.1. The level of tax rates in

Table 3.1. Provincial Tax Rates, 1969 and 1978

Province	Sales Tax Rate[a]		Personal Income Tax Rates[b]		Corporate Income Tax Rates[c]	
	1969	1978	1969	1978	1969	1978
Newfoundland	7%	11%	33%	58%	13%	12/14%
Prince Edward Island	7	8	28	50	10	10/14
Nova Scotia	7	8	28	52.5	10	12
New Brunswick	8	8	38	53.8	10	9/12
Quebec	8	8	50	50–60	12	12
Ontario	5	7	28	44	12	10/13
Manitoba	5	5	33	54	11	11/15
Saskatchewan	5	5	33	53	11	11/14
Alberta	—	—	33	38.5	11	11
British Columbia	5	5	28	46	10	12/15

Source: Statistics Canada, Principal Taxes and Rates, no. 68–201.

[a] Under the sales tax reduction indemnification program of the federal government in 1978, all of the provinces except Quebec and Alberta reduced their sales tax by 2–3 percentage points for a period of 6–9 months. Alberta has no sales tax, and Quebec sales tax was eliminated for one year on purchases of clothing, footwear, textiles, and furniture.

[b] Personal income taxes are expressed as a percentage of federal tax liability. Thus with a federal marginal rate of about 40 percent in the top bracket, the highest marginal income tax was of the order of 60 percent in 1978 when both federal and provincial tax claims are combined. Quebec levies its own income tax which in 1978 was approximately 50–60 percent of the federal tax.

[c] The lowest corporate rate applies to small businesses in some of the provinces above. In addition, there are separate provincial mining and mineral taxes.

all provinces was noticeably higher in 1978 than in 1969, due in large part to the federal government's agreement in 1977 to reduce its share of taxes collected in each province. With a lower federal tax take, provinces were required to raise their rates in order to maintain their revenue. Rates tend to be generally higher in the four poorer maritime provinces of eastern Canada, but on the whole there is no marked disparity in income tax rates from one province to another. The lowest rates are found in Alberta, which also has no sales tax, due to that province's primary reliance on natural resource revenues. It is also not possible to draw any inferences about which areas have high tax costs, since income taxes in some provinces are used to finance services that in other provinces are paid out of user fees. Manitoba, for instance, utilizes the income tax to pay for its share of the costs of the national Medicare program, while Ontario depends on family premiums to cover the same costs.

In contrast to the personal income tax, the vertical and horizontal coordination of corporate taxes has been a much thornier issue to settle, no doubt because it requires agreement on when a company is liable for provincial taxation (nexus rules) and how a company's total profit shall be divided among the provinces in which there is a nexus (allocation rules). Both sets of rules are required to avoid overlapping tax claims. The permanent-establishment criterion (a fixed place of business or the employment of substantial capital or labor) is used to determine jurisdiction under the tax collection agreements.[7] The same agreements specify a two-factor apportionment formula that weighs payrolls and gross receipts equally. A province's share of a company's total profit therefore consists of that profit multiplied by the factor of one-half the sum of that province's fraction of the firm's total payroll and gross receipts. Special, but equally arbitrary, rules have been drawn up for companies which operate in the financial, insurance, and transportation industries. Foreign-source income is excluded from the definition of taxable total profit.[8]

Until 1962 the provincial taxation of multiprovincial companies was not very well coordinated. Ontario levied a separate tax on the total profits of corporations with their head offices located in that province, even though much of those profits were generated in other provinces. Quebec, for a long period of time, used only a sales factor to apportion profits and attributed to itself sales made to another province unless the company operated a plant there. In 1961 Quebec followed Ontario and the

7. The personal income tax base, for reasons of administrative convenience, is allocated on the basis of residence on December 31 of each year. This rule favors provinces which are experiencing significant amounts of immigration.

8. A comprehensive and detailed description of how these rules evolved over time is given by Smith (1976).

other provinces by adopting the same two-factor formula in which payrolls and sales at destination were given equal weight. Although they operate their own corporate tax systems, Quebec and Ontario also adhere closely to the federal definition of taxable income and ordinarily adopt any changes in definition introduced by the federal government.

Despite a clear recognition by Smith (1976) and other writers that a uniform set of rules, regardless of specific content, is required to prevent horizontal tax overlapping, there has been some discussion in Canada of whether the exact elements of the apportionment formula can be determined on the basis of scientific principles. Frequently this question is posed: Does profit arise when the product is made or when it is sold? As McLure (1974) has stressed in his numerous articles on the subject, this is a meaningless question, because any spatial partitioning of an income stream generated in many different jurisdictions is inherently arbitrary.[9] The point is that both production and sales are needed to create a profit: if a product, once made, could not be sold there would be no profit to allocate. It is probably true that this debate over the appropriate elements in the formula has served to obscure the more fundamental issue of whether source or residence is the most desirable principle for the provinces to adopt. If the corporate income tax were integrated, for instance, it would be more plainly evident that a provincial tax on corporations falls explicitly on nonresidents.

A glimpse at Table 3.1 confirms that, at least until very recently, nominal corporate tax rates have been imposed at similar levels in all of the provinces. Unlike the personal income tax, the tax collection agreements allow the imposition of multiple rates. Most provinces have exercised this option and operate with a dual rate structure that confers a lower rate of tax on small businesses. As discussed in the next section, recent legislation in several provinces has offered even more significant tax subsidies to small corporations. Aside from this size distinction, rates are uniform across industries within each province. In addition, a number of provinces impose capital taxes on the paid up value of corporations operating within their jurisdictions. However, these rates are relatively small, on the order of .2 to .3 of 1 percent, and would add perhaps two or three percentage points to the rates displayed in Table 3.1.

As a result of the tax reform of 1972, the federal government abandoned the gift and estate tax fields to the provinces and allowed them to tap this revenue source as they wished. All of the provinces, except Alberta, responded by introducing succession duties and gift taxes that

9. McLure (1979) has also shown that the uniformity of apportionment rules fails to eliminate the distorting effects of nonuniform tax rates and is therefore an imperfect harmonization technique.

were poorly coordinated. Ontario's gift tax, for instance, reached out to nonresidents if they decided to make a gift of real property situated in Ontario. Because of its relatively low yield and the pressure of tax competition, one province after another has withdrawn from this tax field until now only Quebec remains. Ontario candidly admitted that it withdrew so that businesses contemplating a location in that province would not consider the taxable status of their estates in arriving at a decision. Harmonization achieved by voluntary withdrawal could hardly have been foreseen at the time of the 1972 tax reform. Even Quebec's solitary death and gift taxes are unlikely to be distorting, since they exempt the transmission of assets outside the province to Quebec residents.

The first attempt by the provinces, specifically Alberta in 1936, to introduce sales taxation was struck down by the Supreme Court on the grounds that direct taxation was not involved. Other provinces—Saskatchewan in 1937, Quebec in 1940—worded their legislation more carefully so that the tax fell "directly" on the province's consumers with the seller being viewed as the party that collected the levy on behalf of the province. Only Alberta does not now have a retail sales tax. The other provinces have similar definitions of the tax base. All nine taxing provinces exempt food for home consumption and prescription drugs, eight exempt children's clothing, and seven exempt school supplies. Many of them, however, do not provide complete exclusion of intermediate and producers' goods. As can be seen in Table 3.1, the tax rates of the taxing provinces are reasonably similar and have tended to move in unison.

One of the difficulties in adopting a destination principle sales tax is that its effective administration requires border stations to control the flow of imports into the taxing jurisdiction. Without this control some interprovincial transactions may escape tax entirely when purchase and delivery occur in different jurisdictions; some may be taxed twice if tax is paid both to the jurisdiction of purchase and that where usage occurs; and some may result in payment to the wrong tax collector where only a tax at the point of purchase is paid. As Johnson (1973) has noted, however, these problems are not of an overwhelming nature in Canada because there are few border towns with sizeable populations (Hull, adjacent to Ottawa, is the major exception), thus restricting consumer mobility, and also because the incentive to import is slight in view of the similarity in tax rates.[10]

10. Johnson (1974) describes the interesting tax situation of Lloydminister, Saskatchewan, which straddles the border with Alberta. No sales tax in the latter province has forced Saskatchewan tax officials to cease trying to collect any tax from Lloydminister retailers.

In addition, most provinces have developed their own administrative procedures to minimize instances of evasion and double taxation. Registration of motor vehicles brings out-of-province purchases to the attention of the sales tax authorities. Audits of business firms also detect purchases made in other provinces. If sales tax has already been paid, the province where the commodity is used may invoke the origin principle and decide to forego collecting the tax. There is no mechanism for granting a tax credit under the provincial sales tax. Another device consists of agreements with large mail-order stores to collect tax on the basis of a customer's residence and of efforts to persuade or require extraprovincial firms to register with the province and collect the tax on purchases made by residents. Finally, most provinces have agreed to the regular exchange of information on interprovincial transactions, and all have agreed on how to harmonize the taxation of interprovincial carriers.

A recent example of vertical commodity tax coordination is seen in the 1977 reciprocal taxation agreement between the federal government and six of the provinces. Under the agreement, the federal government makes payments in lieu of retail sales tax on its purchases of goods and services in the province. On their part, the participating provinces refrain from claiming refunds of federal sales and excise taxes under the Excise Tax Act. In addition, the federal government extends annual grants in lieu of property taxes to municipalities, school authorities, and provinces which levy these taxes.

Table 3.2. Average Tax Payments per Family by Region and Income Class, 1969

Income Class dollar amounts in thousands	Atlantic	Quebec	Ontario	Manitoba-Saskatchewan	Alberta	British Columbia
less than $1	$ 576	$ 610	$ 816	$ 768	$ 757	$ 658
$ 2–2.9	988	1,029	1,158	1,129	1,190	1,044
3–3.9	1,750	1,449	1,597	1,599	1,629	1,634
4–4.9	1,982	1,955	2,139	2,095	2,126	2,195
5–5.9	2,530	2,316	2,516	2,253	2,473	2,392
6–6.9	2,985	2,914	3,253	2,817	2,876	3,329
7–7.9	3,668	3,225	3,454	3,341	3,538	3,193
8–8.9	4,071	3,812	4,049	3,520	3,736	3,642
9–9.9	4,507	4,205	4,382	4,019	4,719	4,278
10–10.9	5,625	4,890	4,994	4,491	5,205	4,858
11–11.9	5,625	5,364	5,220	4,692	5,166	5,351
12–14.9	6,994	5,932	6,196	5,838	6,080	6,084
more than $15	12,574	11,026	11,949	13,865	11,546	15,106

Source: Maslove (1972)

The information in Table 3.1 is insufficient for any inferences to be drawn concerning the geographic distribution of household tax burdens, since it is a comparison of overall tax bills, not tax rates, which is allocatively important. Using a number of plausible incidence assumptions, Maslove (1972) has calculated comprehensive provincial tax burdens. His estimates of average family tax payments by province and income class for the year 1969 appear in Table 3.2. Although average tax burdens seem to be somewhat greater in the four Atlantic provinces, there is surprisingly little provincial variation in tax bills paid by any given income class and hence little motivation to change residence or province of work because of tax disparities.[11] One of the reasons for this small degree of variation in tax bills is the federal government's equalization program started in 1957, which makes payments to fiscally weak provinces. Federal transfers are received by provinces if, at an average tax rate, their per capita revenues fall short of what would be obtained by applying that rate to the per capita national average tax base.[12] This revenue sharing program is an important harmonization instrument, for it keeps unequal provincial fiscal capacities from exerting a strong allocative influence.[13]

To briefly summarize this section of the chapter, Canada has until recently enjoyed a relatively high degree of tax and fiscal harmonization. As I have observed in an earlier paper (Thirsk, 1980), efforts aimed at harmonizing subfederal tax structures have been notably more successful in Canada than in the United States. It is the result of the federal government's equalization program, its insistence on maintaining a reasonable level of tax base and even tax rate uniformity, and its long-standing concern with the problem of horizontal tax coordination. As provinces begin to flex more of their economic muscle in this era of decentralization and attempt to use the fiscal tools at their disposal to achieve greater mastery

11. This conclusion requires qualification in several respects. First, only if taxes financed approximately the same mix of pure public goods in each region would it be safe to ignore expenditure influences on the choice of residence. Secondly, the estimates pertain to a period prior to the energy crisis. Since the rapid escalation of oil prices, there is little doubt that a strong incentive exists to move to Alberta in order to enjoy the fiscal bonanza experienced by that province. Moreover, the pattern of marginal tax rates in Quebec has risen steeply in that province since the Parti Quebecois took power. For a person earning $80,000 it has been estimated that his personal income tax liability would be $5,405 larger in Quebec than in Ontario. Finally, the estimates themselves are based on particular assumptions regarding tax incidence.

12. For a useful survey of the equalization program, see Boadway (1980).

13. From a different perspective, Scott (1952) has argued that these transfers may interfere with dynamic efficiency by inducing a smaller rate of labor migration from poor regions. The issue is clearly an empirical one, whether, in the absence of unconditional transfers to poor regions, migration from poor-to-richer regions would be excessive or not.

over their economic destiny, the challenge for the future will be to find ways of preserving the measure of harmonization that already exists.

IV. Storm Signals Brewing—A Postscript

In the years ahead the federal government faces the enormously difficult task of maintaining and improving the state of fiscal harmony in the country. It must first of all block and defuse certain provincial fiscal initiatives which threaten to destroy the current, albeit imperfect, fabric of intergovernmental fiscal relationships. Secondly, and perhaps of lesser urgency, it must press for some structural reforms of the current fiscal system which promise to result in even greater fiscal harmony and which may also operate to thwart the erosion of the present system.

On the side of structural reform, the most attractive federal strategy is to maneuver the provinces away from source- and origin-based taxation and towards greater, if not exclusive, reliance on residence- and destination-based types of taxes. Because of the scope for fiscal retaliation, the provinces might be persuaded to restrict their tax efforts largely to the personal income and sales tax bases and surrender, with suitable federal compensation possibly in the form of greater revenue sharing, their occupancy of the corporate tax field. Short of this kind of gentlemen's agreement, the federal government could challenge the constitutional basis of provincial profits taxation before the Supreme Court on the technical ground that it fails to meet the requirement of being a "direct tax within the province." It is arguable that in the rural setting of a hundred years ago the fathers of confederation could not have adequately foreseen the growth of multiprovincial companies as an avenue of tax exporting and, if they could have, some restriction on the provincial use of the profits tax base would have been forthcoming. Further steps of reform would include refinement of both the provincial income and sales tax bases so that they would be more in accordance with residence and destination principles. For example, to the extent that the personal income tax strikes unincorporated businesses and the sales tax extends to capital and intermediate goods, they represent imperfect applications of the residence and destination principles, respectively.

An even more compelling case can be construed to have the federal government obstruct or set aside repugnant beggar-thy-province policies which have proliferated in the last few years. Within a short period, provinces have erected a host of nontax barriers to interprovincial trade and factor mobility.[14] These include protectionist government purchas-

14. See Shoup (1977) for a more complete description of these barriers.

ing policies, preferential hiring and occupational licencing policies, and residence requirements for land ownership. This philosophy of provincial autarky has also begun to seep into the design of new and discriminatory tax measures, which herald the replacement of fiscal coordination by a new round of fiscal competition.

The province of Alberta, for instance, withdrew from the tax collection agreements in 1981 and introduced its own corporate tax system. The purpose of the move was to allow "flexible taxation policies, made in Alberta and tailored specifically to strengthen the competitive position of growing Alberta businesses." Alberta's treasurer complained about the lack of flexibility to offer incentives or to levy differential rates of taxation and indicated that under the new system companies are encouraged to move their head offices to Alberta or to have a larger segment of their research, administration, or other activities there. Incentives for Alberta business now encompass selective tax cuts, new deductions, and refundable tax credits.

Other provinces have joined the struggle to capture a larger share of new investment and business activity. In 1979 British Columbia offered a dividend tax credit of 5 percent for B.C. residents receiving dividends from companies with head offices in that province. Quebec in 1979 introduced a stock savings plan allowing a deduction of 20 percent of earned income, up to a ceiling of $15,000, for the purchase of common shares in Quebec-based companies. Ontario has replied with a 30 percent tax credit on equity invested in small business development corporations and has established a special fund of $200 million to create jobs and to assist provincial industries to be more competitive. The treasurer of Ontario emphasized that the province has to offer incentives to industry that are comparable to those provided by other jurisdictions.

Some provinces have also displayed deftness in manipulating their sales tax in a discriminatory fashion. In 1978 the federal government tried to persuade the provinces to join Ottawa in a nationwide reduction in sales taxes as part of the central government's new stabilization program. Quebec refused to comply with the federal appeal and instead abolished sales taxes on selected items whose production was concentrated in the province. This temporary adjustment in exemptions has now become a permanent feature of Quebec's sales tax policy. In Ontario, the center of the automobile industry in Canada, a temporary sales tax exemption on all cars produced in the province was proposed in a recent budget but was later withdrawn when it became challenged in the courts as a trade-restricting measure. Instead, the policy was revised so that purchases of all automobiles, no matter where they were made, were exempt for a six-month period.

It is at least questionable whether the federal government can forestall this recent trend towards fiscal fragmentation. The dire forebodings made by the Rowell-Sirois Commission about the effects of fiscal disorganization in the 1930s may have had to wait forty years to be realized. No matter whether history is repeating itself, there is a worrisome resemblance between the fiscal chaos so lucidly described by the commission in the 1930s and what appears to be happening today.

Some restraint on provincial fiscal behavior, whether imposed from above or negotiated voluntarily, seems necessary. After all, provinces impose fiscal uniformity on their own municipalities and do not allow them to use property tax variations to compete for industry, so, if fiscal competition is undesirable within a province, how can it be desirable between provinces? Either Canada is one country, and there should be some concern with the efficient spatial allocation of resources over that area, or it is not. There is a point beyond which efforts at province-building become nation-wrecking.

References

Ballentine, J. G., and W. R. Thirsk. 1982. *Taxation Without Representation: The Consequences of Taxing Non-residential Property,* pp. 1–77. Ottawa: Canada Mortgage and Housing Corporation.

Boadway, Robin W. 1980. *Intergovernmental Transfers in Canada.* Toronto: Canadian Tax Foundation.

Dosser, D. 1975. "Economic Analysis of Tax Harmonization." In *Fiscal Harmonization in Common Markets,* ed. Carl Shoup, Vol. 1, Ch. 1, pp. 1–144. New York: Columbia University Press.

Johnson, James A. 1974. "The Treatment of Interprovincial Transactions Under the Sales Tax." *1973 Proceedings of the Sixty-sixth Annual Conference on Taxation.* Columbus, Ohio: National Tax Association.

McLure, Charles E., Jr. 1971. "Revenue Sharing: Alternative to Rational Fiscal Federalism." *Public Policy* 19 (Summer): 457–78.

McLure, Charles E., Jr. 1979. "The State Corporation Income Tax: A Lamb in Wolf's Clothing?" In *Essays in Honour of Joseph Pechman,* ed. M. Boskin, Washington, D.C.: Brookings Institution.

Maslove, Allan M. 1972. *The Pattern of Taxation in Canada.* Ottawa: Economic Council of Canada.

Report of the Royal Commission on Dominion-Provincial Relations. 1940. Ottawa: Queen's Printer.

Scott, A. 1952. "Federal Grants and Resource Allocation." *Journal of Political Economy* 60: 534–38.

Shoup, Carl. 1977. "Interregional Economic Barriers: The Canadian Provinces." In *Intergovernmental Relations,* pp. 81–100. Toronto: Ontario Economic Council.

Smith, E. H. 1976. "Allocating to Provinces the Taxable Income of Corpora-
    tions: How the Federal-Provincial Allocation Rules Evolved." *Canadian Tax
    Journal* 23: 543-71.
Thirsk, W. R. 1980. "Tax Harmonization and Its Importance in the Canadian
    Federation." In *Fiscal Dimensions of Canadian Federalism,* ed. Richard M.
    Bird, pp. 118-42. Toronto: Canadian Tax Foundation.

4 *Frederick C. Doolittle*

Federal Grants
for Urban Economic
Development

Introduction

Federal grants to state and local governments have been an important policy tool in efforts to combat poverty in the United States. Currently grants for income security, medicaid, education, training, employment, and social services amount to more than 60 percent of all federal grants.[1] The bulk of these programs has either provided income or in-kind aid to low income people or attempted to increase their job related skills.

In the last few years, much of the efforts of antipoverty advocates have shifted to a new strategy, which might be labelled "urban economic development." Although there is great variety among the proposals which would fall under this label, many have a theme in common; they address the employment problems of low income people by stimulating the demand for labor in low income areas through subsidizing one or more of the costs of doing business there. These urban economic development programs downplay the supply side of the labor market, reasoning that the primary source of employment problems is an insufficient demand for labor in low income areas.

1. In 1980, income security grants, Medicaid, and grants for education, training, employment, and social services totaled nearly $55 billion. See Office of Management and Budget (1979). Estimates for spending in fiscal year 1982 are slightly higher. See Office Management and Budget (1983).

These lobbying efforts have led to a wide variety of federal expenditures. New urban economic development grant programs have been established, for example, the Urban Development Action Grant (UDAG) program, and existing programs such as the Community Development Block Grant program have been changed to encourage economic development projects. The federal government has also offered grants to community-based nonprofit organizations which undertake economic development projects. The strategy has had impacts outside grant programs; Congress at one time considered a major expansion of the Economic Development Administration's loan programs, and SBA loan and loan guarantee programs increased dramatically in the late 1970s and early 1980s.[2] In addition, most states and many local governments now have agencies which issue tax exempt bonds to fund low interest loans for businesses, resulting in tax expenditures by the federal government.[3]

This chapter addresses some of the policy issues raised by this antipoverty strategy and outlines a framework for evaluating these grants. The following section briefly describes the reasons for the recent interest in this antipoverty strategy. Next is a discussion of how these grant programs could in theory be evaluated using a cost-benefit framework. This is followed by a review of the difficulties in actually conducting cost-benefit analyses created by disputes over the proper perspective to adopt in evaluating these programs and the limitations of current theory in addressing some key issues. The next section discusses in some detail the grant review process in the UDAG program, an important example of current evaluation practice. The final section offers suggestions on how this review could be improved.

The Case for Urban Economic Development

Theoretical Arguments

After the War on Poverty, a growing body of program evaluation literature led many to conclude that training programs and other supply-

2. See Office of Management and Budget (1979, Ch. F). E.D.A. outstanding loans rose from about $720 million in FY 1978 to $900 million in FY 1981, while S.B.A. outstanding loans rose from $1.8 billion to $2.6 billion in FY 1981. E.D.A. loan guarantees rose from about $300 million in FY 1978 to $900 million in FY 1981, while S.B.A. guarantees increased from $6.9 billion to $10.3 billion. Reagan administration efforts to cut the programs have resulted in a small drop in outstanding loans and guarantees. See Office of Management and Budget (1983).

3. In spite of changes in the tax laws in 1969 limiting the use of industrial development bonds, the use of tax exempt bonds to finance "urban economic development" programs is common. See Office of Management and Budget (1979, Ch. F) for a brief discussion of the tax revenue lost because of tax exempt state and local bonds. Reagan administration efforts to limit drastically the use of tax exempt bonds have so far proved unsuccessful.

side interventions into the labor market did not promise major increases in the income of low income people, especially minorities. Though several recent reviews of the program evaluation literature argue persuasively there were many success stories,[4] the stigma of failure was already present and liberal support lessened. More radical analysts condemned supply-side employment programs for implicitly "blaming the victims" for their poverty.[5]

During the early 1970s, a new analysis of low income labor markets tried to explain the low payoff to training and high job turnover for low income workers, especially minorities.[6] This dual labor market literature focused on internal labor markets and other demand-side barriers to entry into stable, well-paying jobs.

The continuing suburbanization of jobs and geographic concentration of low income and minority populations in central cities increased their employment problems.[7] A debate arose between those who favored efforts to allow people in need to move to available jobs and those who argued for stimulating employment growth in the central cities.[8] Proponents of decentralized employment argued for vigorous housing programs and a decentralization of low income housing. They argued that reversing long-term trends of job decentralization based on clear cost differences would be difficult and success would lead to inefficient (i.e., higher cost) production methods. They also warned that employment growth in the central cities could well come at the expense of suburban areas and not be an increase in total employment.

Proponents of urban economic development conceded the force of long-term trends, but asserted that lessening housing discrimination would be even more difficult. They also challenged the efficiency of decentralized job growth, arguing that capital market institutions improperly evaluated the risk of projects in low income areas or do not consider the positive externalities of investment in the area.[9] They also argued that decentralization of minority populations would inhibit the development of minority community institutions and prevent minorities from acquiring political power at the local level.

Political Support

Political support for older antipoverty approaches has eroded since the mid-1960s. Efforts by the last three administrations to reform the

---

4. See, for example, Aaron (1978) for a review of the debate.
5. See Gordon (1972) for an example of this approach.
6. The most important early work was Piore and Doeringer (1971).
7. For a recent discussion see Black (1980).
8. An early review of the debate and a presentation of one position is in Edel (1972).
9. See, for example, Daniels and Kieschnick (1979).

welfare system have been unsuccessful in assembling a winning coalition. Proposals to strengthen fair housing legislation rarely garner strong political support.

Urban economic development programs have important political advantages over previous programs. Many perceive them to be a painless way to help the disadvantaged through income *creation* rather than *redistribution*. Economic growth and work–based antipoverty programs still enjoy widespread popular support despite environmental concerns and the apparent decline of the work ethic. Business interest can be expected to the extent the goal of increased employment is pursued through incentives for business rather than sanctions. Individual members of Congress, especially in the House, may see clear opportunities to claim credit for funding economic development projects, while seeing only trouble if they seek to expand welfare or civil rights enforcement.

This combination of academic debate and political reality has shifted attention away from antipoverty efforts based on income maintenance and employment training to urban economic development. These new programs present a number of complex evaluation problems which are the subject of the remainder of this chapter.

Cost Benefit Analysis of an Urban Economic Development Grant

Cost-benefit analysis provides a framework for evaluating a program on efficiency grounds. The central question in cost-benefit analysis is whether the use of scarce resources for the project increases the total resources available to society. In addition, the policy analyst can determine the income distribution effects of the program by identifying who bears the costs and who reaps the benefits.

Cost-benefit analysis is a suitable framework for evaluating urban economic development grants. These grants are intended to create efficiency gains through increased output and employment. They also may redistribute income if the increased production in the central city is not an increase in total production but comes at the expense of other locations.

Cost-benefit analysis of these grants will not yield a clear answer to whether the grant should be undertaken; that decision may only be made by policymakers who can balance efficiency and equity considerations. Cost-benefit analysis can identify the quantifiable costs and benefits, point out the existence of unquantifiable benefits and costs, and analyze the consequences for income redistribution. A value judgment must then be made whether to undertake the program, considering the quantifiable efficiency gains or loses, the likely magnitude of unquantifiable factors, and the income effects.

Undertaking cost-benefit evaluation of an economic development grant involves several steps:

1. *Definition of the relevant population.* In many evaluations the policy analyst adopts a particular perspective and does not consider all the costs or benefits of the project. This choice of perspective is normally made by limiting consideration to those impacts of the program which affect a certain population. Often the relevant population coincides with the citizenry of the political jurisdiction evaluating the grant.

2. *Identification and valuation, if possible, of the costs caused by the grant.* The opportunity-cost concept is key: What other opportunities must be foregone in order to undertake the program? To the extent the program uses resources which were previously unemployed, there is no opportunity cost. The analysis should include only costs actually caused by the offer and acceptance of the grant.

3. *Identification and valuation, if possible, of the benefits caused by the grant.* Given the efficiency focus of the analysis, only those effects which represent an increase in the total of scarce resources available to the relevant population should be counted. The analyst must determine whether an increase in resources for one group cancels out a decrease for another group and thus does not represent a net benefit. Again the analysis should include only benefits actually caused by the grant.

4. *Identification of the income distribution effects caused by the grant.* This information supplements the efficiency analysis, since in many situations political decision makers do not weigh costs and benefits equally for all groups.

5. *Presentation of the information to the policymaker.*

Application of this framework to an urban economic development grant is complicated because the grant has a wide range of possible effects. Working through an example of a typical grant will simplify presentation of the issues.

A Typical Urban Economic Development Grant

City A is a distressed central city with considerable unemployment and some unused manufacturing facilities. Output Inc. contacted City A's economic development department and told the director it was considering building and operating a plant in a low income neighborhood. The firm said that it was also considering several suburban locations. Output Inc. produces a product which is sold in a regional market in competition with other firms in City A and in the surrounding suburban communities. At this time there was virtually no unemployment or unused plant capacity in these suburban communities, though there was vacant land. The economic development director knew that the total costs of operating the plant in a central city location would be higher than in other possible suburban sites, but was not sure if Output Inc. would be able to make a profit without subsidies, even in the suburban areas.

Output assured the city that a large portion of its labor force would be hired from City A residents. Many of the jobs required few skills and would be open to the city's unemployed. The unemployed of City A receive welfare and unemployment insurance, financed through federal taxes.

City A applied for and received a federal grant to help subsidize some of Output's costs of doing business in the central city. The grant allowed the city to acquire and renovate an unused plant and sell it to Output below the market rate. The city also spent some of its own money upgrading streets and sewer facilities adjacent to the plant and agreed to lower property taxes on the site for two years.

Output Inc. moved into the renovated plant, hired a workforce, and began to produce its products. Output hired many of its workers from among the unemployed of City A. Output now has a fairly stable production level; future costs and output are reasonably predictable. It is paying City A property taxes. City planners anticipate that in the future there will be increased maintenance and operating expenses for roads and sewers because of the plant. They also expect the existence of the plant and the increased employment to stabilize the neighborhood surrounding the plant, leading to less crime and vandalism and fewer fires.

The sample grant contains many simplifications. Many of the costs of the program have already been incurred. The project is operating and many of its impacts are outlined. Some key future impacts are identified and can be fairly accurately estimated. Yet the problem of program evaluation is difficult even in this simplified case.

Application of the Cost-Benefit Framework

This section will trace through the wide variety of possible impacts of the grant program and categorize them as likely costs, benefits, or effects that will cancel out. To simplify discussion of the income redistribution effects, people affected by the program are grouped into categories within which the impact is likely to be similar. A societal perspective is adopted here in order to assemble a complete list of effects, including costs and benefits, which arise outside City A. The perspective issue will be addressed later.

Table 4.1 summarizes the likely effects of the program. Possible effects of the grant are listed along the left margin of the table. They are grouped into those that are expected to be costs, benefits, and transfers from a societal perspective. The column labeled "society" summarizes the net societal impact and contains zeroes designating transfers in which benefits to one group are canceled out by costs for another. Groups potentially affected by the grant are listed across the top of the chart. Entries in the matrix indicate whether the effects are clearly costs ($-$), clearly benefits ($+$), possibly costs ($-?$), or possibly benefits ($+?$).

Societal Costs of the Program.—Some of the costs of the grant program are incurred at the beginning of the project. The federal government offers the grant which finances some of the set-up expenses. The local government improves the streets and sewage system serving the project. These expenses will be listed in government budgets. Output Inc. also incurs start-up expenses, but this analysis should consider only those in excess of what it would have spent without the grant.

Not all of these expenses are real resource costs of the project. To the extent the resources used on the project were previously unemployed, the expenses do not represent real opportunity costs. No other activity must be sacrificed to undertake that part of the project. The money spent on the unemployed resources should be deducted from the expense to show real resource costs. Alternatively, these employment gains might be seen as benefits of the project. Either way the result is the same: the net costs are lowered.

Not all costs of the project are incurred immediately. Local government services are expected to increase because of the project, and Output will incur operating expenses over time. To the extent this represents an increase over the level would have occurred had Output Inc. made its production and location decisions without the grant, these are costs of the grant program. Again, to the extent unemployed resources are used to produce the local government service increase and the firm's output, there are no real opportunity costs. Since these costs occur in the future, their present value at the time the project begins should be used.

Other costs may fall on nonparticipants in the grant program. Some firms and residents may have to relocate because of Output's plant. If they are compensated by the federal government, the costs are borne by federal taxpayers, but otherwise those who move will bear the costs. Residents in City A may also suffer increases in pollution and congestion.

Societal Benefits of the Grant.—One of the major benefits which could arise from the grant program would be an increase in total produc-

Table 4.1. Cost-Benefit Summary

Possible Effects	Society	National Taxpayers	Jurisdiction A		
			Citizens as Taxpayers	Citizens as Service Recipients	Participating Firm
Costs					
Grant	−?	−			
Local gov't. subsidy	−?		−		
Private firm start-up	−?				−
Local gov't. service increase	−?		−		
Firm operating expense	−?				−
Relocation	−			−	
Increase in pollution, congestion, etc.	−			−	
Benefits					
Increase in output	+?				+
Less crime, fire, etc.	+?		+	+	
More neighborhood confidence, etc.	+?			+	
Other					
Decrease in welfare, UIB payments	0	+	+		
Tax abatement	0		−		+
Change in local tax revenue	0		−	+	
Increase in federal taxes paid in jurisdiction A	0	+	−		
Decrease in federal taxes paid elsewhere	0	−?			

− clearly costs
+ clearly benefits
−? possibly costs
+? possibly benefits
0 transfers from a societal perspective

	Jurisdiction A			Other Surrounding Jurisdictions		
Other Firms	Previously Unemployed Labor	Previously Unemployed Capital	Citizens as Taxpayers	Citizens as Service Recipients	Newly Unemployed Labor	Newly Unemployed Capital
	+	+				
	+	+				
	+	+				
	+?	+?				
	+	+?				
−	+?	+?				
−						
−?					−?	−?
+			−	−		
				−?		
	−		+			
			+?	−?		
			+?			

tion. Output's production is apparently higher than it would have been without the grant. However, this increase may be cancelled out by decreases for Output's competitors within City A and in the surrounding communities. It might also be cancelled out by decreases for producers of products which are close substitutes.

Other benefits might accrue to residents of City A. The plant might actually stabilize the neighborhood, leading to an increase in neighborhood confidence and pride and a decrease in vandalism, fires, and crime. If Output's production led to a cut in production in other firms, the neighborhood surrounding these firms might suffer a decline which would partly or completely cancel out these benefits.

Other Effects.—A number of other commonly mentioned impacts of urban economic development grants are not costs or benefits from a societal perspective. Decreases in welfare and unemployment benefits are not societal benefits, since no new resources are created. The decreases merely mean that one group—taxpayers—are able to retain control over resources which would otherwise be transferred to the unemployed in City A. Changes in the tax base should not be counted as benefits, since the increases in property values would arise because of the increase in production or services which could be derived from property. These increases are counted directly and, including the increase in tax base, would be double counting.

Increases in revenues from local, state, and federal taxes are also often counted as "benefits," but within a cost-benefit framework they are really transfers. Collection of taxes does not create new resources; it means a shift in the control of existing resources. It is important to consider tax revenue increases when evaluating the income distribution effects of the project, but they are not efficiency gains. Similarly, the tax abatement offered by the city as part of the subsidy package is not a real resource cost. The abatement means that fewer resources (i.e., taxes) will be transferred from Output Inc. to the city government.

This section used a cost-benefit framework to examine a number of possible impacts of an urban economic development grant. The analysis is far from clear-cut. There are several different ways in which impacts can be counted, for example, employment gains can be seen as a benefit or a decrease in costs. The magnitude of many effects is still unclear. Despite these difficulties, cost-benefit analysis does focus on what should be central questions in evaluation of this type of program: What are the efficiency gains and income redistribution effects? The following section discusses three important problems which arise in practice in evaluating this type of grant.

Problems in Applying the Cost Benefit Framework
The Perspective of the Evaluation

In most urban economic development grant projects, the choice of perspective will matter. In our typical grant, for example, different definitions of the relevant population lead to very different tabulations of costs and benefits. If the population of City A is chosen as the relevant one, the societal cost of the grant is ignored, since it is not a cost to the city. Because the grant would be available only for the specified project, there are no alternative uses of the funds from a city perspective and thus no opportunity cost.

With urban economic development grants, tracing through the possible impacts of the grant suggests that the very process which generates the benefits may also generate costs outside City A. The employment and output increase in City A may be partly cancelled out by a decrease elsewhere because of declines in sales by the subsidized firm's competitors. This is ironic, since one of the normal justifications for categorical grants is to encourage activities which generate external benefits (Break 1980, Ch. 3). These costs will be ignored if City A's perspective is adopted.

The decision by City A and the participating firm to apply for and accept the grant and to proceed with the project constitutes an implicit, favorable cost-benefit analysis from two perspectives. The firm has decided that acceptance of the grant will improve its profit position over its operations without the grant. The city has also implicitly decided the grant improves some politically relevant measure of welfare. Should a third perspective be substituted as proper in the evaluation of these programs?

A strong affirmative case can be made. Resources from outside the participating city are being devoted to the program, partly because of a desire to increase the income of City A's disadvantaged residents. Program support comes also from a belief that this increase in income can be accomplished by stimulating growth in the city which does not come at the expense of others—an efficiency rationale. If income redistribution were the sole societal goal of the program, adopting City A's perspective might be appropriate. Addition of the goal of increasing total employment/output makes the national perspective more appropriate.

Causation in the Grant Program

Many of the societal costs and benefits of the grant in our example are uncertain, and part of the reason is uncertainty about the impact of the grant-funded subsidy on the behavior of the participating firm. It is unclear whether Output would have been able to operate a profitable business without the subsidy. It is also unclear if the subsidy actually influenced the location of the plant and how much the grant increased Output's production. Output might have chosen the site, despite its higher current costs, because the firm was optimistic about economies of agglomeration because of proximity to other related firms or anticipated future market advantages from the location.

This uncertainty is common in practice. Cities which negotiate agreements with developers often do not know what the firm would do in the absence of the grant. The firm has incentives to provide selective information supporting its request for the subsidy, and the city may not have the skilled personnel or resources to investigate independently.

Social science research has also been unsuccessful in predicting industrial location, though some generalizations do emerge from the research.[10] Research on plant location using both survey techniques and large data sets seems to indicate that many of the elements of common economic development agreements do not influence location decisions. Local taxes are a prominent example. Demand-side market factors and the availability of labor seem to be much more important. Some factors within the control of city governments are potentially important; the ability to expand a facility and predictability in the development process are sometimes cited as important in survey research.

It may be that the impact of factors which make up common subsidy agreements can influence location more than what is suggested by the research. The experience of many people in the economic development field is that firms often quickly narrow down possible locations to a relatively short list. They then collect more detailed information on this short list of sites and often may encourage, or at least take advantage of, competing subsidy offers. This search behavior is consistent with optimizing behavior with limited information under certain conditions and is also consistent with satisfying models of search (Richardson 1979, pp. 65–70). Urban economic development subsidies may be relatively ineffective at getting a city onto the short list but may be able to reorder the short list.[11] The short list is probably chosen with demand-side factors and raw material requirements in mind, and cities on this list may be similar on these grounds. The subsidies could then make a difference.

Though this general location model has some theoretical support and is consistent with the observations of economic development practitioners, it still does not answer the tricky questions of causation which must be sorted out before the costs and benefits *caused by the grant* can be tabulated with certainty. The firm might have done nearly the same thing

10. For a recent review of the literature see Richardson (1979, Ch. 3) or Carlton (1979).
11. For a related argument see Mulkey and Dillman (1976).

without the grant. If so, the externalities connected with its operations, costs of start-up and operation, and much of the employment gain and output increase would have occurred without the grant.

Employment Growth versus Shifting

Growth in employment is one of the goals of urban economic development grants. Achievement of this will be prevented if gains in participating firms are offset by decreases elsewhere. Ideally, the policy analyst could draw on models of metropolitan economies to consider the effects of the injection of capital (i.e., the grant) on the performance of other factors in the metropolitan economy. In fact, such models do not exist and are not likely to be developed soon.

Several types of regional economic models are commonly used.[12] Some focus on macroeconomic demand in the region and are closely related to Keynesian models at the national level. Others are neoclassical models of growth, which emphasize supply side factors more. None of the models really addresses the questions which arise in grant evaluation.

The demand-side models require vast data sets to be operational, which are not available at the regional level or below. They do not have spatial detail and do not predict impacts at particular points within a region. The neoclassical models do seem more appropriate for addressing the impact of increases in the supply of capital, but they also are not available for areas below the metropolitan level.

The available research results do not make one expect large net gains in employment. Demand-side theories suggest low multipliers for the increase in aggregate demand because of the grant, since the metropolitan economy is so open and much of the money would be spent outside the local economy. If the grant leads to an increase in the export base, more employment might be predicted. Engle's neoclassical model of the Boston metropolitan area suggests that an exogenous increase in investment would lead to a short-run increase in income and employment followed by a decline (Engle 1979). Engle notes that the result reflects the inelastic nature of the demand for Boston's exports, which is not typical of most of the cities he has studied. This result seems intrinsically related to the impact of grants; subsidizing capital should lead to some output gain but also to a longer term shift to more capital intensive production.

Grant Evaluation in the UDAG Program

Program administrators cannot be paralyzed by the theoretical confusion just discussed; they must evaluate grant proposals and allocate

12. For a review see Richardson (1979, Ch. 4–8).

their limited funds. Comparing actual program review with the ideal will illustrate how administrators cope with limited information and theory and may lead to suggestions for improvement of current practice.

The UDAG program, administered by HUD, operates much like the typical grant program described above.[13] "Distressed" cities or cities with "pockets of poverty" may apply for federal grants to support discrete projects for economic development and neighborhood revitalization. Grants may be used for many of the permitted purposes under the Community Development Block Grant program and for housing. Some urban governments are eligible to apply for grants based on their physical and economic distress as measured by age of housing, per capita income, population growth, unemployment, job growth, and poverty. Small cities and cities with "pockets of poverty" must meet slightly different criteria.

If eligible, a government may apply for a UDAG. The application must describe local problems and planning to combat them and discuss the part the UDAG would play. It also must include an analysis of project feasibility, including information on the developer, site, administration, and financing.

Current Evaluation Practice

The application and review process also addresses some of the issues discussed above.

Causation. The applicant must provide "convincing evidence" that an Action grant is needed for the project to proceed.

Job growth. The applicant must list the expected number of low, middle, and upper income jobs likely to be created by the project, distinguishing between permanent and temporary, and subsidized and unsubsidized. The applicant must also predict the likely increase in dollar volume in sales "in the community" and must normally guarantee that the grant is not being used to finance the relocation of a plant *from outside the metropolitan area.* If a firm is moving from another nearby jurisdiction, the application must include a statement by the chief official of the affected jurisdiction describing the effect of the loss.

Targeting on the disadvantaged. The eligibility rules do target aid somewhat, though the pockets-of-poverty amendment may lessen this targeting. The application requires information on disadvantaged groups affected by the project and an employment plan to assure jobs created by the project will go to the unemployed.

13. The UDAG program was passed in 1977 and operates under regulations at 24 CFR section 570. Reagan administration budgets have lowered budget authority for the program, but it has continued to operate.

Subsidizing inefficient production. The application requires calculation of a leverage ratio, which is a very crude measure of the relative inefficiency of production. This leverage ratio is the ratio of private funds to the Action grant.

Problems and Suggestions

The UDAG review process does address many of the issues which would be examined in an ideal cost-benefit evaluation, but there is room for improvement on several counts.

Perspective adopted in the review. The UDAG review seems to adopt an odd mixture of perspectives. It considers the cost of the grant a societal cost, and worries to some extent about output and employment expansion and income redistribution within the participating community. It ignores for the most part costs imposed on surrounding communities and possible external benefits and income redistributions. If a societal perspective is appropriate, the review should not ignore a part of society likely to be affected.

Causation. The review takes a direct approach requiring an assurance of the necessity of the grant. The assurance however is a limited one—that this particular project would not be possible without the grant. The applicant is not required to provide evidence that a similar but unsubsidized project would not occur elsewhere in the absence of the grant.

The existing review seems too willing to accept job shifting in order to redistribute jobs to the disadvantaged in eligible cities. If other alternative sites are being considered, the grant evaluators could make a more informed decision on the job/income redistribution with some background information on the alternate sites. It may well be difficult to enforce a requirements that cities describe possible alternate sites and projects, but any information which does emerge would be useful.

Job growth. HUD's claims about the success of the program in creating jobs make the assumptions that no smaller project would have been built without the grant and no jobs elsewhere were lost because of the grant. The first assumption really relates to the causation problem addressed above, but the second might be investigated indirectly.

The review process could require that the applicant describe the likely competitors of the project within the applicant's area and in surrounding communities. The applicant could be required to provide basic data about nearby employment in related industries and explain briefly how this project would appeal to customers different from these existing suppliers. The required feasibility analysis does not necessarily serve the same function; the project might be feasible because it can capture a large part of the existing market. The A-95 review process might also be strengthened here. In many situations regional-planning-commission reviews are rather cursory, and jurisdictions often avoid criticizing others' proposals in the hope that their own proposals will receive similar treatment. HUD might make it mandatory that jurisdictions with competing firms provide comments on the project in the application or that the A-95 comments address the issue.

Grant evaluators should also consider the type of project and the likelihood that it will bring outside dollars into the regional or metropolitan economy. As an example, hotel facilities catering to the national convention market or specialized manufacturing might draw many more outside dollars than retail projects.

Subsidizing inefficient production. Some type of "leverage ratio" makes considerable sense. When costs and benefits of production are internalized at all alternate sites and no other subsidies are present, then the percent of total costs covered by the grant is a measure of the relative inefficiency of the UDAG site.

The leverage ratio currently used by HUD—private funds divided by grant—has a confusing meaning. Since other forms of subsidy are allowed and encouraged in the UDAG program, the current leverage ratio does not measure the proportion of costs subsidized. A much better measure would be total costs divided by subsidies, or even total costs divided by UDAG grant.

Conclusion

Evaluators of urban economic development grant programs face a difficult problem. They must evaluate a grant having efficiency and equity goals and complicated, poorly understood impacts. Social science theory does not answer many key questions, and data are limited. The choice of a proper perspective for the evaluation is controversial. Cost-benefit analysis provides a useful framework for organizing the available information, but the limits of data and theory require a less complete review, as the UDAG review process illustrates. Comparison of UDAG-program review with the ideal analysis leads to several practical suggestions for improvement.

References

Aaron, Henry. 1978. *Politics and the Professors.* Washington, D.C.: Brookings Institution.

Black, Thomas. 1980. "The Changing Economic Role of Central Cities and Suburbs." In *The Prospective City,* ed. Arthur Solomon, pp. 80–123. Cambridge, Mass.: MIT Press.

Break, George. 1980. *Financing Government in a Federal System.* Washington, D.C.: Brookings Institution.

Carlton, Dennis. 1979. "Why Do Firms Locate Where They Do: An Economic Model." In *Interregional Movements and Regional Growth,* ed. William Wheaton, pp. 13–50. Washington, D.C.: The Urban Institute.

Daniels, Belden, and Michael Kieschnick. 1979. *Development Finance, A Primer for Policy Makers.* Cambridge, Mass.: Harvard Department of City and Regional Planning.

Edel, Mathew, 1972. "Development vs. Dispersal: Approaches to Ghetto Poverty." In *Readings in Urban Economics,* ed. Mathew Edel and Jerome Rothenberg, pp. 307–25. New York: Macmillan.

Engle, Robert. 1979. "The Regional Response to Factor Supplies: Estimates for the Boston SMSA." In *Interregional Movements and Regional Growth,* ed. William Wheaton, pp. 157–96. Washington, D.C.: The Urban Institute.

Gordon, David. 1972. *Theories of Poverty and Underemployment.* Lexington, Mass.: Lexington Books.

Mulkey, David, and B. L. Dillman. 1976. "Locational Effects of State and Local Industries Development Subsidies." *Growth and Change* 7 (April): 37–43.

Office of Management and Budget. 1979. *Special Analyses Budget of the United States Government, Fiscal Year 1980.* Washington, D.C.: U.S. Government Printing Office.

Office of Management and Budget. 1983. *Special Analysis Budget of the United States Government, Fiscal Year 1984.* Washington, D.C.: U.S. Government Printing Office.

Piore, Michael, and Peter Doeringer. 1971. *Internal Labor Markets and Manpower Analysis.* Lexington, Mass.: Lexington Books.

Richardson, Harry. 1979. *Regional Economics.* Urbana, Ill.: University of Illinois Press.

5 *Richard P. Nathan*

Research Issues in the Evaluation of Broad-Gauged and Multipurpose Grants-in-Aid

For the past eight years, a group of policy analysts at the Brookings Institution and the Woodrow Wilson School of Princeton University have been conducting field network evaluation studies of three major federal grant programs—general revenue sharing, community development block grants, and the public service employment component of CETA. All three are broad-gauged, multipurpose grants which distribute large amounts of money to hundreds, in some cases thousands, of state and local government jurisdictions. In the dynamic, pluralistic setting of contemporary American federalism, the job of obtaining systematic information about the uses and effects of these fiscal subventions is both important to policymakers and challenging to policy researchers. In addition to these three major studies of individual programs, we are also preparing a set of twelve uniformly organized case studies, showing how all types of federal grants have affected major cities included in the Brookings-Princeton field network.

Many publications are available on the methods and findings of this research.[1] For each of the three field network studies, we have issued two

This chapter was prepared for the Committee on Taxation, Resources, and Economic Development, September 26, 1980, Cambridge, Massachusetts. The views expressed are the sole responsibility of the author.

1. See the references provided at the end of this chapter for a list of some of these pub-

93

books or reports, articles, and congressional testimony. The findings from these studies have contributed to the policy discussion of federal grant-in-aid issues and programs. This chapter discusses some of the lessons learned and implications of the research.

Evaluating the New Federalism

American domestic policy is made in spurts. The spigot is opened widest in the early years of a new administration. A classic case is the outpouring of new social legislation following Lyndon Johnson's election in 1964. A similar spurt of new domestic laws came in the first term of the Nixon administration.

It is now commonplace for observers of the Great Society period to say that these programs failed to deal with the nation's social ills. Indeed, I believe, but can't document, that the role of social scientists in the Great Society period focused too much on policy formulation and not enough on the evaluation of programs once they were adopted.

I was a participant in the spurt of domestic policy making in President Nixon's first term. When I returned to the Brookings Institution in 1974, I decided to work on the evaluation of these New Federalism programs. My attitude was that if they fell apart or worked badly, at least these conclusions would be reached with the input of systematic information from social scientists.

How can a participant in the policy process (presumably a person committed to what came out) evaluate the results? I would answer in several ways. One response is that social scientists should be serious about the second word of the title—science—and should exercise objectivity in conducting evaluation research. Second, I would point out that our studies, as it turned out, involved many participants (approximately thirty economists and political scientists from around the country for each study). Even the most extraordinary research manager would have been hard put to insert a bias deliberately into the findings of the thirty social scientists who were part of these field networks.

The third reason I felt comfortable, at least personally, in the role of evaluating programs I had helped design has to do with the way the evaluation research industry operates. Many flowers bloom. Other studies

lications. Since this essay was presented, a fourth field network evaluation study has been undertaken of the effects of the budget cuts and related changes in domestic policy made under the Reagan administration. The first publication on this study is *Reductions in U.S. Domestic Spending, How They Affect State and Local Governments,* edited by John W. Ellwood (1982). The study is similar to those described in this chapter. The sample includes fourteen state governments and forty local jurisdictions.

give users an opportunity to compare and cross check results. The existence of multiple studies, while sometimes excessive, helps to keep the evaluation industry honest and aboveboard.

Once it has been decided to conduct evaluation studies of the New Federalism programs, the question—a very hard one—was raised: How should this be done? The New Federalism programs, as is true of many federal grants which existed prior to the New Federalism, have qualities that make them exceedingly difficult to evaluate.

The purposes of these programs are not always clear, a characteristic typical of American intergovernmental subventions. On the whole, the New Federalism involved broader and less conditional grants than the "categorical" grants of prior periods. This approach was designed to increase the recipient government's flexibility and opportunity for discretionary action. This was the *decentralization* aim of the New Federalism.

But other goals entered the picture. The more goals there are, the more difficult it is to say what a given program is supposed to do and to evaluate whether it actually does what it is supposed to do. Was general revenue sharing supposed to enable recipient governments to cut taxes? Was it supposed to equalize aid among jurisdictions? Was it supposed to spur innovation?

The problem of competing goals is even more pronounced with the block-grant components of the New Federalism. The community development block-grant program is an example. Was decentralization its principal purpose? Was it supposed to aid the poor, the downtowns, the uptowns, the suburbs, the construction industry? Was it, as the law stated, supposed to give priority to achieving "spatial deconcentration"?

The goals are not only broad but frequently shifting, which presents both a problem and an opportunity. The problem is deciding what to evaluate. The opportunity is that, in such a setting, evaluators can evaluate whatever they want. Hence there is always the opportunity, often subtle and not recognized as such, for the evaluator—or worse yet, the government agency paying his or her bills—to set up the design in a way that biases the research.

But this is by no means the only obstacle to the evaluation of broad-gauged, multipurpose subventions. There is also the problem of "universality." Every jurisdiction with certain specified statistical characteristics receives a grant under these programs. There is no opportunity to select a comparison group of similar jurisdictions to determine the difference a grant has made.

The very nature of our intergovernmental system causes further difficulties. So many different jurisdictions receive revenue sharing and block grants that the "treatment" (that is to say, what recipients do with the money) is highly varied.

Another barrier to evaluation research on federal grants warrants mention. The grants themselves are often relatively small—that is, small in proportion to what state and local governments spend in the aided functional area. We are often looking at a thin margin of federal aid. This, too, complicates our task.

There is, finally, the issue of "contamination," which applies in this case to the individual recipients of service under grant-in-aid programs. Here, the problem is the possibility that a supposedly unaided control or comparison group of individual recipients under a given program was aided under a different but similar program. Let me illustrate with the CETA programs. Efforts have been made, for example, using Current Population Survey data, to construct not a control but a comparison group of persons eligible for various CETA-funded employment and training services. But how do we know that the persons in these groups were not aided under another program just like, or very similar to, the CETA program? There are a number of similar programs that help low income persons through local job-creation, training, and special school programs.

We have, then, five problems. First, the grant-in-aid programs have multiple and sometimes conflicting objectives, and it is not easy to decide what to evaluate. Second, we cannot study control jurisdictions because under formula systems all similarly situated jurisdictions receive funds. Third is the problem of pluralism: different governments use federal aid in very different ways. Fourth is the problem of marginality: federal grants often are small proportionate to the total amount spent for the aided functional area of the program. Fifth is the contamination problem, which makes it difficult, even with great ingenuity, to obtain or construct an unaided comparison group of individual program recipients.

There are other complications, too, but I think this list is long enough. In this diverse and constantly changing political and administrative environment, how does the social scientist get a handle on whether "grant A" brings about different results from "grant B" or from no grant at all?

Since entering this area of research, I have been approached by various certified experts on research design with patented remedies to overcome these problems and others. Consider one example: What can be done, I am told, is to recognize all of this messiness and instead of evaluating "programs" evaluate "projects." That is, go out and find jurisdictions that do the same things under a particular grant and compare them to jurisdictions that do different things under the same grant program. I am not sure why anyone would want to do this, but one thing I do know is that, while it may sound nice in a textbook, it would be exceedingly difficult to execute in the field.

Words are just that—words. Recipient jurisdictions draw up elaborate plans to satisfy federal officials. But what goes on in a program can be very different from what is on paper. Even if a jurisdiction says it is going to do "A," it may in fact do "B," or it may shift to "B" midway through the program. What looks even semi-orderly from Washington or the regional office, we have learned from hard experience is frequently a very different animal out in the corral.

Despite these problems, if social science is to be "relevant," we have to go after the hard questions that are important to policymakers. Does it make a difference that we now have revenue sharing, that the grant system was changed to provide block grants for community development or employment and training services, or whatever?

It is not easy, furthermore, to define "making a difference." Are we interested in whether "grant A" changed the way the recipient governmental jurisdictions do their business or whether it changed the business they do? Or should we focus on whether "grant A" made a difference to the man or woman who got a public service job, or to the homeowner who got a housing rehab loan under the community development block grant, or to the taxpayer who felt better because the general revenue sharing program cut his property tax bill?

The Tools of Social Science

Social scientists have three major types of tools for evaluating grant programs. First are statistical and mathematical techniques. With these we can construct models of how the world would look without "grant A." We can then say something about how the real world—the world *with* "grant A"—compares to the model. But the available statistics are weak and limited. They are collected infrequently. Often they are not available for the units of analysis we want to work with. And the regression techniques applied involve many definitions that require assumptions, which, to say the least, are very difficult to make and often are not sufficiently well understood or accepted by the users of a program evaluation study.

The second tool is survey instruments. We can go out and ask people: Did "grant A" make a difference? But whom do we ask and how do we ask them? Suppose we ask officials of the recipient governments. Shouldn't we expect the respondents to give us back chapter and verse of

what the law says, or what they think we want to hear, or what they want
to tell us (whether true or not)? What if we go out and ask the final recipients: What do you think of CDBG or CETA? No matter how we spell
it, the man in the rehab house or the woman in a CETA job is often
unlikely to have the foggiest idea of what we are talking about.

The third instrument available is the case-study approach. We can
have smart people look closely at specific cases. But no matter how smart
a person is, he or she can study only so many cases. And if different
people study different cases, they are likely to do so in different ways. So
we don't have comparability.

To recapitulate, we have now looked at problems in evaluating multipurpose formula grants-in-aid that distribute funds widely. We have
looked briefly at the instruments that can be used to evaluate these grants
and the kinds of problems involved in using the three types of instruments. It has also been asserted that the game is worth the candle—that
policymakers want to have and need to have answers to the question of
whether a given program has made a difference, and, if so, what kind of
difference.

Field Network Evaluation Research

The emphasis of our research has been on the intergovernmental effects of New Federalism and other broad-gauged grants—that is, their
effects on the recipient governmental jurisdictions. Our orientation is
both *analytical* and *descriptive*. We are interested in the effects of large
and important grant programs in three main areas: (1) the finances of the
recipient jurisdictions; (2) the program mix and program content of the
aided activities; and (3) the political processes and system for determining their allocation and specific program use.

Our view from the outset has been that formal survey research is not a
good instrument for evaluating these types of effects of grant programs.
It is our view, furthermore, that the other two approaches mentioned—
econometric and case studies—work best if they are used together. This
is the essence of the approach urged in this chapter. It is the idea of the
"complementarity" of the econometric and case-study research methods. We have used such a tandem approach in one of our studies, the
general revenue sharing study (Adams and Crippen, 1978). We are currently in the process of using this dual approach in another, the study of
the CETA public service jobs program. I know of several other cases
where parallel studies, using both the econometric and field network
approach, are underway.

Note that in the last sentence, I changed the term from "case studies"
to "field network approach." There is a difference.

The way we have adapted the case-study approach at Brookings and Princeton is not unique, but it is noteworthy, because we have used this approach on an extensive scale. What we have done is build networks of indigenous field researchers along with a central management group to work with the researchers so that they use a common approach to a common set of questions. The field researchers (called "associates") *do* the analysis. They make *their* assessments of the effects of a given grant. The central group then compiles these assessments, with the close involvement of the field associates, into a report that cuts across a representative sample of recipient jurisdictions.

Two points in the above paragraph need to be elaborated. First, I used the word "effects" in referring to what is studied. The term is important. Because the objectives of grant programs, especially broad-gauged programs, are diverse, frequently shifting, and sometimes inconsistent, we cannot in a precise way define the aims of a particular program. Instead, we have concentrated on studying their effects. The second point introduced in the paragraph above has to do with the samples used for these studies. We have chosen "representative" samples. These samples of forty to sixty recipient jurisdictions are much larger than can be included using the comparative case-study approach. They are not random samples.

The main reasons for using representative samples have to do with cost and logistics. To have a manageable research group, in many cases we need to ask an associate to report on more than one field site. In addition, in order to make sure that the associates are familiar with the field sites and have good access to the best sources of data about them, we have often organized the field sites in clusters. Such a cluster might, for example, include three or four rural jurisdictions close to a university research center, a central city and one or two of its suburban jurisdictions, or a state capital and a nearby small city. It would not be possible to do this with a random sample.

If the research design for one of the field network evaluation studies had focused on a dominant governmental type, we might have been able to use a random sample. Our experience suggests that locating competent field researchers on this basis would be possible if such a study focused on large governmental jurisdictions, for example, cities above 50,000 population. The trade off here is between a random sample focused on one jurisdictional type and a larger stratified sample that permits researchers to compare various types and groups of recipient jurisdictions —central cities and suburbs, large cities and small ones, cities and counties, rich and poor communities.

Yet, even a random sample of the larger units—for example, a sample of 1,072 cities and counties above 50,000 population—would fail to take adequately into account the layering of some of these units (cities within counties and the functions of state governments and various special districts, township governments, and small municipal governments). In the combined field and statistical study of the general revenue sharing program cited earlier, Charles F. Adams, Jr. and Dan Crippen conducted an econometric analysis of the fiscal impact of revenue sharing using a sample of 1,424 local units. They compared these findings with those from the field network research and found a close fit between the results under the two studies. The size of their statistical sample was determined by the availability of time-series data from the Bureau of the Census. We could have used a smaller random sample of local units, but it still would have been too large in relation to the resources available for a monitoring study. Not everyone will agree, but I believe that local governmental units in America are too diverse and too numerous to warrant using a random sample in a field network evaluation study of the intergovernmental effects of major federal grant programs.

Field network research is longitudinal. We have made three rounds of field observations on revenue sharing. There will be four each for the CDBG and CETA job studies. Although the basic research design has not changed, we have changed the emphasis of our reports on these programs to reflect current issues and the specific stage of a particular program—just starting, changing, or resulting in actual expenditures. For example, in the CDBG study, the first report concentrated on what was being planned and how it was being planned; the second report concentrated on whether the program had a decentralization effect; the third report concentrated on whether CDBG funds were being "targeted" at the poor within jurisdictions; the fourth report will emphasize how CDBG money actually has been spent, that is, program implementation.

Associates in a field network study submit a completed field research "Reporting Format" for each round of field research. These reports include extensive specific data which associates use to reach and justify their analytical findings.[2]

Impact Issues

From a methodological point of view, the most interesting issues we have dealt with in the field network evaluation studies are *impact* issues: Did jurisdictions that received revenue sharing money spend more, or did they substitute these funds for locally raised money they would have spent anyway and cut back their own revenue? Did the CETA jobs pro-

2. Analytical findings and the supporting data are reviewed with the central staff; however, as noted earlier, a field associate's analytical findings are not changed without the associate's involvement and concurrence.

gram result in the creation of new jobs, or did it result in displacement—
that is, the substitution of CETA funds for funds that would have been
paid to workers who would have been hired anyway?

These are tough yet very important questions. They have been studied
with both the field network and econometric approaches. In our research, these issues are being studied with the two approaches married to
each other. May they live happily together.

Synthesis

Think of it this way. In evaluating a program that is operating every-
where, we must find a way to study the counterfactual state. We need to
determine what the world would be like if the program were not operating. There are two ways to do this: the econometric approach and the
field network approach. Both approaches build a model of what would
have happened if the program did not exist, then they compare that
model to the real world in which the program does exist. The econometric approach does this modeling in a computer with a system of equations. In constructing these equations, the researcher must make judgments about economic conditions, program conditions, administrative
structures, etc. The field research associate in a field network study does
this modeling in his head, also making many assumptions. The field researcher can use more variables and can define and manipulate them in
more ways. The human brain is a powerful instrument. But there is a
catch. The computer model can be replicated. The process (no matter
how bad it is) can be specified for other researchers to review. Although
I believe the human equations can deal more effectively with the tre-
mendous diversity and complexity of American federalism, they cannot
be specified in replicable form. So what should we do? *We should do
both.*

We should do field network evaluation studies, for one thing, because
they can be conducted while a new program gets underway. Field researchers can begin when a new program is started, whereas the statistics
needed for econometric modeling often lag years behind the starting date
of a new program.

There is, however, a more important reason for doing both. We
should do both, because they can *reinforce* each other. Information and
insights gained from a field network evaluation study can be used to
develop and refine the equations for manipulating the program and
census data that go into an econometric evaluation of the impact of a
particular grant-in-aid program. With the aid of field network research,
it can produce better and more refined answers than econometric research by itself.

Why Do Evaluation Research?

There are two more issues I want to deal with in this chapter. Why should we do grant-in-aid evaluations? If we do them, how should they be organized and funded?

On the first issue, useful lessons can be learned by comparing practices in different countries. In a study recently initiated by the Woodrow Wilson School on comparative policy research, we have found that evaluation research is much less common and much less public in Europe than in the United States. When such studies are done in European countries, they are often done for internal use by agency officials, who hold the results closely.

By contrast, the combined effect of the existence of privately funded evaluations in the United States, plus the Freedom of Information Act applying to publicly funded studies, produces a veritable cacophony of commentary on the merits and demerits of public programs. Some observers believe we have too much evaluation research in the United States and that, in some situations, this impairs our ability to get things done in the domestic public sector.

My view as a practitioner in the field of program evaluation is the one you would expect. I do not think there are enough thoughtful studies by social scientists who do their best to deal with what is described in this chapter as the kinds of obstacles that must be overcome in sensibly evaluating the effects of intergovernmental grant-in-aid programs in the fluid environment of American federalism. It may not be orderly or beautiful to behold, but the pluralism of our political system is a fact to be reckoned with. If everybody can play government and there are lots of levels and players, then we had better do as much as we can to provide systematic, well-developed information about the effects of intergovernmental programs and actions.

A Proposal for the Joint Sponsorship of Some Evaluation Studies

This brings me to the final subject of this chapter: Who should do evaluation studies? One of our field network studies (the general revenue sharing study) was funded by the Ford Foundation. The other two, plus the twelve-city case-study research, have been funded by U.S. government agencies. We have had good relations with the government agencies that have funded our studies. This has happened in no small part because, in keeping with Brookings policy, we have insisted on explicit language in our contracts, which gives us independence in designing and executing these studies and in presenting and interpreting our findings.

Despite our good experience with these contract provisions, and taking into account the experience of other evaluation researchers, I believe that consideration should be given to alternate ways of organizing and conducting some government-funded evaluation studies.

The evaluation of multibillion-dollar government programs is expensive. The result often is that the only funding source big enough and interested enough to pay for an evaluation study is the government agency responsible for administering the program to be evaluated. And, to phrase a point badly, their interest is not always disinterest. No matter how scholarly the research managers in a given agency may be (and some have very high standards), bias can enter, or be thought to have entered, the relationship between agencies that sponsor and fund research on their own programs and the evaluation researchers who conduct such studies. This can happen in many ways that are not easily recognized or dealt with.

These difficulties are made more serious by the fact that in recent years we have seen the growth of large contract-research houses. They have to think about the future—a future in which they continue to get contracts.

If we add back into this picture the problems and issues discussed earlier that have to be dealt with in doing evaluation research on broad-gauged, multipurpose grant programs, what we have is a situation in which problems relating to the design and execution of evaluation studies may arise, even with the best of intentions.

There are, I believe, relatively simple administrative devices that could be adopted to avoid these problems. I can envision a system in which a government agency in a neutral position would play an intermediary role in contracting for certain evaluation studies. A good candidate for this role would be the National Science Foundation. The National Science Foundation, or some similar organization, might be given a charter to cosponsor evaluation studies, along with an appropriate amount of funding to do this. An agency that administers a program would specify the type of evaluation that is needed and provide a share of the money to conduct such a study. The National Science Foundation, or whatever intermediary agency is chosen, would then work with the program agency in preparing a "request for proposals" and would provide the rest of the funds required. Either on its own or through a special panel, the NSF (or other chosen agency) would then oversee the research. Along with officials of the program agency, it would receive and review the reports on all studies conducted on this basis.

The essential aim of this proposal is to create a mechanism which, under certain circumstances, can be used to insulate the evalua*tor* from the evaluat*ee.* Not all evaluation studies would need to be undertaken through such a joint sponsorship. Such a mechanism might, for example, be limited to impact studies or very large studies. It could be made optional to the program-administering agency.

Regardless of the specifications, a system of this general character would serve a number of major purposes. It would (1) help to advance the art and science of evaluation, (2) stimulate efforts to develop new and better evaluation research designs and techniques, (3) help to identify the most talented evaluation researchers, and (4) give the public greater confidence in the results of evaluation studies.

References

Adams, Charles F., Jr., and Dan Crippen. 1978. "The Fiscal Impact of Revenue Sharing on Local Governments." Report prepared for the Office of Revenue Sharing. Washington, D.C.: U.S. Department of the Treasury.

Cook, Robert F., and V. Lane Rawlins. 1978. "Job Displacement under CETA Public Service Employment." American Statistical Association, *Business and Economic Statistical Section Proceedings,* pp. 86–94.

Cook, Robert F., and V. Lane Rawlins. 1979. "Local and National Objectives in Public Service Employment." Industrial Relations Research Association, *Proceedings of the Thirty-Second Annual Meeting,* December 1979, Atlanta.

Dommel, Paul R., and Jacob M. Jaffe. 1978. *Report on the Allocation of Community Development Funds to Small Cities.* Report prepared under contract with the Department of Housing and Urban Development, Office of Policy Development and Research. Washington, D.C.: U.S. Government Printing Office.

Dommel, Paul R., Richard P. Nathan, Sarah F. Liebschutz, and Margaret T. Wrightson. 1978. *Decentralizing Community Development.* Report prepared under contract with the Department of Housing and Urban Development, Office of Policy Development and Research. Washington, D.C.: U.S. Government Printing Office.

Ellwood, John W., ed. 1982. *Reductions in U.S. Domestic Spending: How They Affect State and Local Governments.* New Brunswick, N.J.: Transaction Books.

Hall, John Stuart. 1980. *The Impact of Federal Aid on the City of Phoenix.* Case Studies of the Impact of Federal Aid on Major Cities, No. 3. Washington, D.C.: U.S. Department of Labor.

Liebschutz, Sarah F. 1980. *The Impact of Federal Aid on the City of Rochester.* Case Studies of the Impact of Federal Aid on Major Cities, No. 5. Washington, D.C.: U.S. Department of Labor.

MacManus, Susan A. 1980. *The Impact of Federal Grants on the City of Houston.* Case Studies of the Impact of Federal Aid on Major Cities, No. 2. Washington, D.C.: U.S. Department of Labor.

Manvel, Allen D. 1975. "The Fiscal Impact of Revenue Sharing." *The Annals* 419(May): 36–49.

Nathan, Richard P. 1980. "Public-Service Employment." In *Employing the Unemployed,* ed. Eli Ginzberg, pp. 60–72. New York: Basic Books.

Nathan, Richard P., Charles F. Adams, Jr., and associates. 1977. *Revenue Sharing: The Second Round.* Washington, D.C.: Brookings Institution.

Nathan, Richard P., and Paul R. Dommel. 1978. "Federal-Local Relations Under Block Grants." *Political Science Quarterly* 93, 3(Fall): 421–42.

Nathan, Richard P., Allen D. Manvel, Susannah E. Calkins, and associates. 1975. *Monitoring Revenue Sharing.* Washington, D.C.: Brookings Institution.

Nathan, Richard P., Robert F. Cook, Richard Long, and Janet Galchick. 1978. *Job Creation Through Public Service Employment, Vol. 2, Monitoring the Public Service Employment Program, An Interim Report to the Congress.* Washington, D.C.: National Commission for Manpower Policy.

Nathan, Richard P., Paul R. Dommel, Sarah F. Liebschutz, and Milton D. Morris. 1977a. *Block Grants for Community Development.* Report prepared under contract with the Department of Housing and Urban Development, Office of Policy Development and Research. Washington, D.C.: U.S. Government Printing Office.

Nathan, Richard P., Paul R. Dommel, Sarah F. Liebschutz, and Milton D. Morris. 1977b. "Monitoring the Block Grant Program for Community Development." *Political Science Quarterly* 92, 2(Summer): 219–44.

Nathan, Richard P., Robert F. Cook, V. Lane Rawlins, Janet M. Galchick, and associates. 1979. *Monitoring the Public Service Employment Program: The Second Round.* Washington, D.C.: National Commission for Manpower Policy, Special Report No. 32.

Orlebeke, Charles J. 1980. *The Impact of Federal Grants on the City of Chicago.* Case Studies of the Impact of Federal Aid on Major Cities, No. 6. Washington, D.C.: U.S. Department of Labor.

Schmandt, Henry J., George D. Wendel, and E. Allan Tomey. 1979. *The Impact of Federal Aid on the City of St. Louis.* Case Studies of the Impact of Federal Aid on Major Cities, No. 1. Washington, D.C.: U.S. Department of Labor.

Steib, Steve B., and R. Lynn Rittenoure. 1980. *The Impact of Federal Aid on the City of Tulsa.* Case Studies of the Impact of Federal Aid on Major Cities, No. 4. Washington, D.C.: U.S. Department of Labor.

II. STATE/LOCAL POLICY OPTIONS

6 R. Charles Vars, Jr.

Informational Problems in Land-Use Planning and Natural Resource Management

Introduction

The increasing demands placed on state and local government to improve land use planning and management of natural resources have revealed significant weaknesses in the inventory and analysis systems used by many agencies. Data obtained by conventional means have become increasingly costly, and new responsibilities have created demands for large amounts of new and repetitive data. No less than a dozen recent federal acts and programs place significant data collection responsibilities on state government. These include, for example, the National Environmental Policy Act (1969), the Clean Air Act (1970), the Water Pollution Act (1972), and the Forest and Rangeland Renewable Resources Planning Act (1974). Further, nearly every state has enacted land use planning legislation that requires local government to compile, maintain, update, and use data on a greatly expanded scale.

Nowhere have the increasing demands for information about land use

This chapter summarizes the larger study reported in Donald H. K. Farness, Rebecca S. Roberts, and R. Charles Vars, Jr. 1978. *Economic Evaluation of Landsat-Based Resource Analysis for the Pacific Northwest,* a Phase IV report of the Land Resources Inventory Demonstration Project to the Technology Transfer Task Force of the Pacific Northwest Regional Commission (Corvallis, Oregon: Department of Economics, Oregon State University).

and natural resources created greater problems than in the three states of the Pacific Northwest region, where the economic base is highly dependent on forest and agricultural products, where urban areas are experiencing rapid changes in population and land use, and where residents actively seek to preserve those qualities of life in the region that are closely tied to its natural resource base and current land use. The three governors, through the Pacific Northwest Regional Commission (PNRC), recognized the need for a stronger information base and jointly sponsored with NASA and the U.S. Geological Survey (USGS) the Land Resources Inventory Demonstration Project (LRIDP). This project sought to determine the applicability of information obtained from Landsat satellite and high-altitude aircraft remote sensing to regional resource and land use inventory, planning, and management problems.

The first section of this chapter describes the LRIDP, and the second outlines the economic evaluation conducted as part of the project. The LRIDP economic study evaluated alternative operational systems to provide Landsat-based land resource inventory data and analyses to state and local government agencies in the Pacific Northwest. The third section of the chapter explains why agency demands were so low that no Landsat-based system for the region could be economically justified for the 1978–82 period. The results of interviews with twenty-eight agencies participating in the LRIDP are summarized to indicate the factors that affected agency decisions to adopt or reject modified or new land use and natural resource data systems. Such decisions reflect the budgetary, conceptual, and implementation problems that account for much of the poor performance of land use planning and resource management agencies throughout the United States.

The Project

The LRIDP was a cooperative effort of major proportions, involving an aggregate expenditure of about $6 million over a three-and-one-half-year period beginning in 1975. More than forty state and local agencies participated in some twenty different demonstration projects. The demonstration projects sought to strengthen land resource planning and management capabilities within the Pacific Northwest.

All demonstrations made use of remote sensing technology, typically with data from NASA's Landsat satellites. Testing of the technology proceeded in a program of five overlapping phases: regional base map preparation, preliminary digital analysis, demonstration projects, evaluation, and recommendations. Phase III, the major effort in the LRIDP, consisted of user-designed demonstrations in agriculture, forestry, range, and urban disciplines in each of the three states. Favorable response to the demonstration projects led participants and ultimately the PNRC to support a three-year follow-on effort. The second PNRC project is now underway and is designated the "Landsat Application Program."

Officially, the LRIDP had four objectives:

1. to provide an opportunity for resource management agencies to extract, utilize, and evaluate information derived from aircraft and satellite remote sensing;
2. to conduct a comprehensive evaluation of the application of an advanced technology within a realistic setting;
3. to achieve cooperation among federal, state, and local agencies to transfer a technology potentially capable of addressing natural resource problems; and
4. to evaluate alternative institutional means for providing continued and effective use of remote sensing by user agencies.

In practice, the objectives were less clearly defined and reflected the heterogeneous aspirations of the participants. The effort included federal agencies providing and promoting the technology, private contractors, and managers and staff of state, county, and local agencies. Varied viewpoints were embodied in different definitions of success for different participants. Anything from achieving a certain level of accuracy in data to generating support and funds for another round of demonstration projects was considered success by some participants.

One of the most important features of the LRIDP was the diversity of the demonstration projects undertaken. The agencies varied widely in the technical capabilities; they selected demonstration projects of differing difficulty; and the efforts they expended fluctuated over the duration of their projects. In terms of acreage, the Washington Department of Natural Resources (DNR) had the most ambitious project. The Idaho Department of Lands, hoping to learn from the experience of others, began its timber inventory project more than a year later than did the Washington DNR and the Oregon Department of Forestry. The Idaho Department of Water Resources attempted to use remotely sensed information and its Snake River Plain aquafer model to produce estimates of irrigated acreage. The Oregon Water Resources Department worked on two simpler projects: a manual analysis of irrigated lands in the Klamath River Basin and a computer analysis of reservoir surface area. The Oregon Department of Agriculture investigated the distribution of a noxious weed that threatens grazing livestock in western Oregon. Agencies concerned with rangeland-related matters included the Oregon Department of Fish and Wildlife, the Washington Department of Game, and the

Idaho Department of Fish and Game. Their projects emphasized wildlife habitat mapping and large-area rangeland classification.

The urban demonstration projects involved the largest number of users. The Puget Sound Council of Government's project included fourteen participating agencies at its maximum. Other urban projects were initiated by the City of Tacoma, Washington, Ada County in Idaho, and Spokane and Kootenai counties on the Washington-Idaho border. Most urban agencies chose to investigate land cover classification and change detection applications; some attempted to combat this data with geocoded regional management information systems. The level of detail required to assess changes in urban areas pushed the Landsat technology to its limits.

The Economic Evaluation Study

The objectives of the LRIDP Economic Evaluation Study were to project and assess the probable demand for, costs of, and benefits from the unsubsidized operational use of alternative Landsat-based digital resource analysis systems by state and local government agencies in the Pacific Northwest over the period 1978–82. Four features of the study distinguished it from previous evaluations of Landsat-based resource analysis systems:

1. Most agencies interviewed were well informed about Landsat data products, because they had participated in the LRIDP.
2. Agencies expressed their demands for Landsat products very carefully and realistically, because they would have to pay for the products entirely from their own budgets.
3. Costs and benefits of Landsat-based products were compared to the costs and benefits of the alternative products most likely to be selected by agencies. Alternatives which provide information comparable to that provided by Landsat but which would never be selected by the agency were not considered.
4. Total benefits were defined as the area under the aggregate agency demand curve for Landsat-based products, or the total willingness of agencies to pay an operational facility for Landsat-based products.

The conceptual framework, methodology, research procedures, alternatives evaluated, and findings are summarized here:

Conceptual framework. Resource inventory and analysis systems attempt to describe the various resource bases and their use in forms which are useful for management and planning decisions (Figure 6.1). The re-

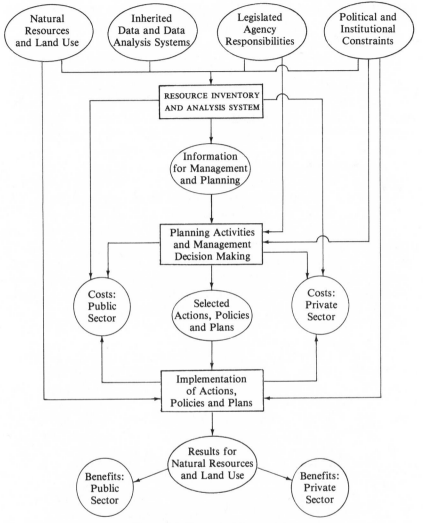

Figure 6.1. Conceptual framework

source base alone does not determine the inventory and analysis system of an agency. Historical practices, legislated responsibilities, budgets, and various political and institutional constraints also affect the resource inventory and analysis system of each agency. Budgets and responsibilities assigned by legislation have impacts that are well known and broadly understood. Political and institutional constraints sometimes affect the inventory and analysis system directly in ways understood by agencies and the public they serve. In other cases, however, political and institutional constraints are so insufficiently defined that agencies can only infer their probable impact.

The resource base and its use always requires some abstraction and conceptualization before its complexity can be adequately and appropriately measured. Agencies must conceptualize and define measureable resource categories and units that allow data to be collected, then present a picture of reality relevant to the agency's responsibilities. In doing this, agencies necessarily see reality through a filter formed by their inherited data analysis systems, legislated responsibilities and budgets, and political and institutional constraints.

Resource inventory and analysis systems abstract reality and cannot provide data better than the basic concepts on which they are built. Improving the quality or usefulness of resource inventory data therefore often requires that conceptualizations change, a process much more difficult than changing the data that are collected. In fact, the usefulness of data collected by alternative resource inventory systems is frequently judged in terms of the concepts of the current system rather than those of the system that provides data with dimensions most appropriate and important for the decisions to be made. As a consequence, changing the data analysis system will improve the usefulness of data only when concepts are changed also.

The purpose of any resource inventory and analysis system is to provide data for use in planning and management. These data are one of many factors, including political institutional factors, which affect the selection and implementation of policies and plans. Costs of various inventory analysis systems to both the public and private sectors are affected by and generated from the costs of the system itself, the planning and management decision-making process, and the implementation of policies and plans. These costs can be incurred by either the public or private sector. For example, the inventory activities of land use planning agencies cost something to perform and may result in implementation decisions which affect costs of public services such as sewers. The same inventory activities may, by collecting the required data indirectly, reduce the costs private organizations incur in the process of supplying public agencies with legally required data. Implementation of policies, actions, and plans produces changes in the use of natural resources in ways that produce benefits, either positive or negative, to both the public and private sectors. For example, effective multi-use management may increase recreational benefits to the public and the flow of timber to private wood-products firms.

Economic method. Alternative regional Landsat-based resource analysis systems were evaluated within the above conceptual framework according to the conventional economic methodology of benefit-cost analysis. This approach required estimation of the total benefits agencies expected to receive from use of Landsat-based products and the costs involved in providing such products under alternative operational systems and institutional arrangements. No feasible means by which agencies might obtain Landsat-based resource inventory products was initially excluded, though not all were formally considered in the final evaluation.

With the assistance of other LRIDP investigators, the economic evaluational team estimated the capital and operating costs to produce products under alternative operational systems and institutional arrangements. Costs were defined as either (1) the costs incurred by an operational facility to do projects for agencies, or (2) the bid prices of private firms or universities to do projects; costs did not include the in-house costs incurred directly by agencies in support of the digital analysis (e.g., the costs to agencies for collecting data to support production of Landsat-based products).

As in conventional applications of benefit-cost analysis to facilities designed to serve particular users, total benefits were measured as the area under the aggregate agency-demand curve for Landsat-based products, or the total willingness of agencies to pay an operational facility for Landsat-based products. The demand curve was estimated from information solicited by interviews and written statements from state and local government agencies involved in the LRIDP. The willingness-to-pay, and hence benefit, estimates reflect the constraints of probable agency budgets and the claims of other agency programs on any increased budgets in the period 1978–82.

One word of caution: Here benefits to an agency are not the total amounts the agency was willing to pay for a Landsat product, but rather that total amount minus the in-house costs incurred to acquire ground truth data and to work with system staff to obtain products with the desired specifications. Benefits therefore equal the maximum amount the agency would be willing to pay to an operational facility. This is appropriate because the economic evaluation was to determine whether the net benefits (total benefits minus internal costs) to agencies were sufficiently large to justify establishing an operational facility in the Pacific Northwest.

Directly asking agencies what they would be willing to pay for Landsat-based products was not expected to be productive, because the question is too hypothetical. A more useful approach was to infer agency willingness-to-pay from cost data. Products with some potential for actual use were divided into three classes distinguished by the relationship of the Landsat product to its alternative. Each class required a different approach to determining agency willingness-to-pay and therefore different cost or other information.

In the first class, the Landsat product was the functional equivalent of its alternative; substitution of one for the other would have no effect on agency performance. Willingness-to-pay for the Landsat product was therefore given by the cost of the alternative product minus the cost of the Landsat product; the agency should be willing to pay for the Landsat product as much as, but not more than, it paid for the alternative.

In the second or hybrid case, the Landsat product was also a substitute for, but not the functional equivalent of, the current product; the two alternatives differed in one or more characteristics that affect agency performance. In this case not only did costs have to be compared, but they had to be weighed against the relative value of the two products to the performance of the agency. Here the agency's willingness-to-pay was given by the cost of the alternative product, minus the cost of the Landsat product, plus the expected incremental benefits (positive or negative) from use of the Landsat product.

In the third case, the Landsat product was a new product; it would not take the place of some currently produced product. The agency in this instance would be willing to pay at most an amount equal to the total benefits received from the Landsat product.

Finally, the willingness-to-pay data for all project types and agencies were combined to estimate a demand schedule for the products of an operational facility. The estimated demand and system cost data were then used in conventional fashion to evaluate operational facilities of different sizes and degrees of centralization.

Research activities. The economic evaluation team investigated all reasonable approaches to collection of the required cost and benefit data. The first step was to survey the literature for both usable data on costs and benefits of Landsat-based systems and approaches used by other investigators to evaluate the costs and benefits of new technologies.

The second activity involved interviews with agencies to explore in detail the probable impact of Landsat-based information on agency performance and therefore on benefits to the agency and the general public. Approaches to quantification of benefits were discussed, and where quantification was not possible, the direction, positive or negative, of the benefit was determined. The team also explored the budgetary, political, and institutional constraints on agencies' resource inventory and analysis systems.

Because agencies would have to consult their files to bring together data on internal costs of the Landsat-based system and its alternatives, the team left a written request with the agency for such information. After summarizing data obtained from agency interviews and cost estimates, the team reviewed their findings and judgments with agency personnel. They also interviewed selected experts to check if their perceptions of agencies or agency perceptions of Landsat accorded with their knowledge.

Alternatives evaluated. Information from all investigations into costs and benefits was brought together in a conventional economic analysis to evaluate four alternative systems of different sizes and degrees of centralization for providing Landsat-based resource analysis products to Pacific Northwest agencies. Three types of regional facilities were considered: (1) centralized systems located at some unspecified location within the region but equally disadvantageous to agencies in the three states, (2) decentralized systems with a complete facility in one state capital and hardcopy computer terminals and staff in each of the other two capitals, and (3) decentralized systems similar to those in (2) but with the addition

Table 6.1. Comparative Advantages of Centralized and Decentralized Systems

Advantages of Centralized Systems	Advantages of Decentralized Systems
Economic	
Lower capital and operating costs	Lower internal costs to agencies because travel costs are lower
Increased and more efficient use of facility and personnel, especially at small scales	Easy accessibility increases demand
Technical	
Greater concentration of expertise gives greater depth and range of capability	Greater availability of input/output machine time and fewer scheduling problems
Communication leading to technological development facilitated	Closer contact possible between analyst and agency
Greater system reliability	
Instant video display times	
Institutional	
Total system easier to manage and coordinate	Little out-of-state travel required
	Easy accessibility increases demand
	More state funds would be spent in-state
	Facility location problem less severe

of color video displays at each of the remote facilities. In the fourth (or zero) alternative, agency demands for digital Landsat-based products would be met by existing facilities at regional universities or by the private sector with or without PNRC arrangements to facilitate communication and information-sharing among agencies in the region and the universities and private sector.

Each of the four alternatives had advantages and disadvantages. Table 6.1 presents the contrasting economic, technical, and institutional advantages of centralized and decentralized regional facilities. Briefly, a centralized system would be more efficient both economically and technically but less acceptable as an institution, whereas the greater physical and institutional accessibility of decentralized systems would probably encourage wider use of the system and higher rates of capacity utilization.

Advantages of the fourth alternative, where projects would be undertaken by the university and private sector, included the following:

Agencies obtained the products they desire while risks inherent in starting a regional operational facility would be avoided.

Major investment expenditures would be postponed, which may be advantageous because the real prices of system hardware and software were expected to decline in the future.

Agencies could take advantage of existing expertise and the relationships they developed during the LRIDP.

There were also disadvantages to the fourth alternative. First, communications and agency participation in the analysis process would be more difficult, because private firms with the appropriate skills were located outside of the region. Second, both the capacity and capability of universities to do complex projects were limited. Third, agencies might have less control over the operation of and services offered by universities and private firms than a dedicated regional facility. Finally, communication of advances in technique could be less than when all projects are completed within the same operational system. Of course, the PNRC could overcome part of this disadvantage by sponsoring activities to increase communication between all agencies and contractors.

Findings. High and low benefit and cost estimates were calculated to indicate the range within which actual benefits and costs might lie if a regional system were actually created and operated. Although the calculated benefit-cost ratios varied according to whether high or low estimates were used, the major findings did not depend on which estimates were selected. Sensitivity analyses revealed that the results were not sensitive to reasonable variation in the discount rate or the time horizon.

Some benefits may have been omitted because some local and smaller state agencies were not interviewed but may have had demands for Landsat products. Agencies representative of this group were interviewed, however, and found to have very limited willingness-to-pay for Landsat products. Omitted benefits therefore could not have been large enough to alter the results significantly.

The benefit-cost ratios for alternative regional systems provided the basis for the following findings:

The high and low benefit-cost ratios for each system at all levels of operation were low, with none exceeding the value of 0.29 for the centralized system. This quantitative evidence, together with qualitative evidence gathered from the agencies, suggested that an unsubsidized regional Landsat-based resource analysis system commencing operations in 1978 was not economically justifiable.

The benefit-cost ratios for a centralized system equalled or exceeded the benefit-cost ratios of decentralized systems at the same level of operations. The increase in total costs to decentralize greatly exceeded the increase in total benefits.

During the LRIDP many agencies worked with a private California firm and ERSAL, the Environmental Remote Sensing Applications Laboratory, at Oregon State University. Both learned the importance of assisting agencies in the design of projects, as well as the need for agency staff to understand and participate in decisions at various steps in the production of Landsat-based resource analyses. The advantages to the region of using private firms and ERSAL were found to be substantial:

The region could postpone (perhaps indefinitely) major expenditures on hardware and software that would probably become less costly in real terms over time.

The private sector and ERSAL could do small numbers of projects, and perhaps all projects identified in the study, at considerably less cost than either a centralized or decentralized regional operational system.

The cost advantages of utilizing private firms and universities could be obtained without state and local agencies in the Pacific Northwest foregoing opportunities to participate in and benefit from a rapidly developing technology.

The Low Demand

Demands for Landsat-based products were low because agencies were uncertain with regard to the characteristics and accessibility of products, the adaptability of their planning and decision processes, and the acceptability of Landsat-based products in the political arena. These uncertainties pertained to what may be referred to broadly as the technical feasibility of the products: Would they do the job for which they were being considered? Other uncertainties pertained to the economic feasibility of the products: Could they be justified on a cost-effective or benefit-cost basis? Finally there were budgetary uncertainties: Would administrators and legislatures provide the necessary funding? Before the adoption of a Landsat product could occur, favorable judgments had been rendered in all three areas—technical, economic, and budgetary.

The views of twenty-eight agencies participating in the LRIDP are summarized here to reveal the specific uncertainties that affected agency decisions concerning operational use of Landsat products. These uncertainties reveal the pervasiveness of conceptual and implementation difficulties in developing new information systems to support more comprehensive land use planning and more effective natural resource management. However, because a summary cannot describe in detail potential applications, performance characteristics, and other matters, the appendix describes in some detail the positions of three representative agencies: the Oregon Department of Forestry, the Oregon Department of Fish and Wildlife, and the Spokane County Planning Department. The materials there indicate why, in 1978, the three agencies had continuing interests in, but limited effective demands for, Landsat-based products.

Product characteristics. Most agencies had seen only a limited number of Landsat data products. For many it was a single product for a single season in a single year. Consequently, questions of both accuracy and ability to detect change had not been fully resolved. Akin to questions of accuracy were questions of resolution and ability to distinguish the required number of data categories at a given level of accuracy.

Uncertainties regarding product quality also arose in instances in which the product had been designed for the joint use of a number of agencies. Some agencies judged products to conform better with the needs of another agency, and until they saw products expressly designed for their needs, they were unable to evaluate the utility of Landsat products for their decision and planning purposes.

Product acceptability. The test of product quality is its impact on the agency performance. Product qualities affect both the recommendations and actions that the agency might undertake and the subjective acceptability of the product by the public. Inaccuracies that do not affect agency recommendations or actions may affect public acceptability and thereby impair agency performance. This situation was illustrated by planning agencies which historically have utilized land use data with a fairly high degree of inaccuracy, primarily because certain parts of their land use inventory were out of date. For such agencies Landsat data could be a considerable improvement for some purposes if accurate only at the 80% level. However, even if the cost of a Landsat product were equal to or lower than its alternative, there was no assurance that the agency would adopt the Landsat product. Planners typically interact directly with citizens and elected officials, and often their tools include maps. A Landsat-derived map deemed superior to maps produced by alternative technologies and adequate to the agency's needs will be inaccurate at certain specific sites. These errors may be identified and become the basis for challenging the use of Landsat products. Thus there was a greater tolerance for errors of the existing system than for the Landsat system. An important reason for this discrepancy was that land cover classification errors are inherent in the Landsat system. If the process were repeated, errors would again appear. In the instance of land use maps developed by ground survey, there also is an inherent source of error. All areas cannot be simultaneously and instantaneously surveyed and therefore cannot be perfect up-to-date. However, correct classification at the time of the survey is possible, and if any errors are detected, the survey process can be repeated so that the errors are corrected. In this sense, error is not inherent in the system.

Thus for political reasons, a planning agency could operate with a data base which is inaccurate because it is out of date and a cost-effective alternative of greater overall accuracy is available. Staff in one agency reported that this could occur because superiors sensitive to public reaction would prohibit use of the Landsat alternative. Other agencies reported that the same choice might be made by the agency in order to maintain the credibility of the planning process and therefore forestall more overtly political decisions which use of Landsat-derived maps might encourage.

Lags in availability. Lags in the availability of Landsat products concerned certain agencies. Both weather and processing factors were involved. Cloud cover interferes with aircraft and satellite remote-sensing activities and is particularly a problem for areas west of the Cascade Mountains. Applications which require frequent products, or products for several seasons of the same year, or products for large areas, were most affected.

The lag between time of the overflight and the delivery of the final data products precluded consideration of Landsat products for applications which require very current data, such as the measurement of reservoir volumes and the detection of forest infestations in time to apply control measures. For other applications the experience of the demonstration projects created doubts concerning the ability of a Landsat system to produce products within the desired time periods.

Certain agencies also expressed concern for the long-run availability of Landsat imagery. Regardless of whether there was any foundation for these fears, until agencies were assured that the system would be available in the long run and produce products of some predictable resolution, they could be expected to be cautious in making large internal expenditures to effect changes in their data systems and related management and planning processes.

Institutional adaptability. Not only were agencies reluctant to make internal adjustments necessary to use Landsat data products effectively, there was some uncertainty as to whether they would be capable of doing so in all instances. In most applications Landsat data products were not identical with the products currently utilized. Where the data were substantially different, significant changes would be required in the agency's management and planning processes if Landsat products were to be successfully integrated into their operations. An example is the incorporation of comprehensive habitat information in game management models. Whether and how soon such changes and incorporations could be accomplished were quite uncertain.

In addition to conceptual changes in management models, more mundane institutional changes were necessary if Landsat products were to become operationally feasible. Old work routines would have to be adjusted to replaced and personnel retrained, reassigned, and possibly terminated. This is hardly a frictionless process. Individuals acquire psychological and economic vested interests in particular work arrangements. Change involves costs to individuals; change also may involve costs to agencies. One agency indicated that for human and technical reasons it would be a matter of years, perhaps as many as ten, before a major new data system could be successfully in place. For that agency to adopt Landsat products, the apparent economic advantage of Landsat products over current data products would have to be truly substantial to offset the costs of institutional inertia.

Accessibility of facilities. The accessibility of regional facilities to produce Landsat products concerned some agencies. Convenience, travel times and costs, and out-of-state travel restrictions significantly affected the demand for Landsat products by state agencies. In fact, the uncertainties concerning the location, capacity, and availability of facilities greatly added to agency inability to make advance commitments to use an operational Landsat system.

Budget. More important constraints pertained to budgets. Most agency budgets did not include funds for data development which could be spent in a discretionary way. Hence legislative or administrative approval would be required if the typical agency were to increase its expenditures for data acquisition, or to merely reallocate funds while maintaining the level of data acquisition expenditures. There was no certainty that such approval would be forthcoming, and therefore no northwest state and local government had made explicit budgetary provision at the time of the study for the acquisition of digital Landsat data products. Of course, caution on the part of legislatures and administrators is the logical outgrowth of the uncertainties inherent in the development and application of any new technology, particularly one that in some instances would provide new information but with a large increase in agency costs.

For example, the in-house costs of complex multistage forest inventory projects would virtually exhaust, if not exceed, the Oregon Department of Forestry's and Idaho Department of Land's budgetary ability to pay for Landsat products. Annual expenditures for forest inventory data in 1977–78 were small relative to the in-house costs that would be incurred to produce the Landsat products. In fact, because the Landsat products for both forestry agencies were not substitutes for current inventory activities, the additional annual budget increases needed to acquire the Landsat products were estimated to be 200 or more percent for the Idaho Department of Lands and, at an absolute minimum, 180 percent for the Oregon Department of Forestry (see Table 6.2). Budgetary increases of these magnitudes were regarded as extremely unlikely by agency personnel. As a consequence the ability of the forestry agencies to pay an operational system was estimated to be zero or less than zero, which is to say some in-house agency activities would have to be subsidized if they were to acquire Landsat products.

A lesser budgetary issue arose where extra-agency funds were available for certain restricted purposes which included data acquisition by non-

Table 6.2. Budget Increases Required for Complex Multistage Forest Inventory Projects, by Agency

Agency	Expenditures Forest Inventory Activities, 1977–78	Estimated Annual In-house Costs for Producing Landsat Products	Annual Budget Increase Required to Cover In-house Costs (%)
Idaho Department of Lands	$75,000	$150,000–180,000	200–240
Oregon Department	58,500	105,000[a]	180[a]

[a] These estimates were based on the costs for a simple rather than a complex multistage project and consequently are low. Judged by the Idaho Department of Land's estimates for a smaller area, but based on experience in doing a complex multistage project, the actual costs to the Oregon Department of Forestry could be as high as $400,000–600,000.

Landsat techniques. For example, CETA (Comprehensive Employment
and Training Act) funds were available in 1978 and earlier years for
labor-intensive activities such as windshield surveys used in the development of land use maps. CETA-financed labor was a free resource to
agencies and consequently biased their choice among data-acquisition
techniques in favor of labor-intensive windshield surveys. Numerous
agencies also indicated that their demands for Landsat products would
be contingent on the receipt of grants-in-aid.

Costs of producing Landsat products by an operational facility. The
budgetary caution of legislatures and administrators resulted from uncertainties pertaining to the costs of producing Landsat products as well
as to what have been broadly termed technological uncertainties. Agencies generally had very little knowledge of production costs, because they
did not bear most costs incurred in the demonstration projects.

Equally in doubt were long-run costs. If Landsat-based products
follow the pattern of other newly introduced products, substantial cost
reductions could be expected in the early years of the system's application. Although these cost uncertainties did not appear to be an important
factor in depressing the demand for Landsat products, they did contribute to the environment of doubt in which agencies responded, and they
certainly added to agency difficulties in making accurate comparisons
between Landsat and alternative data systems.

Benefits. Most agencies were not able to respond well to the question
of how data of a different quality from that presently used would affect
their planning and management decisions and what the implications
would be for the agency's constituent population. At best they could
specify certain effects, but only in terms of their direction, not in terms
of their magnitudes. For example, a game management agency indicated
that better habitat information could lead to harvesting decisions which
would be closer to the optimal policy with the consequent results that
hunting satisfaction would increase, and damage to agricultural, timber,
and range resources would decrease.

Agency decision-makers typically wanted better information, but new
sources were evaluated cautiously because they might imply unacceptable
changes in priorities. An absence of consensus concerning agency objectives led to suspicion of staff expert in a new technology who could be
pushing to achieve their own goals rather than those of the agency. Administrators preferred rejection of a modified, but superior, information
system that might promote priorities other than their own. They also
found rejection easy where Landsat-based information focused on dis-
tant future problems and the political significance of their current concerns was more compelling.

Conclusions

The LRIDP Economic Evaluation Study did not attempt to answer the question of whether a subsidized or unsubsidized operational system would become economically desirable at some time after 1978. The reasons for this limitation derived from the purpose of the study and our understanding of the theories of technological innovation and optimal timing of investments. These theories together predict that the dynamics of technical and operational change have great bearing on when adoption of a new technology will be successful.

The process of any successful technological innovation such as adoption of Landsat-based resource analysis may be divided into three overlapping processes—technological innovation, operational innovation, and adoption for operations (Figure 6.2). Each process produces capabilities which initially grow slowly, gathering momentum for a period of rapid growth that ultimately levels off.

Application of technological innovation theory to the case of Landsat-based resource analysis suggests the following scenario. The first process, resulting in technical capability, has passed through early conceptual developments and achieved rapid development of hardware and software. Operational capability generally follows the development of technical capability, and it is crucially dependent on the development of resource planning and management models, as well as institutional ad-

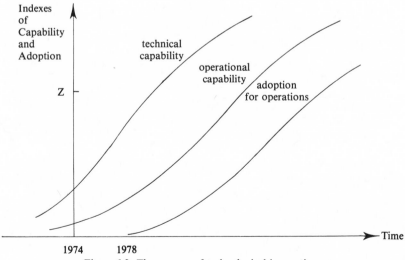

Figure 6.2. The process of technological innovation

justments in response to newly demonstrated technical capabilities. Once
the technical and operational feasibilities of a Landsat data system are
established, actual adoption by agencies could occur, but perhaps only
after a considerable period of time.

Viewed in this framework, developments in technical capability of
Landsat-based resource analysis systems were well advanced in 1978, but
considerable activity continues to today. Operational capability was
clearly less advanced, and the applicability of Landsat products was uncertain for most potential users. Until those uncertainties were overcome, adoption for operational purposes could not be expected to occur
soon. The consequences of these conditions are illustrated in Figure 6.3.
In 1978 the net present value of an unsubsidized regional operational system was negative, and such a system was not an economically efficient
investment. At a future time, however, such a system might be feasible

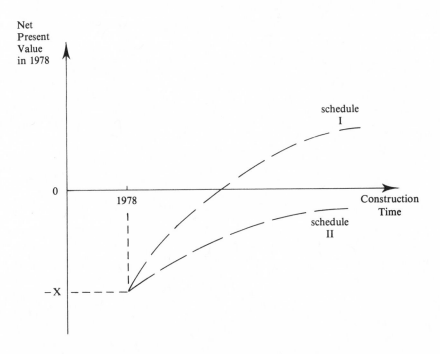

Figure 6.3. Net present value of an unsubsidized regional operational system in 1978 as a
function of the construction time.

depending on the magnitude and timing of developments in the three stages indicated in Figure 6.2. If those developments increase the net present value of an operational system as depicted by schedule I in Figure 6.3, a system would become an economically efficient investment for the region at approximately the time when its present value passes from negative to positive values. However, if the course of development is that depicted by schedule II, an operational system would not become economically feasible over the time range indicated in the figure. Even today the uncertainty associated with the various stages of Landsat developments remains substantial, and no prediction is offered here when or whether an unsubsidized operational system will become economically feasible in the Pacific Northwest.

The economic evaluation study for the LRIDP documented the information problems faced by land use planning and natural resource management agencies in the Pacific Northwest. Most agencies participated in the project because the demands for information placed on them by recent legislation cold not be met satisfactorily by their existing information systems. Repeatedly agencies claimed that the U.S. Congress or the state legislature did not understand the conceptual, technical, and operational obstacles in successfully addressing the problems prompting new legislation. At the time of enactment, legislatures misperceived the current and potential capabilities of agencies. For example, in 1974 when the Forest and Rangeland Renewable Resources Planning Act was passed, the appropriate conceptual models and information and decision systems were in their infancy of development, and considerable innovation was needed before the objectives of the act could begin to be achieved, probably in the mid-1980s. Arguments made by supporters of the act suggested that they perceived the capabilities of agencies to equal or exceed the levels indicated by Z in Figure 6.2, or to be quite above actual capabilities in 1974 and those expected for another decade or so.

Planning and management are especially difficult tasks without information systems based on concepts, measurements, and analyses appropriate for the decisions that agencies must make. Information problems are neither the single nor most important cause of unsuccessful land use planning and natural resource management. Probably more important are agency lethargy and lack of foresight; limited budgets; overly ambitious, inconsistent, and poorly drafted laws and regulations; and private and public conflicts of interests and values. Nevertheless, the experience of the LRIDP demonstrates that information problems must rank as an important factor in the observed poor performance today of land use planning and natural resource management agencies.

Appendix

Oregon Department of Forestry

Highest priority Landsat application. The Oregon Department of Forestry places the highest priority on Landsat products for the development of a state-wide inventory of all forest land in Oregon every five to seven years.

Alternative products. At present a statewide vegetative cover inventory is not available in the number of cover classes desired by the department. The inventory product could replace or could be done in conjunction with the U.S. Forest Service. It could not, and in all likelihood probably would not, replace the current system entirely. The aerial photo interpretation and ground collection would still have to be included when collecting volume information and classifying forest cover.

Significant differences. The inventory product would be similar to the accuracy currently obtained in the U.S. Forest Service/Forest Survey work. The significant difference is that Landsat data could provide in-place mapping of all forest land. Currently, there is scattered, untimely, and varying scales of aerial photography collected in Oregon, and in some cases, there is no photo coverage.

Use of data. The inventory product would be used for broad policy formulation purposes and as a possible first stage in detection of particular activities and conditions for which information is necessary for execution of the department's extensive enforcement, advisory, management, and planning responsibilities.

Performance consequences. Landsat would allow for one-point-in-time resource monitoring of all commercial forest land to help satisfy statute requirements of collecting and publishing information relevant to the forest resource conditions.

Likelihood of use. At this time the department does not have plans to utilize Landsat products. The demonstration project products were not sufficiently accurate or detailed, and until these problems are resolved the products will not be purchased. Use also is contingent on the cost of Landsat products.

Long-run interests. The department has extensive enforcement, assistance, informational, management, and planning responsibilities which require current, uniform, and accurate ground cover information. Available and currently utilized data sources are not satisfactory for fulfilling all of the department's current responsibilities. Consequently the department will continue to be interested in the development of products by Landsat 2 and subsequent Landsat systems.

Oregon Fish and Wildlife Department

Highest priority Landsat applications. The Oregon Fish and Wildlife Department identified two data products for which Landsat is considered a potential source. They are a statewide vegetative cover inventory and a statewide inventory of artificial waters. These inventories would be updated on a periodic basis.

Alternative to Landsat Products. Landsat imagery would be used to update the wildlife habitat component in the agency's computerized resource data base. The current base is the 1970 inventory of thirty ground cover classes compiled by twenty-one district wildlife biologists and other staff specialists. The alternative to Landsat-based data, as determined by a September 1977 agency decision, is to update the data base by a sample revision.

The current inventory of artificial water bodies is being compiled by district biologists. The primary information resource is the knowledge and experience of the paticipants. Consequently the inventory is particularly deficient in timeliness and accuracy, particularly in the smaller standing-water-body component. This product is in the process of refinement by use of existing aerial photos and various agency files.

Significant differences between products. The department believes a Landsat ground cover product would be superior to the product developed for the 1970 base-year inventory. Despite certain imperfectly resolved classification problems, the Landsat product would be consistent in a manner not possible in a product which reflects the individual judgments of numerous specialists working from information gathered at various points in time. Landsat-based products are judged to be more uniform and timely and superior for quantification by areas and ground cover classes.

A Landsat-based inventory of standing water bodies also is believed to be superior for quantification by area and class, more uniform and timely, and more accurate above some minimal size (e.g., five surface acres). However, given the small size of most unmapped standing water bodies, Landsat 2 may be inferior to the alternative data sources.

Use of data. Landsat-based data products are potential management tools for harvest decisions and habitat manipulation. At present, vegetative cover information is not directly utilized in harvest decisions, but rather is used indirectly as reflected in animal populations upon which decisions are explicitly based. There is, therefore, a lag in the recognition of habitat conditions which ultimately affect animal populations. By direct inclusion of this information in the harvesting decision, better decisions may result.

Performance consequences. If Landsat vegetative cover can be successfully integrated into a harvesting model, it may reduce management indecisiveness and thereby enable larger harvests without harming the resource base. This would have consequent benefits in the form of increased hunting activity and success, reduced damage to agricultural crops and timber, and lessened danger of range damage from forage overuse. Similar beneficial consequences also may occur from habitat enhancement activities facilitated by more immediate and comprehensive vegetative cover information.

Better data for standing water bodies may result in increased fishing opportunities, identification of potential bodies for spiny-ray fish propagation, possibly avoidance of the duplication which would result from the construction of new ponds in areas with sufficient but otherwise unknown bodies, and identification of rangeland areas with insufficient supplies for wildlife and livestock. These benefits are, in part, contingent on the fineness of the resolution of Landsat 2 imagery. If not Landsat 2, Landsat 3 imagery may be sufficiently fine.

Likelihood of use in the next five years. Use of Landsat products in the next five years will be contingent on the availability of Landsat products delivery services, costs of Landsat products, quality of the Landsat products which have not yet been fully evaluated, and the ability of the department to incorporate Landsat products successfully into its management and planning process. If Landsat products are utilized, it will mean new costs. It is expected that the data which are currently gathered would continue to be gathered with only a small element of duplication involved.

Long-run interests. The department recognizes the long-run potential of Landsat products, and its interest in Landsat will continue.

Spokane County Planning Department

Data products and alternatives. The desired Landsat data products are Level II land use/cover maps and tabular products to establish an inventory and monitor change. The county would acquire data products every two years to detect change in the Spokane metropolitan area and every three to four years to detect change in the rural portion of the county. An alternative system to produce similar data would use building permit data, windshield surveys, and photo interpretation of U–2 or other overflight images. There is no current system for detecting change; the demonstration project will produce the first countywide land use/cover maps and tables.

Product differences among alternatives. Because the final classification for the demonstration project has not been completed, the desired map and tabular products have not been produced, and the accuracy of Landsat-based classification is not known. Planners do not expect Landsat data products to be highly accurate for small areas. Rather they expect to obtain aggregate data of sufficient accuracy to monitor major changes in the seven planning areas created for the county.

Monitoring change with building permit information supplemented by windshield surveys can provide certain data for limited areas of the county. Photo interpretation of aerial images can be used to classify general vegetative cover in rural areas and land use in urban and suburban areas. Classifications based on photo interpretation, however, do not directly generate the computer tape(s) and statistical data that a Landsat-based process would; further, they cannot provide the uniform countywide classification that Landsat can.

Spokane County planners believe that broadly accurate, uniform, and countywide data are required for the comprehensive planning process in which Spokane County is now engaged. Landsat-based maps and tables are expected to be capable of providing the visual and statistical characterizations of the environment needed for long-range planning purposes.

Use of products. Landsat products are expected to provide important information for (1) the development and implementation of the Comprehensive Plan for Spokane County and (2) the review of environmental impact statements as required by the Spokane County Environmental Ordinance. The future use of Landsat products depends on whether (a) the demonstration project maps, tables, and other by-products are useful inputs to the Comprehensive Plan now being developed, (b) the plan itself is acceptable, and (c) environmental review procedures are successful. If the Comprehensive Plan is accepted, the techniques used to develop data for it will probably be used to implement and update it in the future.

Maps and tables from the demonstration project are expected to characterize for the first time the general environment of major areas within the county, and thereby provide and/or supplement an information base (1) to develop the Comprehensive Plan, (2) to formulate broad policy and implement the plan, and (3) from which to monitor change in land use and cover over time (especially in urban fringe areas). Large-scale Landsat maps and tables would be used in the future to monitor change and provide data to evaluate proposed revisions in county land use policy.

Landsat products are part of a *new* coordinated multiple-component information base now being developed. The components of this information base will be presented by a 25-mm and microfiche display system and include: (1) the USGS map system (1" = 500' with overlays), (2) the USGS land use/cover map system, (3) the Spokane County Comprehensive Plan and data/map system, (4) the Spokane County assessor's file and map system, and (5) Landsat-based maps and tables. Large- and small-scale Landsat products would be used most often in this information system at monthly hearings to represent the environment surrounding the specific sites subject to those hearings. Maps and tables would provide quantitative environmental information for developers and citizens concerned with planning issues.

Budget and other factors. The Spokane County Planning Department has a professional staff of ten, aided by two technicians, four secretaries, and a variable number of part-time employees and volunteers. The budget for the department is tight, but the county commissioners have recently begun to support a map project which will produce data compatible with that obtained from Landsat. Approval to purchase Landsat-based data products from an operational system in the Northwest would require a presentation to the commissioners. An effective presentation would specify the costs of obtaining the products, present examples of the products for examination, demonstrate how the county could reduce its need to rely on other agencies for data, and indicate how the data could be used by the Planning Department, private developers, and citizens concerned with planning-related issues. Budget to acquire Landsat-based data products would depend on how commissioners viewed the benefits of the products to the county and its citizens, the cost of the products, and the net benefits of alternative county activity.

Likelihood of use. The Spokane County Planning Department would request use of an operational Landsat system within the next five years if:

the final classification and map and tabular products from its demonstration project equal or exceed department expectations;
the cost of products obtained from an operational system is not great;
the operational system is user-oriented and functions well in the service mode;
the process of developing an environmentally based comprehensive plan for the county proceeds smoothly; and
the net benefits of alternative county expenditures are not valued highly by the commissioners.

7 *Charles E. McLure, Jr.*

Fiscal Federalism
and the Taxation
of Economic Rents

I. Introduction

Much has been written about the optimal allocation of governmental functions among various levels of government in a federal system. (See, for example, Oates [1968] and Musgrave and Musgrave [1980, Ch. 24].) In the context of Musgrave's three-branch view of government, the stabilization and distribution functions are common agreed to be inappropriate activities for subnational governments. Such governments can, however, effectively handle certain problems of the allocation branch: provision of spatially limited public goods, alleviation of geographically limited environmental costs, etc.

This division of functions among governments at different levels has important implications for the optimal division of fiscal resources in a federal system. Most obviously, progressive income taxes and income maintenance programs intended to implement the redistribution of income are not appropriate for state and local governments. Subnational income taxes that diverge greatly from national averages encourage emigration of the wealthy (or their wealth) and differentials in welfare pro-

The author is a Senior Fellow at the Hoover Institution at Stanford University. When this chapter was written he was Vice President of the National Bureau of Economic Research. The views expressed here are solely those of the author, and not those of either the Hoover Institution or the NBER.

grams induce immigration of the poor.[1] On the other hand, taxes and fees related to benefits received from localized public services and to many environmental costs can be imposed by subnational governments without distorting economic decisions; indeed, in some instances they must be levied in this way if distortions are to be avoided.

Since the beneficiaries of many publicly provided services cannot easily be identified and charged the marginal cost of providing those services, it would often be necessary to go beyond benefit taxes and environmental fees in financing state and local governments, even if an effort were being made to implement the Musgrave layer-cake system of fiscal federalism.[2] One commonly used approach to raising general revenue that probably has relatively little distorting effect is state sales taxes levied on retail sales to consumers residing in particular states.[3] Such taxes are sometimes also used to finance local government, especially through the device of surcharges levied on state taxes.

A more traditional means of financing local government has been property taxation. Under some circumstances it can be argued that property taxes are, on the average, reasonable ways of charging for benefits received, as in the case of residential property taxes used to finance education. But in many cases, especially for mining, manufacturing, and commercial property, property taxes clearly bear no close relation to benefits received and probably exceed them by a wide margin. If the excess taxation of business property were uniform across the nation, it is unlikely that the geographic location of economic activity would be seriously affected. But where differentials of taxes paid in excess of benefits received differ greatly among states, they can cause significant misallocations of geographically mobile resources among states.[4] This has, in

1. Whether it is the wealthy or their wealth that is encouraged to move depends on whether the tax is levied on the basis of the residence of the recipient of income or the source of income.

2. Even if beneficiaries of public services could be identified and benefit taxes were being levied, a balanced budget would generally result only if average cost of the service were constant. For further discussion of the "tax assignment problem," see the papers in McLure (forthcoming).

3. State sales taxes, being commonly levied on the basis of *destination* of sales, probably cause little distortion, except insofar as the choice of residential location is affected by differentials in taxes that do not reflect differences in public services provided to households. If, contrary to common practice, state indirect taxes were based on the *origin* of the production (that is, on production rather than on consumption), interstate differentials in tax rates not justified by differences in levels of public services provided to businesses could be distorting.

4. Among the most celebrated of such effects is the shuttling of inventories of automobiles out of California just prior to assessment day to avoid the tax on personal property. Because it applies only on a given day, this tax entails little waste of resources beyond the fuel and time required for the shuttle. Permanent taxes on property probably induce more serious losses of welfare.

effect, been captured in the normative proscription mentioned above against the use of progressive taxation by state and local governments.

It has been a common belief that property taxes levied on totally immobile factors, such as the rental component of the return from natural resources, are ideal sources of revenue for state, or even local, governments, since they cause no geographic misallocation of resources. Because the resources are, by assumption, immobile, the argument goes, rents can be taxed by subnational governments without causing spatial misallocation of the exploitation or use of the resources.[5] Presumably this argument should be as applicable to income taxes and severance taxes as to property taxes, so long as resource rents are being taxed in all cases.

The purpose of this chapter is to question this traditional result. It is shown that where natural resources are available in different abundances or qualities in various areas, subnational taxation of the differential rents from those resources will generally tend to cause geographic misallocation of other mobile resources. This result occurs not because the taxes are distorting if used by subnational governments, but because unequal access to revenues allows states to engage in tax or expenditure policies that distort resource allocation. In general, only federal taxation of differential resource rents—or quite far-reaching sharing of revenues among subnational governments—will result in an economically efficient solution.

Due to the enormous increases in resource rents created by the actions of the Organization of Petroleum Exporting Countries (OPEC), this issue in the optimal design of fiscal federalism has recently attained substantial practical importance. The states of the northern Great Plains of the United States have imposed severence taxes on coal that appear to be far in excess of anything that could be justified on benefit grounds; the Canadian province of Alberta has reduced personal income taxes, has eliminated gasoline taxes, and has established an "Alberta Heritage Savings Trust Fund" (AHSTF) that has an estimated present value of $30 billion; and Alaska has recently attempted to make lump sum payments to residents from the large royalties and the income and severence tax revenues it has been collecting on natural resources.[6]

5. This argument has been buttressed by administrative considerations. Realty, including natural resources, is more easily taxed by local governments than are, for example, flows of income or even personal property.

6. For a general discussion of severance taxes on coal, especially those levied in Montana, see Krutilla, Fisher, and Rice (1978). Cuciti, Galper, and Lucke (1983) convincingly document the enormous disparities in the fiscal capacity of resource-rich and other states. The Alberta Heritage Savings Trust Fund has recently been the issue of a special conference; see Smith (1980). The present value of the Alberta Heritage Savings Trust Fund has been estimated at $30 billion by Helliwell (1980). The Alaskan scheme of lump sum pay-

There has been a movement in Alberta and its neighboring provinces, motivated by the desire to avoid sharing the largess made possible by extraordinary resource rents, toward the establishment of barriers to immigration or even toward political separation from the rest of Canada. The Canadian national government has countered Alberta's efforts by attempting in several ways to capture for the rest of Canada part of the rents that would otherwise accrue to the province. It has held the domestic prices of petroleum products below world market prices; it has levied an export tax on foreign sales of Canadian oil and gas; it has eliminated the deduction for provincial taxes and royalties in the calculation of fedral income tax liability; and it has adjusted the formula used to equalize fiscal resources among the provinces in a way that penalizes Alberta.[7] These and other initiatives have raised the specter that the uneven geographic distribution of natural wealth will join with "the Quebec problem" in causing Canada to disintegrate.

While this kind of destructive influence has been felt more strongly in Canada, it has not been absent in the United States. The recently enacted federal windfall profits tax will substantially reduce the latitude for state and local governments in producing regions to capture rents arising from exploitation of domestic petroleum resources. This tax does, however, provide for pass-through of state severance taxes and does not apply to royalties on oil and gas produced on state-owned lands, which are especially important in Alaska. In *Commonwealth Edison et al. v. Montana* a number of public utilities in consuming states joined together with coal companies to contest the constitutionality of Montana's 30 percent severance tax on coal, but they were unsuccessful. Bills have been introduced in Congress that would limit the severance taxes the states can levy on coal. Finally, several consuming states have exhibited the desire to "get in on the action" by taxing the major oil companies.[8]

ments has recently been struck down by the courts, because the payments would be conditioned on length of residence in the state.

7. For an analysis of the equalization formula in effect in 1975 and several alternative formulas, see Courchene (1976). It can be argued that over the years the federal government in the United States has followed policies that *increased* resource rents available for capture by the states. Among these are the depletion allowance and import quotas on oil. More recently prohibition of the use of oil and gas in new electrical generating plants may have increased potential rents on coal.

8. S. 2695, introduced in the second session of the 96th Congress, would limit severance taxes on coal produced on federal lands and on Indian lands to 12.5 percent. A similar bill, H.R. 1313, was introduced in the first session of the 97th Congress. Gross receipts taxes on the major oil companies have been combined with price controls in Connecticut and New York, but have been found unconstitutional. See Hellerstein (1983) for a careful analysis of the legal restraints on state action in this area, and McLure (1981) for an analysis of the likely incidence of various types of taxes used by producing and consuming states. Congressional hearings on severance tax disparities are reported in U.S. Congress (1982a, b).

Section II of this chapter presents a simple taxonomy and analysis of different schemes of taxation and public expenditure that might be employed in a two-level federal system. The alternative tax regimes are federal taxation, taxation by the state of source of rents from natural resources, and taxation by the state of residence of owners of (recipients of rents from) natural resources.[9] No distinction is made between various ways of capturing resource rents; though public royalties, income taxes, property taxes, and severance taxes may affect various economic decisions differently, those differences are not of immediate interest. Rather, it is simply assumed that the technical problem of taxing economic rents, and only rents, has been solved, or at least is no more likely to be solved at one level of government than the other.[10]

It is assumed that the tax revenues can be employed for one of six purposes: to provide various kinds of tax cuts or subsidies, to finance pure public goods, to finance public provision of basically private goods (hereafter called "specific" goods), to finance "province building," to finance "country building," or to equalize taxpaying capacity in the various states. The uses that have been made of the AHSTF (described briefly in Collins [1980]) suggest that certain cells in this taxonomy bear a striking resemblance to reality. It will be seen that in general only federal taxation of resource rents is spatially efficient, though under certain conditions federally financed revenue sharing or use of state revenues to finance country building may also be efficient.

This conclusion should not be taken as strong evidence that Alberta should turn its Crown lands over to Ottawa, that state severance taxes should be limited to amounts that can be justified on benefit grounds, or that the Texas permanent school fund should be transferred to the federal government. First, as emphasized in Fieldstein (1976), tax *design* is not the same thing as tax *reform*. Thus the analysis presented here would have been more appropriate in informing those drafting the Spanish land grants, the charter of the Hudson Bay Company, or the Mayflower

9. For present purposes the "owner" of the natural resource is taken to be the entity whose income would be reduced by the tax on rents. While ordinarily this would be the legal owner, in some instances it is not. For example, contractual agreements between a landowner and a firm developing a resource might result in increases in severance taxes being borne by the landowner, by the developing firm, or by both, in a predetermined pattern. Thus in the discussion of state taxes based on residence, we could, in principle, be interested in either the landowner or owners of the developing firm, or both.

10. For an inconclusive exploration of the proposition that taxation of resource rents should be vested in a particular level of government because the taxes used at that level are more appropriate for capturing economic rents, see Bradley (1976). For an analysis of the effects of various tax policies on the time pattern of depletion of natural resources, see Dasgupta, Heal, and Stiglitz (1980). As noted there, the effect of tax policy on depletion depends crucially on expectations of future tax policy.

Compact—the real world analogs of the "spaceship landing on Mars" often employed by economists to conjure up the Rawlsian curtain of ignorance. By now—and perhaps by the time of the U.S. Constitution and the British North America Act—investment decisions have been made on the basis of existing divisions of fiscal resources among the various levels of government. Any alteration of these divisions and the redistributions of revenues they would entail could have substantial windfall effects on property values that must be weighed against the efficiency gains that would result from nationalizing the taxation of resource rents. Second, we should emphasize that the analysis presented in section II is concerned primarily with only one aspect of the question of the optimal assignment of revenue sources in a federal system, the locational effects of various uses of revenues from natural resources.[11] Section III explicitly considers various qualifications and complications to the simple neutrality analysis of section II.[12]

II. Taxonomy and Analysis

A simple conceptual model is employed to evaluate the geographic neutrality of various combinations of sources and uses of tax revenues from resource rents. In order to simplify the analysis initially, we abstract from many complications. But when certain of the simplifying assumptions are relaxed in section III, many real-world problems are highlighted.

A. The Model

It is assumed that two states constitute a nation. Since analysis focuses on effects of geographic differences in availability of revenues from natural resources, we assume for convenience that one state (A) contains

11. Mieszkowski and Toder (1983) and Mieszkowski (forthcoming) present preliminary estimates of the economic cost of the distortions described here. We do not even consider other questions of economic efficiency, such as distortions of the labor-leisure choice, the saving-consumption choice, and the optimal supply of public goods. It can be argued, for example, that the AHSTF provides a large pool of saving that would not exist if the taxation of resource rents were centralized in Ottawa. A more complete analysis would, of course, consider such issues.

12. As originally presented, this chapter also contained an extensive section on "Legal Developments and Limitations," based largely on Hellerstein (1978). The decision in *Commonwealth Edison* 101 s. ct. 2946 (1981) renders this discussion largely obsolete. Similarly, the accord between Alberta and Ottawa makes much of the original discussion of institutions determining the split of revenues between the provinces and national government of Canada outmoded. See Mieszkowski and Toder (1983) and Mieszkowski (forthcoming) for an analysis of such institutions in the U.S.

natural resources but the other (B) does not.[13] We assume that exploitation of natural resources requires such a minimal amount of factor inputs that its cost can be ignored and that no external social costs or benefits are involved; thus the entire proceeds from sale of the natural resources are economic rent for society, as well as for owners of the resource. In section III we modify this assumption that exploitation of natural resources involves no environmental degradation or other social costs. We begin the analysis with the assumptions that exploitation can be painlessly begun at the optimal level and that the natural resource in question is inexhaustible, but is exploited at an exogenously determined annual rate. Thus we abstract from the problem of determining the optimal rate of extraction the effects of taxation on extraction and the social problems that result from "boomtowns" and subsequently declining regions. But in section III, we discuss the public financial implications of boomtowns.

To simplify the analysis further, it is assumed that the two states contain equal amounts of equally fertile land and are characterized by identical production functions for nonresource products, the arguments of which are labor, capital, and land. Since, as indicated by this specification of the production function, natural resources do not enter into the production of nonresource products, and the resource industry has been assumed to involve no real costs, the natural resource can best be seen as a perpetual flow analogous to manna from heaven that can either be consumed or traded for other goods.

Because our primary interest is, in the long run, efficiency of allocation of economic resources, we assume initially that both labor and capital are completely mobile between states. But in section III, we comment on the equity effects of short-run immobility and barriers to migration.

The nation is assumed to be open to foreign commerce, but foreign influences are not modelled explicitly. Rather, we simply assume (a) that natural resources are exported from the country in exchange for other goods and (b) that prices of all goods are determined on international markets, so that they are fixed so far as the nation under discussion is concerned. It is worth noting at this point that we have carefully assumed away the possibility of tax exporting to consumers in the state that has no natural resources. This is not to say that tax exporting does not actually occur. But as I explain more fully in part D of this section, it is important to recognize that the efficiency results to be presented initially do not depend on tax exporting.

13. Reality has conveniently provided Alaska and Alberta as examples of "state A." Boston does fairly well as the archtypical "state B."

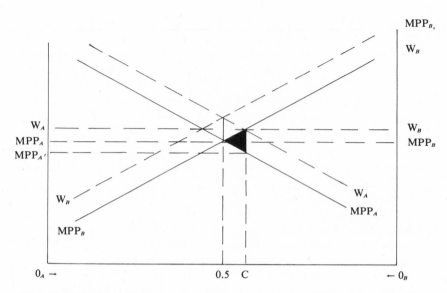

Figure 7.1. Marginal physical product of labor (or capital) as function of interstate allocation of labor (or capital)

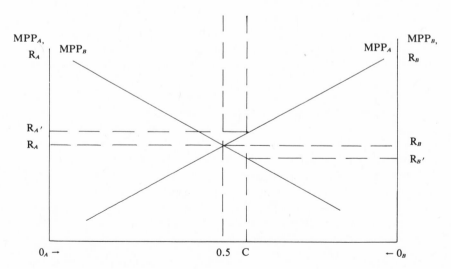

Figure 7.2 Marginal physical product of land as function of interstate allocation of labor (or capital)

We begin the analysis with a world in which natural resources are privately owned and untaxed. It is assumed that the rentiers who receive resource rents will employ those rents in a way that maximizes their utility and that, by standard theoretical reasoning, this results in the optimal allocation of the mobile resources (capital and labor) across states, as well as across industries. Rentiers are assumed initially to be divided between the two states in a way that depends on historical accident. They may be concentrated in the resource-rich state, but that is not inevitably the case and not really relevant for the present analysis. We also assume initially that there are no taxes on capital and labor that do not reflect benefits of government services. Relaxing this assumption will, of course, complicate the analysis.

The initial equilibrium in the situation just described can be illustrated heuristically as in Figure 7.1. This diagram can be thought of as illustrating the optimal interstate allocation of labor (or, with relabeling, capital). The horizontal distance between the two origins represents the total labor supply of the country at any given time. The amount of labor used in state A is measured to the right from 0_A and that in state B to the left from 0_B. The marginal physical product (and revenue product) of labor in the two states is given by the two curves (MPP$_A$ and MPP$_B$).[14] Because of the assumption that labor pays no taxes not related to benefits and is completely mobile between states, the allocation of labor is determined by the intersection of these two curves, at which point the wage rates and marginal products of labor in the two states are equal and total national output is maximized. Given the initial assumptions of identical production functions and endowments of land, this occurs where employment in the two states is equal, but this fact has no real consequence, stemming as it does from a special assumption. Analogous reasoning applies to the interstate allocation of capital.

The two curves (MPP$_A$ and MPP$_B$) in Figure 7.2 indicate how the marginal productivity of land (and land rent) in each of the two states depends upon the allocation of labor (and capital) between the states. Given the special assumptions underlying this analysis, the two curves are mirror images and intersect at the point at which labor is evenly divided between the two states and land has the same marginal produc-

14. If, as is assumed, capital is mobile, the marginal physical product of labor will generally depend on the amount of capital with which it is combined in each state. Strictly speaking, these curves showing the MPP of labor can thus be drawn only for a given investment of capital in each state or for "packages" of capital and labor used together in fixed proportions. Though not rigorous, this simple diagram is nevertheless useful in gaining an intuitive understanding of the geographic misallocations that can result from subnational use of revenues from taxation of natural resource rents.

Table 7.1. Taxonomy of Sources and Uses of Revenues from Resource Rents and Effects on Geographic Allocation of Resources

	Province Building						Country Building			
	Public Goods (a)	Specific Good (b)	Wage Subsidy (c)	Portfolio Investment[a] (d)	Direct Public Investment[a] (e)	Capital Subsidy (f)	Debt Retirement or Portfolio Investment (g)	Direct Public Investment (h)	Capital Subsidy (i)	Revenue Sharing (j)
1. Federal	potentially efficient	potentially efficient	efficient	distorts	distorts	distorts	potentially efficient	potentially efficient	efficient	potentially efficient
2. State taxation										
a. Source based	distorts	distorts	distorts	distorts	distorts	distorts	potentially efficient	efficient	efficient	fosters efficiency
b. Residence based	concentration of rentiers and mis-allocations	misallocations to states where rentiers are concentrated					efficient	efficient	efficient but unlikely	efficient

[a] Assumed not to be made in accord with dictates of capital markets

tivity and earns the same rent in each state. More generally, whereas in the initial equilibrium, mobility assures that both labor and capital would have identical marginal productivities in the two states, the marginal productivity of land and rents in the two states could differ, depending upon the relative abundance of land and the production functions of the states.

Imposition of a tax on resource rents would reduce the amount of income available to rentiers. To the extent that the drop in income may be reflected in reduced saving, there would be less capital at any point of time, and the various curves involved in this analysis would be altered. But the tax would not, in and of itself, alter the tendency for the resources to be allocated optimally between the states. The locational distortions at issue in this chapter result from the way tax revenues are spent.

B. Federal Taxation

Consider various alternative uses that might be made of revenues raised by a federal tax on resource rents. Federal revenues from resource rents could be used to subsidize wages uniformly throughout the country, say, by reducing payroll taxes (see Table 7.1, line 1, column c). In such an event net wages would rise by the amount of the subsidy in both states, but the gross wages paid by firms would be unaffected. This result is shown by the intersection of the two broken curves (W_A and W_B) in Figure 7.1. The choice between labor and leisure might be affected, but no geographic misallocation of labor or other resources would result.

Similarly, using revenues from a tax on resource rents to subsidize all investment in the country, say, through a uniform tax reduction or negative tax on capital income, might affect the total amount of investment in the country by affecting saving (or, in a more complete model, by stimulating capital inflow). Depending on how the capital stock may be affected, the various curves in Figure 7.1 and 7.2 might shift. These effects are beyond the scope of this analysis. But a uniform national tax reduction or capital subsidy would result in identical shifts for each of a given pair of curves, so that no geographic misallocation of capital (or labor) between the two states would result (see Table 7.1, line 1, column i). Thus this solution would also be geographically neutral.

Of course, there is no reason to believe that federal revenues from resource rents would be used entirely to subsidize investment or wages. A somewhat more likely result is that at least part of revenues would be devoted to increased public provision of goods and services. If specific goods and services were provided to households in amounts that did not depend on the location of the beneficiary, the result might, however, be analytically indistinguishable from payment of a wage subsidy, since, by assumption, specific goods are simply private goods provided by the public sector. In the extreme case the publicly provided specific goods would simply replace privately purchased goods, freeing private purchasing power for other uses.[15] Thus, as in the wage subsidy case, no geographic misallocation of resources would necessarily result. Pure public goods are different, in that once provided they can be enjoyed by everyone. But if the benefits of public goods are uniform throughout the nation or if equal per capita amounts of public goods that do not have benefits that extend beyond state borders are provided in the two states, everyone receives benefits that are independent of state of residence. Again, the result could be geographic neutrality.[16] These results are shown in Table 7.1, line 1, columns a and b.

Another approach might be simply to run a federal budget surplus and make the resulting financial resources available through capital markets (via retirement of public debt or private portfolio investment) for investment in the private sector (Table 7.1, line 1, column g). In theory, the result in this case could be economically efficient, particularly under the scenario of debt retirement. In that case, one would expect a result similar to the counterfactual result in which private rentiers use resource rents for private investment. Another alternative would be to have the federal government invest directly in economic activities (Table 7.1, line 1, column h). Provided federal investment were subject to the same taxes and regulations as private investment and were made with the objective of maximizing national social welfare, this use of federal funds could also be efficient.[17] In fact, because of failures of incentives, direct government investment and perhaps even portfolio investment are likely to produce a result inferior to the private welfare-maximizing outcome.

The results to this point can be easily summarized. Except insofar as distortions of the choices between labor and leisure and between present

15. This extreme result would occur only if specific goods were inframarginal to the amount of the good desired. Otherwise, households would have more of the good than they would voluntarily buy, given its price and their incomes.

16. The analysis is somewhat different if services are provided to firms rather than households, but efficiency effects are not fundamentally different.

17. For a further elaboration of this line of reasoning, see Gillis and McLure (1976). Strictly speaking, it is not necessary that federal investment actually be subject to the same taxes and regulations as private investment; what is necessary is that public decisions on investment are made *as if* the same taxes and regulations apply. Country building might, of course, involve investments that would be justifiable on social grounds, but not on the basis of returns to private investors. Examples of such social considerations might be income distributional objectives, and external economies and diseconomies that would not be relevant to private investors. These could, in principle, be incorporated in the pricing signals to which both public and private managers respond. These issues are not considered further.

and future consumption are concerned, wage and capital subsidies financed by a national tax on natural resource rents do not distort the allocation of resources, so long as the subsidies are uniform throughout the nation. Nor does federal provision of either pure public goods or specified goods financed by revenues raised from taxes on natural resources distort the geographic allocation of resources. If a budget surplus is made available for private investment, the result should be locationally neutral. Finally, if public investment is made in accord with the dictates of economic efficiency, the use of resource rents for country building need not be spatially inefficient. But the "if" in this proviso is a big one.

If, on the other hand, federal revenues were employed to spur development in the resource-rich state (or in the other state, for that matter), the geographic allocation of resources would be distorted (see Table 7.1, line 1, columns d–f). Since this case is analytically similar to the "province building" considered in the next subsection, it is not discussed in detail. But it may be worthwhile to note here that federal subsidies for the consumption of energy distort locational choices toward cold climates, as well as cause too much energy to be consumed in total.

Revenue sharing plays an interesting role in this analysis. Sharing of federal funds with the states, based on either population or the origin of capital income, would be neutral toward the spatial allocation of resources in this model.[18] Perhaps more important is the role to be played by federal equalization schemes if revenues from resource rents are *not* nationalized. As noted in the remainder of this section, it can be expected that state command over resource rents results in geographic misallocation of resources. In this situation, grant schemes that go beyond merely sharing resource rents toward the equalization of fiscal capacity can help to reduce the distortion of the allocation of resources toward the resource-rich state.

C. State Taxation

Having presented these benchmarks for the efficient private and federal use of revenues from resource rents, we turn now to the primary issue of interest, the geographic neutrality of state taxes on rents from natural resources. We distinguish between taxes collected by the states in which rentiers reside and those collected by states where resources are located.

18. Strictly speaking, this result would hold for revenue sharing based on population only if the ratio of population to workers were the same in the two states, since it is actually revenue sharing based on labor income that would be spatially neutral. We ignore demographic complications such as this in the remainder of this section. Similarly, we ignore the difficulty of determining the source of capital income for the purpose of revenue sharing; but see McLure (Ch. 2, this volume).

Source Taxation.—It has been suggested that the Alberta Heritage Savings Trust Fund should be invested in part in country building as well as in province building. If Alberta (or a state of residence of rentiers, for that matter) were simply to engage in portfolio investments in financial securities of Canadian institutions or if it were to engage in direct investments but followed the same principles as private investors, there is little reason to believe that the results would differ considerably from those in columns g and h of line 1, Table 7.1, provided that provincial investments were taxed and regulated like private investments.[19] Thus, as with the use of federal revenues, it appears that the state use of revenues for country building would not necessarily be geographically inefficient. Similar comments might apply to Table 7.1, column i of line 2a, country building via a nationally uniform capital subsidy financed by the source state, but this use of state funds seems rather unlikely, except as a form of payment intended to forestall even more adverse policies mandated by the federal government.[20] Of course, to the extent that source states share their revenues with other states (Table 7.1, line 2a, column j), geographic neutrality is fostered.

All the other uses of revenues from taxes on resource rents collected by source states produce geographic misallocations. This can be seen most clearly in the case of a wage subsidy limited to the producing state. Immigration into the resource-rich state is stimulated to the point that the sum of the marginal product of labor in that state and the wage subsidy equals the marginal product of labor in the resource-poor state. This is illustrated in Figure 7.1 by assuming that the schedule showing wages received by workers in A shifts to W_A, but that in B remains at MPP_B. Equilibrium occurs at allocation C, where W_A and MPP_B intersect. The marginal product of labor is greater in B and less in A than in the optimum situation without distortion. Due to this misallocation, society suffers a loss equal to the shaded area between the two marginal product curves. A similar result holds for a subsidy to capital invested in the

19. It is, of course, unlikely that direct state investments would be taxed like those of private investors. Thus, an institution such as the Alberta Heritage Savings Trust Fund might constitute an enormous new component of tax-exempt investment. The implications of such a development are worthy of further study but are not considered here.

20. There is, however, something artificial about the blurring of the distinction between country building investments and a provincially financed nationwide subsidy to capital. The capital subsidy seems unlikely because it involves relinquishment of the provincial claim to rents. If the lending of funds seems more palatable, it may be because the rents remain legally vested in the province. But inherent in the presumed difference seems to be a perception that residents of the province may reap some future benefit from the invested funds, even if returns on the investment are continually being reinvested. If this is true, that use of funds may not be geographically neutral after all.

resource-rich state. The result is quite analogous in the case of public funds used to provide private (specific) goods, and is only slightly different if revenues from the tax on natural resources are used to finance pure public goods with benefits that do not spill across state lines. In this case the benefits that can be provided are independent of the number of persons for whom they are provided, but excess population is encouraged.

Once we consider other state or provincial tax and expenditure policies it is necessary to specify what is meant by "province building" investment. If it merely means that the fiscal authorities of the state or province must invest directly in the state or province or indirectly, via securities of firms operating there, misallocations need not occur. No distortion would occur, for example, if public investment were made on sound principles and replaced inframarginal private investment that would have otherwise occurred. (Private funds would simply be invested elsewhere, perhaps outside the state or province.) But such a result seems hardly to be of practical relevance, for it could occur only if so few funds were involved that private investment *could* be replaced without significantly affecting returns to capital (and land and labor). Far more relevant is the case in which investment is limited to the state or province, but sound economic principles would *not* dictate investment there.[21] Naturally enough, province building, thus defined, results in the uneconomical misallocation of resources to the taxing jurisdiction.

Residence Taxation.—Rents from natural resources are usually taxed most heavily by states in which the resources are located. But they do not toally escape taxation by states of residence, since income of rentiers is so often subject to state income taxes. It is thus useful to consider this alternative, especially since one prominent bit of analysis of the taxation of economic rents has been based on the taxation of rents by states of residence, rather than states of origin (see Flatters, Henderson, and Mieszkowski [1974]). For this purpose assume that resource rents are the only source of income of rentiers.

If taxes on resource rents are confiscatory in all states, rentiers are totally indifferent about where they reside, so long as no public goods or other benefits are provided to them. Thus, whether or not state taxation based on residence is geographically efficient would depend upon the initial distribution of rent payments among states of residence. If, as is likely, rentiers are concentrated in one state, a wage subsidy, for example, could be higher in that state than in the other, and both capital and labor would be misallocated. A similar result would apply if public funds

21. See the comments in Collins (1980) about the difficulty of finding investment outlets for the AHSTF that would both spur development in Alberta and provide a reasonable rate of return.

were used to provide specific goods to workers within the state.[22] Province building in this context produces a similar result. Either subsidization of capital investment within the province or direct or portfolio investment targeted to the province that cannot be justified by standard economic analysis would result in a misallocation of capital toward the states in which rentiers were concentrated.

There is, of course, something unnatural about this result. If the state that had relatively few rentiers were to levy a tax of less than 100 percent on natural resource rents, it could attract rentiers if the latter are mobile. Indeed, unless there are barriers to migration of rentiers that have not yet been specified, the low tax state would attract *all* rentiers, and competition between the states could be expected to bid the tax rate down until it approached zero. This is, of course, one of the reasons it is expected that states cannot effectively use redistributional tax policies.

Once we allow for the provision of pure public goods by states of residence of rentiers, the analysis becomes somewhat different. With confiscatory taxes rentiers can, by assumption, consume only public goods or specific goods. In the latter case competition between the states would result in the tax on rents being essentially a benefit tax, and therefore not distorting.[23] If public goods are supplied to rentiers, it is in the best interest of rentiers to concentrate in one of the two states in order to maximize the total amount of public goods provided for them. Once this happens, one state has the entire natural resource tax base, as noted by Flatters, Henderson, and Mieszkowski (1974). Since workers can also consume the public good, this concentration means that labor will be misallocated between the two states until the point at which the marginal product of labor in the state that has no rentiers equals the sum of the value of public goods and the marginal product of labor in the state where rentiers concentrate. This, of course, produces a geographic misallocation that resembles those in the cases where state taxation is based on the location of natural resources. (It is worth noting that this result occurs independently of whether or not states compete for rentiers, unless competition drives the tax on rents to zero.)

D. Conclusions

The implications of the analysis presented here are clear. Source taxation of rents from renewable natural resources, to the extent that

22. If specific goods were provided to rentiers, as well as to workers, there would be an incentive for them to concentrate where provision is greatest. Even with confiscatory taxes, competition of the type described in the next paragraph of the text, but on the expenditure side, could be expected.

23. It might be argued, however, that rentiers would not be in equilibrium in the allocation of income between private and specific goods.

revenues exceed what is necessary to compensate for benefits of public services and environmental degradation, almost certainly results in the geographic misallocation of resources toward the resource-rich state. The primary exception to this conclusion is the case in which revenues are shared with resource-poor states or used for country building. Taxation based on the state of residence of rentiers is also likely to result in misalloation, though through a different mechanism. Again, country building and revenue sharing provide exceptions. Only in the case of federal taxation is it generally likely that geographic misallocation can be avoided.

E. Distributional Effects

Much of the contemporary debate over the allocation of power to tax resource rents is couched in terms of income distribution, not geographic misallocation of capital and labor. Even where arguments refer to effects on the location of industry induced by the ability of resource-rich states to offer attractive nonresource taxes, the concern appears to be basically distributional, not allocational. As indicated in the next section, there are good short-run reasons for this emphasis, aside from the generally observed phenomenon that economic neutrality is a goal espoused almost solely by economists. But it may be worthwhile to emphasize that in the perfectly competitive, complete mobility model of this section much of this concern about distributional effects would be misplaced. The reason is simple. By assumption both labor and capital move to the point where there is no further gain from movement, no matter what policy is followed. Hence it makes little difference to them, from a distributional point of view, whether a given policy (wage subsidy, capital subsidy, provision of public goods, etc.) is uniform across the nation and therefore neutral, or confined to a state and nonneutral.

The result can, of course, be quite different for landowners. Because land is immobile, the geographic allocation of complementary factors can be an important determinant of land rents. This is illustrated in Figure 7.2. Because of the reallocation of resources toward A made possible by the use of resource rents to subsidize wages in A, rents in that state are R_A' and those in B are R_B', rather than what they would be under a neutral use of revenues from resource rents, R_A and R_B, respectively.[24]

24. A more conventional analysis would be to use a diagram for land analogous to that of Figure 7.1. In the cases of no taxes or the use of resource rents to finance neutral policies, equilibrium in this special case would occur where the demand curves for land in the two states intersect at the fixed point of interstate allocation of land. The reallocation of labor and capital resulting from non-neutral use of revenues from resource rents would shift the demand curve for land (MPP) up in A and down in B, producing the changes in rents shown in Figure 7.2.

Of course, as noted above, there is no reason that the two states should actually be mirror images. Most of the natural resources of the United States are located in the largely unsettled states of the Rocky Mountains. Thus it may be that the real-world diagram corresponding to that of Figure 7.2 would show a quite flat curve for state A, relative to that for state B, with land rents being substantially higher in B than in A. Under these conditions, a shift in the location of industry would have a more severely detrimental effect on land rents in state B than the corresponding gain it would produce in state A.[25] This could help explain why non-neutral use of revenues by the resource-rich states is so annoying to those living elsewhere, at the same time that exploitation of natural resources is not popular in the energy-rich states.[26]

A final point deserves emphasis, since it may help to clarify further the nature of our argument. It is sometimes said that the resource-rich states unfairly take advantage of the consuming states by levying severance and other taxes that are exported to consuming states and then using the proceeds to replace other taxes or provide extraordinary public services and thereby attract industry away from the consuming states.[27] The use of revenues from natural resources to attract industry is, of course, the subject of this chapter. But note that there is no presumption that the tax on natural resources examined above is shifted to consumers of the natural resource in state B. We have, on the contrary, assumed from the outset that the price of the resource is set in world markets and that the entire proceeds from the resource are rents. Thus there is no possibility of shifting the tax to consumers; by assumption, the tax is a burden on economic rents. (Whether rentiers live in the producing states or elsewhere we have left unspecified in the discussion of source-based taxes, since it is of little relevance in that context). Moreover, we have assumed that none of the resource is consumed in state B, either directly or indirectly as an input to goods traded between the states.[28] Thus there would be no burden on consumers in state B, even if conditions were such that the tax could be passed forward.

25. Under certain conditions the rise and fall in aggregate land rents in the two states will be approximately equal in magnitude. But the change would be spread over a much larger surface area in state A, producing smaller effects on rent per unit of area.

26. Implicit in this statement is an assumption that the residence of landowners is concentrated in the state in which they own land. Of course, the great majority of those living in resource-rich states are not substantial landowners.

27. For a clear statement of this view, see Appleton and Kingsley (1980, pp. 58–65).

28. Under the assumed initial conditions of the model, identical production functions and endowments of land, there would not even be any interstate trade. Once the allocation of labor and/or capital was distorted toward state A, it would specialize in goods requiring relatively intensive use of the artificially cheap factors, and B would specialize in land intensive products and in goods using the unsubsidized factor. This trade creation would be another symptom of the uneconomic misallocation of resources.

The point is not that the absence of forward shifting is the most realistic assumption, though for many purposes it probably is.[29] Rather, the point to note is that the unequal geographic distribution of natural resources makes it quite likely that nonresource factors of production will be misallocated toward resource-rich states and away from other states. This is at least as likely if, as assumed here, revenues come from rents as if they come from taxes that are shifted to those in consuming states.

III. Qualifications and Complications

The analysis of the previous section was admittedly extremely oversimplified; it omitted numerous characteristics of the real world that require qualification of the previous conclusions. Among these is the fact that we do not live in static long-run equilibrium; resources that are exhaustible are discovered and exploited, and production eventually declines. As this dynamic process occurs, public investment in infrastructure is required and may then be abandoned, and boomtowns, with their social costs, spring up and eventually may fade away, leaving aging populations ill-suited for the demands of the postresource economic environment. Moreover, contrary to the simplifying assumption of section II, exploitation of natural resources can involve other important social costs, the most important of which are various forms of environmental degradation. Finally, much of life is spent during the time frame in which there are substantial immobilities of people and of capital. Thus there are many important distributional consequences that are not captured by the simple complete-mobility model of section II. This section addresses the issues raised by these and other complications. It ends with a brief discussion of an elusive topic that can be labelled the "birthright" issue— the claim that producing states are entitled to revenues from taxes on resource rents so that they can convert the mineral wealth in the ground into financial wealth.[30]

A. Boomtowns

Exploitation of natural resources often requires extraordinary "lumps" of public investment in infrastructure that would not otherwise be needed. Roads to remote places may be needed and even those to less

29. For elaboration of this statement, see, for example, Gillis and McLure (1975), Gillis (1979), or McLure (1978). This earlier literature is synthesized and extended in McLure (1983).

30. We do not consider the important problems of designing taxes to capture rents in a world in which natural resource rents and revenues from exploitation of natural resources are not identical. As indicated earlier, in order to focus on questions of fiscal federalism, we ignore any differences that might exist in federal and state abilities and proclivities to levy taxes that burden only rents.

remote destinations may need to be upgraded in order to carry the heavy equipment used in the resource industry. Once exploration ends—and certainly once deposits are exhausted—the transportation network may be more than is needed for the more normal demands placed on it. Similarly, schools may need to be expanded rapidly in the exploration phase and then contracted as the industry matures and declines. Other examples could be cited, but these serve to illustrate the problem and the policy question it raises: whether and to what extent this need for extraordinary public investment in infrastructure justifies a claim of producing states to revenues from resource rents.[31]

Analysis based on the theory of benefit taxation and public utility pricing is of value in helping to answer this question. Both equity and efficiency demand that taxes cover the cost of publicly provided services. But whereas equity suggests that *average* costs should be covered, efficiency requires that *marginal* cost be covered. There is, of course, no reason these mandates need yield the same solution.

By ignoring temporarily the fact that much of the present problem seems to result from the growth and subsequent decline of the demand for public infrastructure, we can reformulate the analysis in such a way that the literature on peak-load pricing is instructive, especially in the case of demand for transportation. The demand for highways that far exceed the carrying capacity that would be needed in the absence of the natural resource industry is analogous to peak-load demands for services of public utilities. The industry should therefore carry the lion's share (if not all) of the entire marginal cost of providing the highways.[32] For the present purpose it seems most relevant to interpret this as long run marginal cost. If highway construction can be accomplished at constant cost, as may be likely in the present context, average costs would also be covered. Similar statements can be made about other public services.

If one accepts this reasoning, there may still be problems of timing, fiscal imbalance between local communities, and risk. Since requirements for infrastructure will generally precede the flow of tax revenues, boomtowns may experience temporary difficulties in financing public services and the quality of life may deteriorate. This is true even though one could hardly imagine better average credit risks than some of the resource-rich western states and localities. States and even local governments that will eventually be resource-rich may therefore seem to need federal "impact aid" to get them over the hump. But this approach seems illogical. Presumably what is required for efficiency is that the

31. For more on this issue, see Schulze et al. (1981).

32. An extreme version of this result can be seen from inspection of a map of northern Maine, where nearly all the roads are owned privately by the large timber firms.

present value of tax receipts from resource rents equals the present value of costs of infrastructure, not that expenditures be financed by current revenues to the extent possible and be subsidized by federal aid beyond that. Thus, in principle, infrastructure could be debt-financed and then the debt amortized from the revenues from resource rents. But since the eventual fiscal strength of state and local governments often depends on the vagaries of public policy, as well as on the risks inherent in the natural resource sector, even potentially rich governments may be unable to borrow to finance needed facilities. The above reasoning suggests that the boomtown problem is largely one of institutional failure—failure of present institutions to adapt to the mismatch of the timing of revenues and expenditure needs. This problem is aggravated where the government that experiences the costs of boom is not the one that obtains increased tax revenues. This can occur either because the governments are spatially separated (in some cases even by state boundaries) or because mismatch occurs between the tax revenues and fiscal needs of cities, counties, school districts, etc., within a given area.

A number of institutional responses are possible. For example, the federal government might provide credit on market terms—but not aid. Funds raised from prior exploitation could be channeled from state governments to the various local units that need them on a revolving-fund basis. Alternatively, governments might borrow from the energy companies that are largely responsible for the increased costs. Or the energy companies could be called on to finance infrastructure directly.[33] It is likely that imaginative institutional responses will be necessary at the state level if the temporary mismatch of fiscal resources and responsibilities is to be overcome.[34] But that does not affect the basic economic reality that the fact that the infrastructure may outlive the natural resources is of no particular relevance; it would have already been financed (fully amortized from tax revenues), just as private investment will have been.

The above provides more of a framework for thought than a totally satisfactory analysis. Clearly what is required is a calculation of the present value of the incremental social costs that can be attributed to the natural resource industry and recovered from it over time. But casual observation suggests that the need to finance infrastructure cannot justify state capture of a large proportion of the total rents from natural resources.[35]

33. As Schulze et al. (1981) note, there is much to be said for the long discredited "company town" as a means of internalizing the costs of developing infrastructure.

34. For a far-ranging description and appraisal of the response of Wyoming, including especially an analysis of the constitutional constraints that need to be considered in six of the coal-producing western states, see Daley (1976).

35. For confirmation of this view, see Schulze et al. (1981).

B. External Costs[36]

The literature of environmental policy analysis suggests that an efficient outcome requires that firms be charged for the marginal damage their activities cause. In a few cases this requires a relatively straightforward analysis in order to quantify the relevant social costs. Closing and disguising the opening of a mine shaft is a trivially simple case. Analysis of reclamation of strip mines is substantially more difficult, for the terrain will be permanently altered (for better or worse), no matter how careful and conscientious efforts are to be socially responsible. Costs of mine tailings, especially where the tailings go beyond merely being unsightly to causing serious water pollution and health hazards, are more difficult to assess. But *if* the costs of the mineral industry could be quantified, effluent and similar charges could be levied to compensate for them. Though debate still exists about whether efficiency requires that injured parties be compensated from the revenues from effluent charges, it does not seem unreasonable that states be allocated enough resource rents to cover the social costs under discussion, rather than having all funds flow to the federal government.[37]

Finally, it should be noted that some of the complaints often heard about costs of development of natural resources involve pecuniary externalities, not technological externalities such as those just mentioned. Examples are scarcity of water and higher land rents. Increased demand for water can create important issues of income distribution, as noted in the next part of this section, but not the kind of economic distortions that are created by external social costs such as pollution of water from tailings. This issue, along with the "birthright" question, is discussed in part D of this section.

C. Immobilities and Barriers to Migration

Even casual observation indicates that there are substantial barriers to the complete mobility of labor assumed in the model of section II. So long as this is true, labor in producing states will benefit from higher wage rates generated by inflows of capital and complementary labor (but

36. See also Schulze et al. (1981).

37. Several points should, however, be made. First, it might appear that if taxation of *rents* is really at stake an effluent charge would serve no purpose, so far as efficiency is concerned. But from a social point of view, rents are measured accurately only if account is taken of all social costs. Second, there would be relatively little problem with compensating injured parties if they do not respond perversely to the compensation. But reducing the private cost of settling in a place where settlement aggravates social costs may make little sense; see also Schulze et al. (1981) for further discussion of this application of the "Coase theorem." Newbery (1980) provides a more general discussion that reaches different conclusions.

not competing labor) induced by the local disposal of state revenues from resource rents. On the other hand, they may be disadvantaged by higher residential rents created by increased competition for a temporarily limited and slowly expandable supply of housing and by various kinds of environmental degradation for which they are not compensated. Contrary influences may be felt in resource-poor states.

On the production side, owners of capital employed in sectors where supply cannot expand as rapidly as demand will realize increased quasi rents. But for others, such as those involved in water-intensive production outside the resource sector, the boom may be no boon. Increased prices for inputs such as land, labor, and water will make them less competitive in world or national markets and reduce quasi rents. Such effects may, of course, extend to some labor that is specific to such disadvantaged sectors. Although the region may be generally prosperous, those whose skills are not relevant to the resource-induced expansion may not share directly in the prosperity, though they may share indirectly via lower state and local taxes. Because effects such as these are commonly not lost on the general public and on politicians, efforts have occasionally been made by producing areas to limit migration and thereby accentuate the natural immobilities that create the positive effects.

D. Whose "Birthright"?

A person or firm owning substantial mineral wealth could reasonably be expected to want to convert part of the wealth to financial assets as the deposits are depleted, rather than simply consuming it, and might even be judged profligate for failure to do so. The same reasoning has been applied to the wealth of states; failure to conserve the state's share of resource rents is often viewed as inexcusable fiscal irresponsibility.[38] Moreover, this notion of the birthright of the state, bolstered by consti-

---

38. Thus for example, the report of the Montana legislative subcommittee underlying the 30 percent severance tax contains the following language: ". . . A state's natural resources, particularly its mineral resources, are non-renewable. When the resources are mined the state loses a valuable asset forever. The levying of a severance tax is one manner by which the state can share the profits associated with the extraction of a mineral asset" (Rosen 1979, p. 677).

A similar sentiment has been expressed by Governor Link (1978, p. 264) of North Dakota:

. . . [W]e considered the consequences for future generations of North Dakotans who will not have coal available to them as an energy source—we considered the consequences of relinquishing this one-time harvest of coal.

We concluded that the burden must fall on our generation to become the planners for our children and our children's children. We affirmed that North Dakota coal should be developed only if . . . we would receive in return . . . [j]ust compensation for losing forever a one time harvest.

tutional silence on such matters, is taken as evidence that the state, rather than the federal government, should have the power to capture resource rents, even if one ignores the arguments based on public provision of infrastructure and services and on environmental and other costs discussed in parts A and B of this section.

This issue is troublesome at two levels, at the very least. First, whether the "birthright" is properly that of the individual states or should be seen as that of the nation is a fundamental constitutional question that has no easy answer. That the U.S. Constitution is essentially silent on the matter is unfortunate.[39] But experience in Canada, where the British North America Act deals explicitly with the issue, is not as encouraging as one might hope; certainly federal price controls, export taxes, and the disallowance of deductions for provincial royalties in calculating liability for federal income tax raise important questions of the attributes and extent of the provincial ownership guaranteed by the BNA.

Second, it is meaningful to speak of the "birthright" of a person, a family, or even a nation, especially if the latter controls immigration. The concept is far more elusive for a state, since the possibility of uncontrolled migration makes it difficult to know *whose* birthright is at stake. This is highlighted by various schemes that have been implemented or proposed to define beneficiaries of the patrimony of various states and provinces. Alaska has conditioned benefits on proof of native (Indian or Eskimo) blood. More recently it attempted to base tax rebates on the length of residence in Alaska; it is interesting that this approach has been deemed unconstitutional. Finally, as part of a proposal to prevent the kind of geographical inefficiencies discussed in section II, McMillan and Norrie (1980) have proposed "privatizing" the AHSTF by distributing shares in it to residents of Alberta. While there is little doubt that this approach would eliminate many of the allocational problems created by provincial ownership, one might wonder about McMillan and Norrie's claims for the equity of this approach, especially since other alternatives, including federal ownership, are available.

The possibility of federal ownership brings us back to where we started. If constitutional issues are not treated satisfactorily at the outset, considerable centrifugal tensions can be expected to develop when significant fiscal disparities arise or pre-established ownership patterns are changed.

39. It is interesting to note that (1) the Texas permanent school fund predates the sate joining the Union, and (2) when Texas surrendered its sovereignty in 1845 to become a state, it reserved (with the assent of Congress) its ownership of public lands. This does not, of course, mean that it retained sole power to tax natural resources on private lands. But it does raise interesting questions of the power of the federal government to extend the windfall profits tax to oil produced on state land in Texas. Similarly, Alaska, in choosing lands for state ownership, took those known to contain petroleum resources.

IV. A Legal Postscript

The enormous increases in resource rents generated by the actions of OPEC seem to have inspired lawmakers at all levels of government in the United States to unprecedented levels of covetousness. The federal government has levied a windfall profits tax estimated to yield revenues of $227 billion over its first eight to ten years; states in which oil, gas, and coal are found have dramatically increased severance and other taxes; local governments have raised property taxes. Nor has the desire to skim off some of the cream been limited to producing states and localities. New York and Connecticut have attempted (unconstitutionally, the courts have ruled) to siphon off some of the rents of the oil companies by combining a gross receipts tax with a prohibition of price increases, and other states have considered similar steps. Consuming states have also been considering restructuring their corporate income taxes to use the "unitary method" for much the same purpose.[40] Finally, Philadelphia has considered levying a tax on the two refineries located there. Perhaps more worrisome, some states are sifting through their economies to see what they can tax in retaliation for the taxes imposed by resource-rich states.

Leaving aside the challenges that might be made under the constitutions of the various states, there appear to be two important legal limits to efforts of state and local governments to tax natural resources: those contained in the U.S. Constitution and those that could be passed by the U.S. Congress pursuant to the Commerce clause. In the wake of *Commonwealth Edison et al. v. Montana,* it appears that the Constitution offers little hope to those who would find in it a bar to imposition of heavy severance taxes by the producing states. So long as such taxes are not facially discriminatory against out-of-state consumers of resources, they will probably be found legal.[41] On the other hand, it also appears that there is little in the Constitution that would prevent Congress from passing legislation that would limit severance taxes. Indeed, the Supreme Court has, in effect, reminded Congress that it has this power.[42] Presumably the same conclusions would apply to other means of capturing rents, such as property taxes.

The lack of federal limits on state severance taxes may soon be elimi-

40. On this issue, see McLure (Ch. 2, this volume).

41. For an excellent discussion of legal limits on state powers to tax, see Hellerstein (1983).

42. In *Commonwealth Edison v. Montana* (101 s. ct. 2959) the Court said:
 . . . [T]he appropriate level or rate of taxation is essentially a matter of legislative, and not judicial, resolution. . . . Under our federal system, the determination is to be made by state legislators in the first instance and if necessary, by Congress, when particular state taxes are thought to be contrary to federal interests.

nated. Already legislation has been introduced that would limit state severance taxes applied to coal produced on federal land and on Indian lands to 12.5 percent, and there is little reason to believe that once passed similar legislation would not be extended to coal produced on private lands and to other resources. Judging whether such legislation is desirable is beyond the scope of this chapter, although it is the purpose of the chapter to help inform a decision on the matter. But it should be noted that little purpose would be served by limiting only severance taxes, leaving states the opportunity to accomplish much the same effect through other fiscal means.[43]

References

Appleton, J., and J. Kingsley. 1980. "Western Energy Production: Related Taxes, Subsidies, and the Impact upon the Northeastern Region." Report prepared by the Governor's Office of Policy and Planning. Trenton: State of New Jersey.

Bradley, Paul G. 1976. "Governments and Mineral Resource Earnings: Taxation with Over Simplification." In *Natural Resource Revenues: A Test of Federalism,* ed. Anthony Scott, pp. 214–31. Vancouver: British Columbia University Press.

Collins, A. F. 1980. "The Alberta Heritage Savings Trust Fund: An Overview of the Issues." *Canadian Public Policy* 6 (February: 158–65.

Courchene, Thomas J. 1976. "Equalization Payments and Energy Royalties." In *Natural Resource Revenues: A Test of Federalism,* ed. Anthony Scott, pp. 74–96. Vancouver: University of British Columbia Press.

Cuciti, Peggy, Harvey Galper, and Robert Lucke. 1983. "State Energy Revenues." In *Fiscal Federalism and the Taxation of Natural Resources,* ed. Charles E. McLure, Jr. and Peter Mieszkowski, pp. 11–63. Lexington, Mass.: Lexington Books.

Daley, James B. 1976. "Financing Housing and Public Facilities in Energy Boom Towns." *Rocky Mountain Mineral Law Institute* 22: 47–144.

Dasgupta, P., G. M. Heal, and J. Stiglitz. 1980. "The Taxation of Exhaustible Resources." In *Public Policy and the Tax System,* ed. G. A. Hughes and G. M. Heal, pp. 150–72. London: George Allen and Unwin.

Drugge, S. E., and T. S. Veeman. 1980. "Industrial Diversification in Alberta: Some Problems and Policies." *Canadian Public Policy* 6 (February): 221–28.

Feldstein, Martin. 1976. "On the Theory of Tax Reform." *Journal of Public Economics* 6, 1,2(July–August): 77–104.

Flatters, Frank, Vernon Henderson, and Peter Mieszkowski. 1974. "Public Goods, Efficiency, and Regional Fiscal Equalization." *Journal of Public Economics* 3, 2(May): 99–112.

43. Note also, that such a limit would have no effect on the royalties received by Alaska, by far the greatest source of fiscal disparities in the country.

Gillis, Malcolm. 1979. "Severance Taxes on North American Energy Resources: A Tale of Two Minerals." *Growth and Change* 10, 1(January): 55–71.

Gillis, Malcolm, and Charles E. McLure, Jr. 1975. "Incidence of World Taxes on Natural Resources with Special Reference to Bauxite." *American Economic Review* 65 (May): 389–96.

Gillis, Malcolm, and Charles E. McLure, Jr. 1976. "Tax Policy and Public Enterprises." Staff Paper 8, prepared for the Bolivian Mission on Tax Reform and summarized in *Fiscal Reform in Bolivia: Final Report of the Bolivian Mission on Tax Reform,* Richard A. Musgrave, Dir., pp. 197–200. Cambridge, Mass.: International Tax Program, Harvard Law School, 1981.

Hellerstein, Walter. 1978. "Constitutional Constraints on State and Local Taxation of Energy Resources." *National Tax Journal* 31, 3(September): 245–56.

Hellerstein, Walter. 1983. "Legal Constraints on State Taxation of Natural Resources." In *Fiscal Federalism and the Taxation of Natural Resources,* ed. Charles E. McLure, Jr. and Peter Mieszkowski, pp. 135–66. Lexington, Mass.: Lexington Books.

Helliwell, John F. 1980. "Comment." In *The Alberta Heritage Saving Trust Fund,* ed. Roger S. Smith, a special issue of *Canadian Public Policy* 6 (February): 179–81.

Krutilla, John V., Anthony C. Fisher, and Richard E. Rice. 1978. *Economics and Fiscal Impacts of Coal Development: Northern Great Plains.* Baltimore: The Johns Hopkins University Press.

Link, Arthur A. 1978. "Political Constraint and North Dakota's Coal Severance Tax." *National Tax Journal* 31, 3(September): 263–68.

McLure, Charles E., Jr. 1978. "Economic Constraints on State and Local Taxation of Energy Resources." *National Tax Journal* 31, 3(September): 257–62.

McLure, Charles E., Jr. 1983. "Tax Exporting and the Commerce Clause." In *Fiscal Federalism and the Taxation of Natural Resources,* ed. Charles E. McLure, Jr. and Peter Mieszkowski, pp. 169–92. Lexington, Mass.: Lexington Books.

McLure, Charles E., Jr., Ed. Forthcoming. *Tax Assignment in Federal Countries.* Canberra: Centre for Research on Federal Financial Relations.

McMillan, M. L., and K. H. Norrie. 1980. "Province-Building vs. A Rentier Society." *Canadian Public Policy* 6 (February): 213–20.

Mieszkowski, Peter, and Eric Toder. 1983. "Taxation of Energy Resources." In *Fiscal Federalism and the Taxation of Natural Resources,* ed. Charles E. McLure, Jr. and Peter Mieszkowski, pp. 65–91. Lexington, Mass.: Lexington Books.

Mieszkowski, Peter. Forthcoming. "Energy Policy, Taxation of Natural Resources, and Fiscal Federalism." In *Tax Assignment in Federal Countries,* ed. Charles E. McLure, Jr. Canberra: Centre for Research on Federal Financial Relations.

Musgrave, Richard A., and Peggy B. Musgrave. 1980. *Public Finance in Theory and Practice,* 3d ed. New York: McGraw-Hill.

Newberry, D. M. G. 1980. "Externalities: The Theory of Environmental Pol-

icy." In *Public Policy and the Tax System,* ed. G. A. Hughes and G. M. Heal,
pp. 106–49. London: George Allen and Unwin.

Oates, Wallace E. 1968. "The Theory of Public Finance in a Federal System."
Canadian Journal of Economics 1 (February): 37–54.

Rosen, Mitchell S. 1979. "The Increasing Conflict between State Coal Severance
Taxation and Federal Energy Policy." *Texas Law Review* 57, 4(March): 675–
96.

Schulze, William D., David S. Brookshire, Ronald B. Cummings, and Ralph C.
d'Arge. 1981. "Local Taxation for Boom-Town and Environmental Effects
Resulting from National Resource Extraction." Paper presented at the TRED
Conference on Fiscal Federalism and the Taxation of Natural Resources. September 11–12, Cambridge, Mass.

Smith, Roger S., ed. 1980. *The Alberta Heritage Savings Trust Fund,* a special
issue of *Canadian Public Policy* 6 (February).

U.S. Congress. 1982a. "Fiscal Disparities." Hearings before the Subcommittee
on Intergovernmental Relations of the Committee on Governmental Affairs,
U.S. Senate, 97th Congress. Washington, D.C.: U.S. Government Printing
Office.

U.S. Congress. 1982b. "Coal Severance Tax Limitations." Hearings before the
Subcommittee on Fossil and Synthetic Fuels of the Committee on Energy and
Commerce, House of Representatives, 97th Congress. Washington, D.C.:
U.S. Government Printing Office.

8 *Jon Sonstelie*

The Public Finance of Education: Subsidy versus Supply

I. Introduction

Nonfederal governments spend more money on elementary and secondary education than in any other expenditure category. In the 1976–77 fiscal year, school expenditures constituted 26 percent of the combined budgets of state and local governments and 52 percent of the budgets of local governments (Bureau of the Census 1978). Few people take exception to the notion that governments should play a role in the financial support of education. A literate population is recognized as a necessity for the smooth working of both a democratic government and a market economy. There is less agreement about the form the governmental role should take, however. In the broadest sense, the alternative roles are supply and subsidy. The government can supply education itself and make it available at little or no cost to students, or it can subsidize the provision of education in the private sector. Although public supply has predominated, there have recently been several proposals that would initiate some form of subsidy for private schools.

The first of those is the Packwood-Moynihan bill, which would have provided federal tax credits for private school tuition. The bill passed the House of Representatives in 1978 but was narrowly defeated in the Senate. In California, attempts have been made to put two different subsidy schemes on the ballot. The first was a modified version of the educational voucher; the second was a tuition tax credit for the state income tax. As yet, none of these proposals has been successfully enacted. Perhaps we are merely experiencing a brief and ultimately futile flurry of activity in this area like that of the attempts by the Nixon administration to enact some form of public aid to nonpublic schools in the early 1970s. There are two reasons for thinking that support for these attempts will be wider and more enduring this time, however.

First, the recent reforms of public school finance initiated by *Serrano v. Priest* and other court decisions will, I believe, make subsidies for private education more appealing to many families. Education is not essentially a public good, in that economies of scale in joint consumption are exhausted on a small scale. There is thus little benefit in having a large number of people consume the same quality of the good. On the other hand, there are considerable costs to this arrangement, since all families will not demand the same quality. Families whose tastes and incomes lead them to demand a high level of quality must somehow strike a compromise with those who would prefer to spend less money on education. Given the lack of mutual benefits from common consumption, it would seem unlikely that public education would be a stable institution. It has endured, nevertheless, and part of the credit for that must be given to the local nature of public school finance, which has allowed considerable diversity in spending levels across districts. Because of that diversity,

Table 8.1. Educational Expenditures

	Real Expenditures per Pupil		Real Earnings per Full-Time Employee (all workers)	Average Real Salary per Teacher
	Total	Operating		
1949–50	$ 685	$ 553	$ 7,749	$ 7,961
1951–52	746	581	7,914	8,219
1953–54	817	617	8,446	8,905
1955–56	904	685	9,142	9,682
1957–58	984	747	9,369	10,303
1959–60	1,006	799	9,874	11,029
1961–62	1,104	873	10,263	11,873
1963–64	1,135	934	10,905	12,665
1965–66	1,283	1,053	11,450	13,602
1967–68	1,447	1,211	11,863	14,047
1969–70	1,584	1,353	12,161	14,658
1971–72	1,717	1,507	12,684	15,372
1973–74	2,076	1,837	12,954	15,019
1975–76	1,918	1,704	12,666	14,784
1977–78	1,953	1,739	12,805	14,836

Source: National Center for Educational Statistics, *Digest of Educational Statistics,* 1979

families who demanded high levels of public school spending did not necessarily have to compromise with others who demanded less. They could realize their demands by moving to a community of families with like demands. The recent round of school finance reforms will tend to close that outlet by equalizing expenditure levels across districts. The private sector will then be the only outlet for those who are dissatisfied with the quality of education in the public sector. We should therefore expect to see support from those families for policies that would make that outlet less costly.

The second reason for thinking that support for such policies may grow is the rapid rise in expenditures for public education. In the first two columns of Table 8.1, I have listed expenditures per pupil in the United States adjusted by the Consumer Price Index. Note that expenditures per pupil almost tripled in real terms between 1949 and 1977. In contrast, the earnings of full-time employees, represented in column 3, have not quite doubled in real terms. Part of the explanation for the growth in expenditures may be demand responses to changes in prices and income. In a stimulating paper, Borcherding (1977) has attempted to account for the growth in government spending through just such price and income effects. The following is an application of his approach to the statistics on educational spending in Table 8.1. As Borcherding has shown, assuming that the growth of income and of the price of education is exponential and that the demand of education has constant price and income elasticities, the growth rate in expenditures per pupil can be expressed as $(1 + e_p)r_p + e_w r_w$, where e_p is the price elasticity of the demand for education, e_w is its income elasticity, and r_p and r_w are the growth rates of price and income, respectively. The annual growth rate in expenditures per pupil from 1949–50 to 1977–78 was 5.8 percent, while the growth rate for earnings was 2.8 percent. As an index of the price of education, I have used the average real salary of members of public school instructional staffs, which is listed in the fourth column of Table 8.1. The annual growth rate for salaries was 3.5 percent. Inman (1978) has estimated price and income elasticities for public education at approximately -0.4 and 0.7, respectively. Using those estimates, one can calculate a predicted annual growth rate of expenditures per pupil of 4.1 percent.

These calculations are admittedly crude. Nevertheless, the picture they paint is one of an educational sector growing 1.7 percent per annum faster than the growth rate justified by changes in prices and incomes.[1]

1. In his study of general government expenditures over a longer time span, Borcherding has also found that the growth in expenditures could not be fully explained by changes in prices and income. Shapiro (1981) has applied the same approach to public expenditures in California before Proposition 13. He also has found evidence that the growth in expenditures exceeded that rate predicted by changes in income and prices.

Table 8.2. Annual Growth Rates

	Actual Expenditures per Pupil	Real Salary per Teacher	Real Earnings	Predicted Expenditure per Pupil
1949–50 / 1977–78	5.8%	3.5%	2.8%	4.1%
1949–50 / 1959–60	3.8	3.3	2.4	3.7
1959–60 / 1969–70	4.5	2.8	2.1	3.2
1969–70 / 1977–78	2.6	0.2	0.6	0.5

An even more interesting picture emerges if these growth rates are broken down by decade. In Table 8.2, the growth rates of actual educational expenditures, of prices, and of incomes are given for each of the three decades since 1950. The last column is the predicted growth rate in educational expenditures based on the growth in prices and incomes. Notice that during the 1950s, the predicted growth rate in expenditures was virtually identical to the actual growth rate. During the 1960s, the actual rate exceeded the predicted rate by 1.3 percent, and in the 1970s the actual exceeded the predicted by 2.1 percent. Thus, it appears that in the 1960s the growth in expenditures per pupil began exceeding the rate that can be justified by changes in prices and incomes and that the divergence between the two increased in the 1970s.

There are many possible explanations for this divergence. One possibility is that educational expenditures were below equilibrium levels at the beginning of the period and that they have been catching up ever since. Another is that the total expenditures of school districts grew rapidly in the 1950s to accommodate growing enrollments caused by the postwar baby boom and that the system overshot the equilibrium in the 1960s and 1970s. Critics of public education would make a different case from these figures, however. In their view, public education has become an overgrown bureaucracy with goals of its own that bear little resemblance to the basic concerns of parents. If that view becomes widespread, we should expect to see more attempts to rein in that bureaucracy in the future. Tuition tax credits and educational vouchers may be perceived as ideal tools for this job, because they would make the alternatives to the public sector more competitive.

Subsidies for private education touch many of the issues of central concern to students of state and local public finance. Since such subsidies will reduce public school enrollments, they will also reduce total school expenditures, and thus the need for property tax revenues at the local level. At the same time, the subsidies themselves will either increase expenditures at a higher level of government, as in the case of vouchers, or decrease tax revenues at a higher level, as in the case of tuition tax credits. Thus, the traditional issues of intergovernmental fiscal relations come into play. Moreover, subsidies for private education will affect public expenditure decisions at the local level. If more parents enroll their children in the private sector as a result of the subsidies, political support for public schools will decline, and expenditures per pupil may decline as well. But a decrease in public school enrollments also decreases the tax price of expenditures per pupil in a school district. As a result, the demand for expenditures per pupil would tend to increase for those with children in public schools. The net outcome of these two opposing forces depends on the political process for making expenditure decisions and on the way the property tax distributes the burden of local school expenditures. These also are traditional areas of concern for students of state and local public finance.

In the remainder of this chapter, I have developed a model of the effect of private school subsidies on the finance of local public schools. Section II discusses the basic theory of choice between public school and private school and how that choice is affected by subsidies for private education. In section II, a model of political decisions on public school expenditures is developed. It is shown that even minor subsidies for private education are theoretically capable of inducing dramatic declines in public school enrollments and expenditures. For realistic values of the relevant parameters, this instability is shown to be unlikely, however. The general conclusions to be drawn from the model are summarized in section IV.

II. The Choice Between Public and Private Schools

A family with a school-age child may educate that child either in the public schools in its community or in one of a variety of private schools. The public schools provide an education of a given quality and charge no tuition. The private schools vary in quality, and each charges a tuition which reflects the quality of education it provides.

The choice between public and private schools is represented graphically in Figure 8.1. The curve D is the family's demand curve for education compensated to the utility level the family would obtain if it were to send its child to the public schools in its community. Given that it is compensated to that utility level and given that the price of educational quality in the private sector is p, the family would demand an education of quality q if it were to send its child to a private school. The public sector offers an education of quality $\bar{q}$ at no charge.

The choice between the private and public sectors can be expressed in terms of the family's public school surplus (PSS), which is defined as the

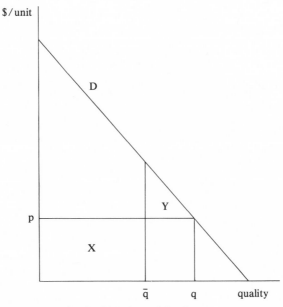

Figure 8.1. Public school surplus for high demand family

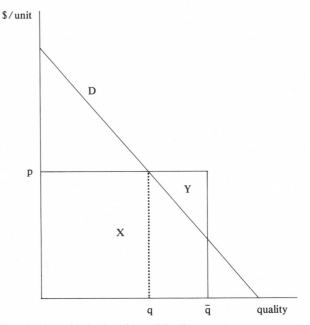

Figure 8.2. Public school surplus for low demand family

minimum amount the family must be compensated to enroll its child in a private school rather than in its local public school. The family's PSS is represented in Figure 8.1 as the area of rectangle X minus the area of triangle Y. The area of the rectangle is the amount the family must pay to obtain an education in the private sector equivalent in quality to that provided in the public sector. This amount overstates the family's PSS, however, because by opting for the private sector the family may choose a higher quality of education than that provided in the public sector. The surplus to be gained in this manner equals the area of triangle Y. The family's PSS is thus the private sector cost of the public sector education less any surplus the family gets by consuming more education in the private sector than it would have consumed in the public sector. If the PSS is positive, the family would enroll its child in the public school. If it is negative, it would opt for the private sector.

Figure 8.1 implicitly assumes that the family would consume more education in the private sector than in the public sector. That is not necessarily the case, of course. In Figure 8.2, a family's PSS is represented for the case in which the family's compensated demand in the private sector is less than the quality of education in the public sector. In that case, the PSS is the rectangle X less the triangle Y lying inside of it. The interpretation of the rectangle is the same as before. The triangle, however, represents the gain to the family by reducing the quality of education it would consume in the private sector below the quality provided in the public sector. That gain occurs because the family's marginal willingness to pay for an education of the quality provided in the public sector is less than the marginal cost of that education in the private sector. By reducing its consumption of education and diverting some of the resources that would have been spent on education to other forms of consumption, the family increases its welfare.

A family's PSS will vary with income. Figures 8.1 and 8.2 demonstrate that the family's PSS is always less than or equal to $p\bar{q}$, which is the private sector cost of the quality of education provided in the public sector. When income is low enough that the family's compensated demand for education in the private sector is less than the educational quality in the public sector, the family's PSS is strictly less than $p\bar{q}$. As income rises, PSS also rises until it equals $p\bar{q}$ at the income level where the family's compensated demand for education in the private sector equals the quality of education in the public sector. As income increases beyond that level, the compensated demand for private education exceeds the quality of the local public schools, and thus PSS will decline. The relationship between PSS and income is therefore an inverted $\cup$-shaped curve (represented in Figure 8.3) with a maximum of $p\bar{q}$. The income w_0 is the income at which the family demands the school quality provided in the public sector. At that income, the PSS equals $p\bar{q}$. For incomes less than w_0, the PSS is less than $p\bar{q}$. It must be positive, however, as long as the family's demand for education is positive. At income level w_1 the family's PSS is zero. For incomes greater than that, the family would choose the private sector over the public sector.

Let me now introduce a subsidy for private education, which takes the form of an educational grant for a certain amount. That grant is received by every family that enrolls its child in a private school, it can only be spent on education, and it may be supplemented by additional expenditures on education by the family. A family's equivalent educational grant (EEC) is defined as an educational grant of an amount just large enough to induce the family to enroll its child in a private school rather than its local public schools.

If a family's compensated demand for education in the private sector exceeds the quality of education in the public sector, the family's EEC will equal its PSS. This follows because a family in that situation would spend more money on education in the private sector than its PSS, since the PSS is never greater than $p\bar{q}$. An educational grant equal to the PSS is thus entirely fungible; it is equivalent to a lump-sum payment with no strings attached. Since the PSS is the minimum lump-sum payment necessary to induce a family to transfer its child from public to private

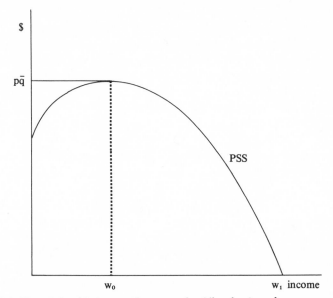

Figure 8.3. The relationship between income and public school surplus

schools, it must also be the minimum educational grant necessary to induce that transfer.

For a family whose compensated demand for education in the private sector is less than the quality of education in the public sector, the EEC will equal $p\bar{q}$. To understand this, consider a case where the family receives an educational grant equal to $p\bar{q}$, the private sector cost of an education equivalent to that in the public sector. The family can now achieve the same utility level it would have achieved in the public sector by enrolling its child in a private school that provides education of the same quality as that provided in the public schools. Its child receives the same quality of education and, as in the case of the public schools, it spends none of its own after-tax income on education. If the family's demand for education in the private sector exceeds the quality provided in the public sector, it can actually increase its utility above that level by sending its child to a school of higher quality than that of the public school. But if the family's demand for education in the private sector falls short of the quality of the public schools, it would not increase its utility by increasing expenditures on schooling. Nor would it do better for itself by decreasing those expenditures, since none of its own income is being spent on education. Therefore, an educational grant equal to $p\bar{q}$ will give the family the same utility level in the private sector as in the public sector. It is thus the equivalent educational grant for a family whose compensated demand for education in the private sector is less than the quality of the education provided in the public sector.

The relationship between the EEC and income is represented in Figure 8.3. For income low enough that the family would demand a lower quality of education than that provided in the public sector, the ECC equals $p\bar{q}$. Once income reaches a point where the compensated demand for education in the private sector exceeds the quality of the public schools, the family's EEC equals its PSS. Both of these curves depend on the quality of the local public schools. An increase in that quality will shift both curves upward and, assuming it is not accompanied by a tax increase, move w_0 to the right.

III. Median Voter Model

Since an educational grant will induce some parents to transfer their children from public to private schools, it will affect political decisions on local school expenditures. Lower enrollments will mean fewer voters with children in public schools and thus less political support for those schools. But lower enrollments will also mean a lower tax price for public school quality, which will increase the demand for quality among those

voters with children in public schools. In this section, I have modelled the
effects of those forces on local expenditure decisions.

Revenues to finance the local public schools are assumed to be raised
by the property tax. The school district's budget constraint is

$$\bar{q} = tv/s \qquad (1)$$

where $\bar{q}$ is expenditures per pupil in the public schools, t is the district's
property tax rate, v is the assessed value of property per school-age children in the district, and s is the fraction of school-age children in public
schools. I have assumed that expenditures per pupil is an index of public
school quality. From the budget constraint, the tax price of public school
quality is sh/v, where h is the assessed value of the family's house. The
family's tax price is an increasing function of s, because higher enrollments mean that the revenues raised by any given tax rate must be spread
across a larger number of public school students.

The level of expenditures is assumed to be determined by majority
rule. The vote of a family with children in public school will be determined by the difference between its demand for public school quality and
the quality supplied. An increase in income will have two effects on a
family's demand for public school quality. Assuming that public school
quality is a normal good, an increase in income will tend to increase the
demand for quality via the ordinary income effect. But because housing
is also a normal good, an increase in income will increase h, which will
increase the family's tax price. It is therefore necessary to distinguish the
partial income elasticity of demand, which is denoted by $e_{q,w}$, from a total
income elasticity, $E_{q,w}$, which includes both the partial-income effect and
the effect of income on the tax price of education. That total elasticity is

$$E_{q,w} = e_{q,p}e_{h,w} + e_{q,w} \qquad (2)$$

where $e_{q,p}$ is the price elasticity of the demand for public school quality,
and $e_{h,w}$ is the income elasticity of housing demand. The first term is the
tax-price effect, and the second is the partial-income effect. Polinsky and
Ellwood (1979) have estimated $e_{h,w}$ to be between 0.5 and 0.8. Inman
(1978) has estimated price and income elasticities of public school quality
to be about -0.4 and 0.7, respectively. According to these estimates, the
partial-income effect dominates the tax-price effect, so that the demand
for public school quality rises with income.

Assume there is a community of families whose demand functions for
public school quality are identical but whose incomes vary. Let $F(w)$ be
the percentage of those families with incomes less than or equal to w. For

families with children in public schools, the demand for public school quality will be an increasing function of income. There will therefore be some income, $\bar{w}$, at which a family would demand exactly $\bar{q}$, the level of public school quality provided. For those families with children in public schools, all with income less than $\bar{w}$ would demand less public school quality than is being provided, and all with incomes greater than $\bar{w}$ would demand more quality. I have assumed that families with children in private schools would oppose marginal increases in public school quality and support decreases in that quality. We therefore have the following political coalitions. The political support for public schools, those families that would favor increased school expenditures, comes from those families with children in public schools and incomes greater than $\bar{w}$. The opposition to those increases comes from those with children in public schools and incomes less than $\bar{w}$ and from those with children in private schools.

In equilibrium under majority rule, the number of voters that oppose an increase in public school spending must equal the number that favor an increase. All families with incomes less than $\bar{w}$ will favor a decrease in public school quality. Those with children in public school will favor it because their demands are less than $\bar{q}$; those with children in private schools will favor it because I assume that all families with children in private schools favor decreases in public school spending. This implies that $\bar{w}$ must be less than or equal to the median income. In fact no family with income less than the median will enroll their children in private schools. As was shown in the previous section, a family's equivalent educational grant decreases with income. Therefore, if any family with income less than the median were to enroll its children in private schools, then all families with incomes greater than or equal to the median must do so. In that case, more than half the families would support decreases in public school spending. Since this could not be a political equilibrium under majority rule, it must be the case that no family with income less than the median enrolls its children in private schools. Therefore, all families with incomes less than $\bar{w}$ enroll their children in public schools and oppose increases in public school spending. Assuming that the fraction of students in public schools, s, equals the fraction of families that enroll their children in public schools, political equilibrium must be characterized by

$$\tfrac{1}{2} = F(\bar{w}) + (1 - s) \tag{3}$$

The first term on the right-hand side of that equation is the fraction of families that enroll their children in public schools and oppose increases in public school spending. The second term is the fraction of families that enroll their children in private schools. Because this constitutes the political opposition to increases in public school spending, half the voters must belong to these two groups.

The effect of changes in student enrollments on the level of public school spending can be determined by equation 3. An increase in s will increase $\bar{w}$, the income of the median voter, since fewer voters will have children in private schools. But an increase in s will also increase the tax price of education, and thus decrease the demand for education by a family with any given income. The elasticity of $\bar{q}$ with respect to s is

$$e_{q,s} = E_{q,w}e_{w,s} + e_{q,p} \tag{4}$$

where $e_{w,s}$ is the elasticity of the income of the median voter with respect to a change in the fraction of students enrolled in public schools. The first term is the positive effect on $\bar{q}$ of increasing the income of the median voter; the second term is the negative effect on $\bar{q}$ of increasing the tax price. Since the first term is positive and the second is negative, the net effect of a change in enrollments on expenditures per pupil is indeterminant.

The way in which the property tax distributes the cost of public schools plays a major role in this result. To see this, suppose that the tax base for school finance were more elastic with respect to income than is housing. To be precise, suppose that the income elasticity of the base exceeded an amount, λ, which is equal to the absolute value of the income elasticity of the demand for education divided by its price elasticity. In that case, demand for educational quality would fall with income, and the political coalitions in support of public education would change.

As before, those with children in private schools would favor decreases in public school spending. But now they would be joined by those with children in public schools and incomes *greater* than $\bar{w}$. For the reasons discussed above, those with children in private schools must have incomes greater than the median. Therefore, the income of the median voter must equal the median income. Those with incomes greater than the median would then be either families with children in private schools or families with children in public schools who oppose increases in public school spending.

An increase in public school enrollments would not change the income of the median voter, since all families with incomes above $\bar{w}$ vote against increases in spending regardless of whether they send their children to private schools. The only effect of an increase in enrollments would be to increase the tax price of education and thus decrease the median voter's demand for public school quality. This is a significant point for those who are concerned with the negative effects that aid to private schools might have on public school quality. The concern is that decreased enrollment caused by such aid will lead to less political support for the public schools and thus less expenditures per pupil. If that possibility exists (and I have examined this in more detail later in the chapter), it must in part be attributed to the way the property tax system distributes the public school tax burden. If the tax base had an income elasticity greater than λ, public schools would not be subject to this danger.

The effect of student enrollments on the public school quality is only half the story, because public school quality will also affect enrollments. As was demonstrated in the previous section, the minimum educational grant large enough to induce parents to switch their children from public to private schools is a decreasing function of posttax income. Therefore, there is a posttax income that divides families who send their children to public schools from those who send their children to private schools. This critical posttax income will be negatively related to the value of the educational grant, g, and positively related to the quality of the public schools, $\bar{q}$. The posttax income of a family with pretax income of w is $w - sh\bar{q}/v$. Thus, the pretax income, $\bar{w}$, at which a family is indifferent to the choice between public and private schools is negatively related to g, positively related to $\bar{q}$, and positively related to s. Let $\bar{w} = W(s,g,\bar{q})$ be this function.

The fraction of students in public schools will be

$$s = F(W(s,g,\bar{q})) \tag{5}$$

Since the right-hand side of equation 5 is increasing in $\bar{q}$, $\bar{q}$ is implicitly defined as a function of s and g. Let $\bar{q} = Q(s,g)$ be this function. The interpretation of Q is that it gives the public school quality necessary to yield public school enrollments of s when the education grant is g. An increase in s has two opposing effects on $\bar{q}$. On the one hand, it decreases posttax income and thus decreases the quality of education necessary to induce a given percentage of students to enroll in public schools. On the other hand, an increase in s, holding posttax incomes constant, means that the quality of education must be increased to induce more parents to enroll their children in public schools. The net effect is indeterminant, although it seems that the later effect is likely to dominate the former.

To summarize, there are two relationships between public school enrollments and public school quality. The first is the effect that public

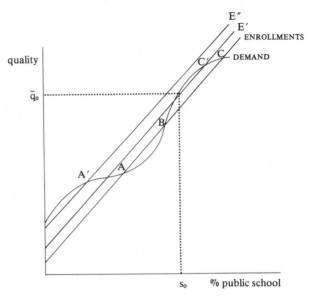

Figure 8.4. Equilibrium public school quality

school enrollments have on the demand for public school spending. This relationship is represented by the curve labeled DEMAND in Figure 8.4. The second relationship is the effect that public school quality has on the families' choice between public and private schools. This relationship is represented by the curve labeled ENROLLMENTS. An equilibrium exists where these two curves coincide. The points A, B, and C are equilibria. The possibility of multiple equilibria exists, because nothing guarantees that one curve is steeper at all points than the other. In fact, nothing even guarantees that either relationship is monotonic. This possibility of multiple equilibria for public school quality and enrollments has been recognized by Barzel and Deacon (1975), Flowers (1975), Ladd (1979), Stiglitz (1974), and Sonstelie (1979).

Points A and C in Figure 8.4 are locally stable equilibria. Imagine, for example, that the quality of education is $\bar{q}_0$. At that quality level, s_0 of the students would be enrolled in the public schools. But if s_0 of the students are enrolled in the public schools, the demand for education exceeds $\bar{q}_0$. Thus, public school quality will increase, and the system will move towards the equilibrium at C. Point B is not a stable equilibrium, however.

The possibility of multiple equilibria makes comparative statistics difficult and also raises the possibility of dramatic, nonmarginal changes in enrollments and public school quality resulting from marginal changes in parameters. Suppose, for example, that the size of the educational grant is increased. That will decrease public school enrollments for any given level of public school quality, and thus the ENROLLMENTS curve in Figure 8.4 will shift to the left. The curve E' represents that new enrollments relationship. If the system was originally in equilibrium at C, it will now adjust to the new locally stable equilibrium C'. A marginal decrease in both public school quality and public school enrollments will result.

Suppose, however, that the increase in the size of the educational grant is slightly larger so that the new enrollments curve is C'' instead of E'. Now the only equilibrium is A', which is a decidedly nonmarginal decrease in both public school quality and public school enrollments. In abstract terms, this is the possibility that appears to concern many opponents of aid to private schools. A rather small level of aid could touch off an unstable adjustment process where declines in enrollments trigger declines in public school quality, which in turn trigger further declines in enrollments. The fear is that the system will ultimately come to rest at an equilibrium characterized by public schools of low quality attended only by students from families of low incomes.

Whether that theoretical possibility could become a reality is an empirical question. A first step towards answering that question is to simulate the equilibrium of this simple model using realistic values for the relevant parameters. For that simulation, I have assumed that the school district consists of nine equally sized groups of families. All families in the same group have the same income, but incomes differ among groups. The income of Group 1 was chosen to be the upper limit of the first decile of the 1970 income distribution of families with school-age children. The income of Group 2 was chosen to be the upper limit of the second decile, and so on. These incomes are listed under the heading "Incomes" of Table 8.3.

Table 8.3. Income Groups for Simulation

	Income	Tax Price
Group 1	$ 5,033	$0.56s
Group 2	6,896	0.70s
Group 3	8,260	0.79s
Group 4	9,488	0.87s
Group 5	10,897	0.96s
Group 6	12,436	1.06s
Group 7	13,974	1.15s
Group 8	16,821	1.31s
Group 9	22,279	1.57s

I have assumed that the income elasticity of housing demand is 0.7, which implies that the share of taxes paid by a family with income w is

$$\frac{w^{0.7}}{(\Sigma w_i^{0.7})/9} = w^{0.7}/695 \tag{6}$$

where w_i is the income of families in group i. Assuming that each family has one child, the tax price of expenditures per pupil is there $sw^{0.7}/695$. These tax prices are listed that heading of Table 8.3. The demand function for education was assumed to take the form $q = p^{-0.4}w^{0.7}$ where q is expenditures per pupil, p is the tax price of expenditures per pupil, and w is income.

Calculation of the public school surplus for each group requires that an assumption be made about the price of educational quality in the private sector. Several empirical studies of services other than education have found that private provision of a good is cheaper than public provision.[2]

In a recent paper (Sontelie 1982), I found that this also appears to hold for primary and secondary education. Accordingly, I assumed that education obeys Borcherding's Bureaucratic Rule of Two—the cost of public provision is twice that of private provision. Thus, the tuition for an education equivalent to $\$X$/pupil in the public sector is $\$\frac{1}{2}X$ in the private sector.

The first task of the simulation is to determine the equilibrium levels of public school expenditures and enrollments when there are no educational grants. To do this, I first calculated the median voter's demand for expenditures per pupil under the assumption that all groups send their children to public schools. In this case, the median voter is in Group 5. Using this value for expenditures per pupil, the public school surplus was then calculated for the highest income group. If that surplus is positive, then this is indeed an equilibrium, since the public school surplus will be positive for all other groups as well, and thus all families will send their children to public schools. If the surplus for Group 9 is negative, it is not an equilibrium.

Next, it is assumed that only Group 9 sends its children to private schools. The median voter shifts to Group 4, since the families in Group 9 will now favor decreases in public school quality. The demand of the voter was calculated, and then the public school surpluses for Groups 8 and 9 were calculated using the level of expenditures per pupil demanded by the median voter. If the PSS for Group 8 is positive and the PSS for Group 9 is negative, this level of expenditures is an equilibrium, with

2. See Spann (1977) for a review of these studies.

Groups 1 through 8 sending their children to public schools and Group 9 sending its children to private schools.

This procedure was repeated with Groups 8 and 9 in private schools, then with Groups 7, 8, and 9 in private schools, and so on. Of course, when Groups 5 through 9 enroll their children in private schools, the median demand for education is zero, and thus a completely private system results.

To calculate the PSS in each case, it is necessary to have the appropriate compensated demand curve. That curve can be found in the following way. Consider a family with posttax income w. Suppose with a price $\bar{p}$ *and compensation* $\bar{p}\bar{q}$ that family would demand the quality of education, $\bar{q}$, which is provided in the public sector. A family facing that price and receiving that compensation must have the same utility it would have if it had sent its children to free public schools of quality $\bar{q}$. Its consumption of education is the same and the amount of income it has to spend on other goods is the same, since it is being compensated for its expenditure on tuition. Thus, the point $(\bar{p}, \bar{q})$ must be on the compensated demand curve with utility equal to that received in the public sector and on the ordinary demand curve with income $w + \bar{p}\bar{q}$. One point on the compensated demand curve can therefore be found by solving the equation $\bar{q} = (\bar{p})^{-0.4}(w + \bar{p}\bar{q})^{0.7}$ for $\bar{p}$. Starting from that point, the rest of the compensated demand curve can be derived from the ordinary demand curve by varying income along with price so as to keep utility constant. That procedure was used in finding the compensated demand curves to calculate the PSS in the simulation.

With no educational grant, an equilibrium occurs with expenditures per pupil of $672, with Groups 1 through 8 enrolling their children in public schools, and with Group 9 enrolling its children in private schools. The first column of Table 8.4 characterizes this equilibrium. The first nine entries in that column give the quality of the school attended by the children in each group. The quality for the first eight groups is the same since they attend the public schools. The children of the families in Group 9 attend private schools and receive an education equivalent to that of a public school spending $1,415 per pupil. The tuition for a school of that quality is only $708, however, since I have assumed that the public schools cost twice as much per unit of quality as the private schools. The second section of nine entries in the first column give the amount that families in each group have to spend on goods other than education. That amount is income less property taxes and tuition for those families that send their children to private schools. The final three entries give government expenditures per family for education. The first of these entries is the expenditure per pupil in public school. Since eight of the nine groups send their children to public schools, the cost per family is eight-ninths of $672. The next to last entry is expenditure per family on educational grants, which is zero, and the final entry is total government expenditure per family.

The theoretical model suggests that multiple equilibria are possible. Indeed there is one other equilibrium which occurs with all children attending private schools and zero expenditures on public schools. I have assumed in what follows that the system is initially in the equilibrium represented in the first column.

The introduction of an educational grant will upset this equilibrium. To determine the impact of these grants, I first calculated the minimum educational grant that would be necessary to draw the families in Group 8 into the private sector, given that the public sector is providing schools of the quality demanded by the median voter when Groups 8 and 9 are

Table 8.4. Simulation Results

Educational grant	$ 0	$ 41	$ 167	$ 171	$ 232
School quality					
Group 1	$ 672	$ 669	$ 660	$ 622	$ 531
Group 2	672	669	660	622	657
Group 3	672	669	660	622	743
Group 4	672	669	660	622	816
Group 5	672	669	660	622	897
Group 6	672	669	660	959	982
Group 7	672	669	1,034	1,040	1,064
Group 8	672	1,166	1,178	1,184	1,210
Group 9	1,415	1,422	1,434	1,441	1,469
Noneducational expenditures					
Group 1	$ 4,697	$ 4,740	$ 4,785	$ 4,838	$ 5,000
Group 2	6,478	6,532	6,587	6,652	6,800
Group 3	7,785	7,846	7,909	7,983	8,121
Group 4	8,965	9,032	9,101	9,183	10,128
Group 5	10,320	10,394	10,471	10,561	10,680
Group 6	11,803	11,884	11,968	11,760	12,177
Group 7	13,288	13,376	13,117	13,226	13,672
Group 8	16,040	15,597	15,821	15,945	16,448
Group 9	20,620	20,780	21,026	21,176	21,778
Government expenditures per family					
Public School	$ 597	$ 520	$ 440	$ 346	$ 0
Grant	0	9	56	76	232
Total	597	529	496	422	232

sending their children to private schools. The resulting expenditure per pupil will then be an equilibrium when educational grants are set at that minimum level. In the model, the minimum educational grant necessary to induce Group 8 into the private sector was $41.

The equilibrium levels of school quality, noneducational expenditures, and government expenditures are listed in the second column of Table 8.4. Note that expenditures per pupil in the public schools decline slightly from $672 to $669, because the median voter is now in Group 3 instead of Group 4. The effect of the reduction of expenditures per pupil on the income of the median voter is partly offset by the decrease in the tax price of expenditures per pupil, because Group 8 no longer sends its children to public schools. This lower tax price is reflected in the higher posttax income of families. Families in Group 1, for example, now have $43 more to spend on noneducational items than they did without the grant. This is more than enough to compensate them for the slight reduction in public school quality.

The same is true for the other groups that still enroll their children in public schools. The families in Group 9 consume more education and have more money to spend on noneducational items. This results because their property taxes are lower and because they now receive an educational grant for sending their children to private schools. The families in Group 8 increase their consumption to education considerably, but their noneducational expenditures actually fall by over $400. Despite this decrease, these families are also better off than before the grant. With a grant of $41, they are marginally better off in the private sector than in the public sector. But, if they were to send their children to public schools of the quality now provided, they would be better off given their present posttax incomes than they were when no grant was provided. Thus, they must also be better off with the grant. In summary, the welfare of all families in increased by the introduction of the grant.

The source of these mutual gains is the aggregate welfare improvement from transferring children in Group 8 from public school to private school. This welfare improvement results because the private schools are assumed to be less costly than the public schools and because the children in Group 8 receive less education in the public school than their parents would optimally choose for them. Thus, there is a deadweight loss from sending these children to the public schools. The gain to society of doing away with their deadweight loss is not captured just by the families in Group 8, however. It is spread among all families, because the aggregate property tax burden is reduced.

These improvements in welfare assume that money to pay for the educational grants comes from outside the system. But even if it were assumed that these grants must be financed by some form of tax applied to these families, it is unlikely that the basic conclusion would change because the cost of the grants is only $9 per family.

An educational grant of $167 is just large enough to induce parents in Group 7 to enroll their children in private schools. The equilibrium with this grant is characterized in the third column of Table 8.4. Again public school expenditures per pupil are reduced somewhat, as are property taxes. As in the previous case, the decline in property taxes appears to be more than adequate to compensate those parents with children in public schools for the decline in public school quality.

The families of Group 6 will be induced to leave the public schools for an educational grant of $172, and the members of Group 5 will do so for a grant of $232. When the families of Group 5 leave the public school system, the median voter is a family with children in private school. Since I have assumed that such a family demands zero expenditure per pupil in the public schools, the public school system collapses and all parents enrolls their children in private schools. School quality declines from $672 to $531 per pupil for families in Group 1, but the disposable income of those families increases by more than $300. Of course, some of that gain may be reduced by the taxes needed to support the educational grant, so the net outcome is in doubt. The results are less ambiguous for families in other groups. For Group 2, educational quality is only $15 less per pupil than with no educational grant, and disposable income is more than $300 greater. For Groups 3 through 9, both educational quality and disposable income are higher. To repeat, the source of these gains is the lower cost of education in the private sector and the opportunity that families have in the private sector to choose the quality of their schools to match their demands.

IV. Conclusion

A public school system gives rise to a deadweight loss, because some families will be induced to consume a different quality of education than they would choose for themselves and because public supply is more costly than private supply. The transfer of students from public to private schools would reduce that loss. Tuition tax credits and educational vouchers are instruments for effecting that transfer and thus for increasing aggregate social welfare. The concern is that this aggregate gain will come at the expense of low-income families, who will be left with publc schools of considerably diminished quality.

I have sought to address that concern in this chapter. The model of public school expenditures developed here suggests that the aggregate gain of policies like tuition tax credits and educational vouchers may fall disproportionately on upper-income families, but it also suggests that such policies may not be as detrimental to low-income families as might be expected. There are two reasons for this. First, because the educational grant necessary to induce a family to transfer its children from public to private schools is less than the cost of educating those children in the public schools, the total tax burden will be reduced, and that will benefit all taxpayers. Secondly, a decrease in public school enrollments will reduce the tax price of public school quality, which will increase the demand for quality among those with children in public schools. In the simulation, this partly offset the effect on public school quality of the declining support for public schools due to reduced enrollments. The net effect was a slight decline in quality. Thus, as the result of the transfer of children of upper-income families from public to private schools, the quality of public schools declined somewhat, but the adverse effect of this on low-income families was offset by an increase in posttax income.

There are several other issues concerning aid to private schools which I have not dealt with in this chapter. The impact of such aid on racial segregation in primary and secondary schools is one of those. That issue and others not considered here are obviously important for any comprehensive discussion of the merits of tuition tax credits and educational vouchers.

References

Barzel, Yoram, and Robert Deacon. 1975. "Voting Behavior, Efficiency, and Equity." *Public Choice* 21: 1–14.

Borcherding, Thomas E. 1977. "The Sources of Growth of Public Expenditures in the United States, 1902–1970." In *Budgets and Bureaucrats: The Sources of Government Growth,* ed. T. E. Borcherding, pp. 45–70. Durham, North Carolina: Duke University Press.

Bureau of the Census. 1978. *Government Finances in 1976–77.* Washington, D.C.: U.S. Department of Commerce.

Flowers, Marilyn R. 1975. "The Possibility of Double-Peaked Preference Rankings for Public School Expenditures: Extensions of the Barzel-Deacon Analysis." *Public Choice* 3: 81–85.

Inman, Robert P. 1978. "Testing Political Economy's 'As If' Proposition: Is the Median Income Voter Really Decisive?" *Public Choice* 33: 45–65.

Ladd, Helen F. 1979. "Tax Limitation and Educational Finances: Comments." *National Tax Journal* 32: 375–80.

Polinsky, A. Mitchell, and David T. Ellwood. 1979. "Empirical Reconciliation of Micro and Grouped Estimates of the Demand for Housing." *Review of Economics and Statistics* 61: 199–205.

Shapiro, Perry. 1981. "Popular Responses to Public Spending Disequilibrium: An Analysis of the 1978 California Property Tax Limitation." In *Tax and Expenditure Limitations,* ed. Helen F. Ladd and T. Nicholas Tideman. Washington, D.C.: Urban Institute Press.

Sonstelie, Jon. 1979. "Public School Quality and Private School Enrollments." *National Tax Journal* 32: 343-54.

Sonstelie, Jon. 1982. "The Welfare Cost of Free Public Schools." *Journal of Political Economy* 9, 4: 794-808.

Spann, Robert M. 1977. "Public versus Private Provision of Governmental Services." In *Budgets and Bureaucrats: The Sources of Government Growth,* ed. Thomas E. Borcherding, pp. 71-89. Durham, North Carolina: Duke University Press.

Stiglitz, J. E. 1974. "The Demand for Education in Public and Private School Systems." *Journal of Public Economics* 3: 349-85.

III. LOCAL POLICY OPTIONS

9 *Richard A. Musgrave*

Private Labor and Common Land

Theories of distributive justice follow three major traditions. Natural law theorists view a person as entitled to the fruits of his labor. Justice prevails if each receives the value of his product. Utilitarians hold that reason calls for distribution based on the maximizing rules of welfare calculus. A third tradition rejects personal talents as a basis for desert. Just distribution is to be deduced from principles of fairness, agreed upon in the original position. My purpose here is *not* to compare these approaches or to choose among the ethical premises on which they rest. Rather I shall deal with the entitlement approach only and take its premises as given.[1] More specifically, I shall focus on the tension which arises within a dual view of entitlement, where private entitlement to the fruits of one's labor is combined with common entitlement to the fruits of land.

The entitlement doctrine is of particular interest to the historian of economic thought who is not embarrassed by the interaction of analysis and value. It has provided an ethical framework for economic theory

The author is H. H. Burbank Professor of Political Economy, Emeritus, Harvard University, and Adjunct Professor of Economics, University of California at Santa Cruz. He is indebted to the Lincoln Institute of Land Policy for support of this research and to Barry S. Clark and Mason Gaffney for helpful comments.
1. For a critique of the underlying premises, see Nagel (1975).

from medieval doctrine on usury over Adam Smith's natural order and
Karl Marx's surplus value to J. B. Clark's view of marginal product as a
just return (Clark 1899). If justice calls for reward in line with value
created, determination of factor shares matters not only for the theory of
production but also for the implementation of distributive justice. Economists, to be sure, have been annoyed by this nexus. Marx wanted his
doctrine of surplus value to be understood as an objective fact of capitalist production, not as a moral basis for social critique. George Stigler in
turn criticizes Clark for having linked marginal productivity theory to
just distribution. Its significance as an economic theory should be seen in
relation to efficient resource use and to the theory of production, not as
legitimization of market ethics.[2] Later welfare economics, be it of the
Pigou or Samuelson-Bergson variety, heeds this separation and bypasses
the relationship between factor pricing and entitlement to distributive
shares.[3] Yet the notion that justice calls for compensation in line with
productive contribution remains very much a part of our social mores.[4]
Indeed, it may well be considered the dominant norm. *Re*distribution by
definition follows distribution and is the exception to the rule.

The same goes for the perception that "land" or natural resources in
general differ from other factors. On the one hand, economic analysis
has extended the concept of rent to all factors, viewing it as a generally
applicable phenomenon of inelastic supply. On the other hand, land has
retained its special place in the common man's view of property rights.
This difference arises not because of differences in supply elasticity or
spatial mobility, but because land is outside man and, as a matter of
"natural right," is seen as held in common. The modern concern with
environment and the right to oil resources and ocean wealth are cases in
point, as is the ongoing debate over property taxation. Traces of the dual
entitlement rule thus remain embedded in popular mores, and a review of
its doctrinal development is more than a historical exercise. We begin
with the seminal presentation by Locke (ed. Laslett 1963),[5] turn to its
recent restatement by Nozick (1974), and then step back to its essential
role in the earlier system of Henry George (1954).

Lockean Entitlement and the Provisos

Locke's theory of property begins with the proposition that man has
the right to self preservation and hence to the things which "nature"

2. See George Stigler's critique of J. B. Clark, whose "naive production ethics" is
blamed for "the popular and superficial allegation that neo-classical economics was essentially an apologetic for the existing economic order" (Stigler 1941, p. 297).
3. This point is stressed in Clark and Gintis (1978).
4. See *President's Economic Report* (1974, p. 137).
5. Page references are to the revised edition, with section numbers of Book II also given.

yields for his subsistence.[6] For this purpose nature was given to mankind to be used in common: "Whether we consider reason or revelation—'tis very clear that God, as King David says, has given the earth to the children of men, given it to mankind in common" (Locke, ed. Laslett 1963, p. 327, §25).[7] But man, so Locke continues, also has property in his person: "... Every man has a property in his own Body and the Work of his Hands, we may say, are properly his" (p. 328, §27). The two entitlements interact because labor yields fruit only when mixed with land. Man, to obtain fruits from his labor, must obtain property in the crop which he raises: "Whatever then he removes out of the State that Nature has provided—he has mixed his labor with, and joined to it something that is his own, and thereby makes it his Property" (p. 329, §27). But there are limits to the produce which a man may extract from land. They are given by two provisos which to me seem among Locke's most intriguing passages.[8]

The first proviso holds that no one can accumulate more goods than he can use without wastage: "As much as any one can make use of to any advantage of life before it spoils; so much he may by his labor fix a property in" (Locke, ed. Laslett, p. 332, §31). Since produce spoils, this limits accumulation and thereby the utilization of land. The second proviso adds that a person has a right to the produce which he extracts from land "at least where there is enough and as good left in common for others" (p. 333, §33). Both provisos are inoperative while land is abundant. Without scarcity of land, the spoilage proviso has no distributive bite but merely prohibits waste as an offense against nature. The "as good" proviso as well is satisfied as long as the supply of land is abundant. Man can freely mix his labor with "new" land without preempting its use by others, thereby satisfying the "as good" condition. Locke thus shows how property could exist in the state of nature prior to civil society, and do so without offending against the common entitlement and its provisos.

But how does Locke deal with the tension which arises when land becomes scarce? Now that the crop becomes the joint product of private labor and scarce (but common) land, can the cultivator still lay sole claim to it? Viewed in the context of a barter economy, Locke's answer would

6. The Lockean doctrine, as presented here, is based on his exposition in chapter V of the *Second Treatise*. For more comprehensive appraisals of the Lockean system which are of special interest in our context, see McPherson (1962), Vaughn (1980), and Clark (1980; 1981).

7. Locke's reference is to Psalm CXV:xvi, which reads, "The . . . heavens are the Lord's, but the earth hath he given to the children of men." Note that the stipulation of "given it to mankind in common" is Locke's own addition and hence hardly unimportant in interpreting his text.

8. For a less favorable view, see Viner (1963).

have had to be no. With land scarce, the "as good" proviso would come into play and restrict the private property in land. But he did not foresee that this condition would occur. The "wild woods and uncultivated wastes of America," he tells us, still beckon with a safe margin of uncultivated land (Locke, ed. Laslett 1963, p. 336, §37).

Land becomes scarce only with the use of money and the resulting drive for accumulation. But the use of money as a means of exchange and store of wealth now permits a person to hold more land than he needs for his own use, and to do so without spoilage.[9] The surplus crop may be sold and wealth may be accumulated in the form of money. The spoilage limitation to private ownership of land is thus removed. True enough, but Locke further holds that tacit consent to the use of money also suspends the common claim to land and permits its unlimited private possession. This conclusion only follows if the "common claim" is viewed as a derivative of the nonspoilage proviso. As we read Locke's earlier invocation of the common claim, be it by "reason or by revelation," this is not a permissible interpretation.[10] A better explanation is needed to show why Locke suspends his principle of common claim.

One possible explanation lies in Locke's observation that private ownership of land increases accumulation and adds to the nation's wealth, which in the end will be to everyone's benefit (Locke, ed. Laslett 1963, p. 343, §50). Perhaps so, but it seems strange for Locke to sacrifice the common claim to land—introduced first as a God-given natural right —to so utilitarian a consideration. This is strange, especially since private accumulation could proceed in terms of money and of capital goods, even though the common claim to land was preserved.

To make Locke's reasoning stick, one would have to reinterpret his initial postulate of common claim to land. Rather than as a natural right in itself, the common claim would have to be seen as derived from the right to self-preservation.[11] One could then argue that with the use of money and trade, self-preservation no longer requires access to land; and thus reinterpret the "as good" proviso as referring to produce rather than to land itself. The objection that a utilitarian argument is used to override a right would then be overcome. But once more, this interpretation seems incompatible with Locke's invocation of scriptures and natural law, when presenting his initial doctrine of common claim to *land in particular*. As we read Locke, he meant to say that the fruits of land only were to be shared, while leaving private entitlement to the fruits of one's

9. For an argument that accumulation without spoilage is possible even in a barter economy, see Weymark (1980, pp. 282–90).

10. For a contrary view, see Vaughn (1980).

11. This explanation is suggested by McPherson (1962, p. 213).

labor. Such a dual entitlement rule does not interfere with the right of self-preservation, but merely influences how total output is to be divided and to what assets private title can be attached.

However this may be, it is not our purpose here to speculate on Locke's precise reason for abandoning the common claim and his "as good" proviso.[12] Rather, let us consider the consequences of strict adherence to Locke's initial model as we read it, that is, consider a situation of scarce land with the "as good" proviso in full force. That part of output which is contributed by labor—a part which Locke considers to constitute most of the total (Locke, ed. Laslett, p. 339, §42)—belongs to the worker. The remainder, which is contributed by land, belongs to the common. The question is how to distribute the common share among the workers. Since God gave land "to the use of the industrious," not to the idle, the Lockean model might distribute rent in proportion to labor input (p. 333, §34). Workers, as it were, participate in two roles: (1) as claimants to the fruits of labor and (2) as co-workers of land and co-claimants to rent. With (2) assigned in proportion to (1), workers receive the entire product in line with wages. Under this rule, the common claim to land would not change the distribution pattern set by wages. Workers cultivating a given plot would divide the output in line with labor inputs, so that in fact there would be no need for splitting the two shares at all. But this conclusion only follows if assignment to the "industrious" is considered appropriate. If instead the common claim were interpreted as, say, an equal per capita division, the distribution of rent would have an equalizing effect. But even then, differential labor income would permit inequality to arise. Acceptance of common entitlement to the fruits of land does not make Locke an egalitarian.

It remains to fit capital into the Lockean scheme. Locke notes the use of financial capital as essential to production with interest a necessary return due to its unequal holding (Vaughn 1980, p. 52). But he does not present a full view of the role of real capital as a factor of production. Rather, the labor that was needed to make the plough must be charged to labor (Locke, ed. Laslett 1963, p. 346, §43). There has thus developed an interesting controversy over whether or not Locke held to a labor theory of value, but we shall bypass this here. Rather, let us consider claims to

---

12. McPherson (1962) suggests that Locke's relaxation of his initial limitation of property rights (limiting property to the fruit of one's *own* labor only) was needed to accommodate his desire to provide an apologetic for the capitalist system. Vaughn (1980, p. 106) suggests that his support of private accumulation only reflected his recognition that everyone would gain thereby. Clark (1980; 1981) views the Lockean system as disapproving of great inequality and claims that Locke is among the originators of the liberal theory of justice.

factor shares in an updated Lockean model, which allows for returns to both capital and labor.

How may entitlement to the return of capital be assigned? Presumably Locke would have argued that the saver is entitled to this return in response to his contribution, just as the worker is entitled to his wages. Labor would no longer receive the entire product other than rent. The consideration remains: How would the claim to rent now be distributed? Should the suppliers of capital share in the bounty of nature, and if so, should rent be distributed in line with capital and labor shares? If labor benefits from "mixing" with land, so does capital. If reward to the "industrious" is now applied to both saving and work, the solution would again be one of sharing rent on a matching basis, leaving rent once again a distributionally neutral factor.

However this may be, a rule is needed to define factor shares. A theory of entitlement in line with productive contribution requires this contribution to be determined. Not only must the common share of rent be separated out, but the remainder must be divided between capital and labor. Assignment in line with factor pricing in a competitive market is one such rule. Moreover, it has the further qualities of (1) being in line with efficient resource use, and (2) being open to implementation through a competitive market.[13] J. B. Clark, when presenting his marginal productivity theory at the close of the last century, believed in this triple union of justice, efficiency, and competitive markets. The requirement of competitive markets, to be sure, is not spelled out in Locke. His discussion of natural price well preceded the modern view of price determination as the function of both cost and demand conditions. Yet he thought of a fair market price as determined by the interaction of many sellers, a formula quite compatible with the spirit of competitive markets (Vaughn 1980, p. 60).

Nozick's Justice in Holding

Similar problems persist in Nozick's reformulation of the Lockean model. Nozick (1974, p. 10) launches his argument from Locke's proposition that man has a right to act freely as he wishes but within the bounds of nature, that is, man is subject to Locke's condition that "no

---

13. An alternative union of justice and efficiency might be obtained by a system in which all rents, including those of land and labor, are taxed away and considered to be held in common. This would still be efficient, because the return at the margin would not be affected. At the same time it would be considered just if the entitlement doctrine were changed to grant entitlement to compensation for work disutility only. But though a possible reformulation, this is not what the Lockean entitlement doctrine had in mind.

one ought to harm another in his life, health, liberty, and possessions.''
Justice in holding exists, so Nozick argues, if possessions are justly acquired in line with (1) the principle of just acquisition and (2) the principle of just transfer (p. 191). The theory of justice is thus formulated as
a process theory. A just state of distribution is one that has come about
through a just process, and his theory of justice is conceived as a historical theory. He then contrasts this with what he calls end-state theories,
according to which a just distribution is one that meets a predetermined
pattern.

But justice in acquisition precedes justice in transfer. The rules of just
acquisition are thus of fundamental importance to Nozick's entire argument and not a mere "additional bit of complexity" as he suggests
(Nozick 1974, p. 174). Nozick does not invoke Locke's proposition that
God has given land to man for use in common, but begins with the
broader maxim that the law of nature forbids actions which harm others.
Property rights in "a previously unused thing" cannot be acquired if
"the position of others no longer at liberty to use the thing is thereby
worsened" (p. 178). The "previously unused things" include Locke's
land and natural resources, but other items such as inventions are added
in. Locke's "as good" proviso, so Nozick notes, was designed to prevent
such unjust acquisition; and he draws the conclusion—avoided by Locke
—that after land becomes scarce, literal interpretation of the proviso
causes the existing entitlement structure to collapse by a principle of
regression (p. 180).

Nozick tries to meet this difficulty in various ways. One of them is to
follow Locke in noting that private property in scarce land contributes to
economic progress which benefits *all,* even those who no longer can
obtain use of land. Thus private property in scarce land is said to be compatible with the *intent* of the Lockean proviso. This consideration, so
Nozick notes, is not introduced as a utilitarian suspension of a basic
right. Rather it is allowed because (similar to a previously noted reading
of Locke) the common claim to land was never meant to be absolute but
derived from the right to "things." As a second line of defense, Nozick
suggests that the share in property holdings which is traceable to unjust
appropriation of land is minor, so that the difficulty applies to only a
small part of the prevailing property structure. Perhaps so, but this
hardly resolves the principle at issue.

Finally, and most interesting, Nozick suggests that the proviso be
restated in less demanding form. A distinction should be drawn between
two ways in which a person's position can be worsened. *A* taking a piece
of land as property may (1) reduce *B*'s ability to use land freely which he
previously so used, or (2) reduce *B*'s ability to acquire new land. A strin-

gent interpretation prohibits both outcomes, whereas a weaker version would prohibit the first one only (Nozick 1974, p. 176). Nozick accepts the weaker version as sufficient for his theory of just acquisition. The regression problem may then be avoided by one further adjustment: the addition of a "base line" date and a general amnesty for unjust acquisitions that preceded it (p. 177). We are left with an interesting but still unsatisfactory solution. Drawing the base line is an arbitrary matter and amnesty begs the issue of justice in original acquisition. Without a just basis from which to start, the concept of just process remains a somewhat hollow construct. However this may be, let us accept the base-line-plus-amnesty version and consider the requirements of just process thereafter.

Clearly, just transactions should be voluntary in nature, requiring the consent of both parties.[14] But this is not sufficient. As Nozick (1974, p. 181) puts it in his colorful way, "each owner's title to his holding includes the historical shadow of the Lockean proviso on appropriation." Transactions must not leave anyone worse off than the base line position. A may not, as formulated in situation (1) above, purchase the only waterhole in existence and then charge what he wishes. If he were to do so, his property in the well would not be justly acquired. But Nozick suggests that the free operation of the market system will not actually run afoul of the proviso, that is, type (1) situations will not be prevalent. At the same time, A may, as formulated in situation (2), manufacture pins and sell them more cheaply than B, thereby driving B out of business and leaving him less well off. The difference between situations (1) and (2) is that the former involves the holding of scarce resources and thus violates the proviso, whereas the latter does not.

But what if a third type of situation arises, where A, after buying out B, establishes a monopoly in pins and thus hurts C who must pay more? This would be no offence against Nozick's concept of just transaction, as I understand it. I have two difficulties with this conclusion. For one thing, the meaning of entitlement, as a matter of natural right, can hardly be made contingent on what market structures happen to develop in the post–base-line period. Yet this will be the case if exchange is defined simply in terms of noncoercion.[15] A person's return is deter-

14. Nozick (1974) recognizes one exception, however, where individuals do not wish to join the voluntary protective association (the minimal state) and are forced to do so. However, compensation must be paid.

15. There is the further question of how the concept of coercion is defined. Nozick's essay (1969) on coercion leaves the answer problematic. Nozick states that exchanges between buyers and sellers cannot "normally" be considered coercion (p. 447), but beyond this no reference to the problem of coercion in market transactions is made. However, in distinguishing between threats and offers in other settings, certain analogies arise. Thus

mined by his real wage, and this depends not only on what is offered but also on the structure of the labor and product markets in which he deals. For another thing, specification of permissible terms of trade is crucial for the relationship between efficiency and justice. Both criteria are met if the permissible terms of exchange are restricted to competitive markets; but they conflict if justice is taken to require noncoercion only. Exchanges may then proceed in noncompetitive markets and the benign scheme of the market as an invisible hand process—both just and efficient—breaks down. This basic issue cannot be avoided by *assuming* that all markets are competitive or that only negligible departures occur. Antitrust policy, for instance, will be just or unjust (as well as efficient) depending on how the concept of just transaction is defined.

Similar problems arise with regard to externalities, be they of the cost or benefit variety. If *A* is damaged by *B*'s activities (such as the construction of a next-door factory which creates a smoke nuisance), does the rule of justice call for compensation?[16] In the modern world, which abounds with externality and third-part problems, it is clearly unsatisfactory to define entitlement and just property rights in terms of a model which consists of contractual relations only. By assuming away market imperfections and externalities, a much too simplified picture is drawn. We can hardly criticize Locke, who wrote 300 years ago, for overlooking these complications. But Locke re-created should allow for them.

Henry George and the Unearned Increment

Nowhere has the antinomy between the common claim to land and the private claim to the fruits of one's labor been carried so far as in the writings of Henry George. His approach differs from that of Locke and Nozick in various ways. For one thing, the common claim to land is given as a fundamental right, as seen in the Biblical-natural law tradition, not as a mere derivative of the right for subsistence. Next, he accepts the full consequences of the proviso by calling for public appro-

---

Nozick considers a situation where *P* announces that he will do such and such if *Q* does *A*. Whether this is to be considered an offer or a threat (coercion) to *Q* depends on whether *P*'s intervention will make the outcome of *Q* doing *A* better or worse than it otherwise would be in the "expected" course of events. The term "expected" is used as a straddle between "predicted" and "morally required."

Given the criterion that expected outcomes render a transaction noncoercive, the question remains whether the transactor is or is not entitled to expect competitive markets. The issue remains unresolved by the expectation criterion.

16. An expectation criterion similar to Nozick's is suggested by Michelman (1966), who proposes that entitlement for compensation be made contingent on the damage being unexpected.

priation of the returns to land. Finally, and most important, he does not see private ownership of land as necessary for economic progress. On the contrary, he is concerned with "the evils which, as modern progress goes on, arise from the greater and greater inequality in the distribution of wealth," and he considers private ownership of land to be the major cause of this evil. Public appropriation of rent offers a simple and sufficient remedy. It "will substitute equality for inequality, plenty for want, justice for injustice, social strength for social weakness, and will open the way to grander and nobler advances of civilization." Expediency joins justice, so he concludes, in the case for abolishing the private ownership of land (George 1954, pp. 329, 367). Note that his immediate case is directed only against inequality which results from the private ownership of *land*. Apart from land, George was a staunch defender of private property and its role in economic progress. However, with private ownership of land the major cause of inequality, its removal would go far to abolish inequality at large.

The rightful basis of property, so George argues, is the right of man to himself: "Thus there is to everything produced by man's exertion a clear and indisputable title to the exclusive possession and enjoyment which is perfectly compatible with justice as it descends from the original producer in whom it is vested by natural law" (George 1954, p. 334).[17] These laws "are the decree of the Creator." Without directly claiming the authority of Locke, George's basic premise of entitlement is the same as that of the 18th century writers, combining natural law with divine sanction.[18] Man is rightfully entitled to the fruits of his exertion by labor only. Property may be transferred legitimately after it has been acquired, but just acquisition of a good has to be based initially on the input of one's labor.[19] The worker cannot claim private property in land, since land does not embody labor. Private ownership of land permits the owner to appropriate the produce of another person's labor as the price that person must pay for permission to labor (p. 341). It is thus incompatible with the very principle of entitlement to the fruits of one's labor. Public appropriation of the return to land is thus just. He proposes that this be done by a confiscatory tax on the rent of land rather than outright public ownership (p. 406).[20] Improvements, however, are not to be taxed, since capital earnings are a just return.

17. See also note 7 above.

18. For a more extensive discussion of values as derived from natural law, see George's controversy with Henry Spencer (George 1955).

19. See also Collier (1979).

20. George does not consider the question of how the market can function as an allocator of land if there is a 100 percent tax on rent, reducing the value of land to zero. However, in one passage (p. 347), he refers to levying a tax so as to "very nearly" absorb rent, which may allow for a management fee.

To show how the evil of private ownership of land increases with economic progress, George must show how the rising share of rent creates poverty. The first step is to examine how factor shares are determined. Rent is defined along Ricardian lines as the excess of product over that which the same labor input can secure from the least productive land in use (George 1954, p. 168). "Wages and interest," so he argues, "do not depend upon the produce of labor and capital, but upon what is left after rent is taken out; or upon the product which they could obtain without paying rent—that is from the poorest land in use" (p. 171). This may be taken to suggest a general equilibrium system in which all factor shares are mutually determined, but the fuller exposition also carries overtones of the physiocratic notion that land is the basic source of output, with the return to land determined first and the other factors receiving what is left.

Turning to interest as a return to capital, George rejects the view that interest is a return to waiting, and that wages are "advanced" by capital. Rather, it is the current output of labor that sustains capital formation. The consequence of an increase in the number of workers is not that a given wage fund must be spread more thinly. On the contrary, increased labor gives rise to increased capital. Interest, according to George, is paid because the use of the tools of production increases the efficiency of labor. "The advantage which is given by the lapse of time springs from the regenerative forces of nature" (George 1954, p. 367). He thus does not admit that capital formation requires a diversion of labor from the production of current output to that of tools and that this involves waiting, which enters as a cost of production. Yet, he considers the return to capital as a legitimate return. It is only the income from land that is to be in common. The reasoning is puzzling. If the "regenerative forces of nature," which stem from capital, are created by the input of labor, why then should not the return of capital also accrue to the worker?

Having developed his theory of factor shares in a static setting, George proceeds to his major theme, which is the rising share of rent in the course of economic growth. In line with the classical tradition, he begins with the impact of population growth. He does not, however, follow the Malthusian doctrine that increasing population, via diminishing returns on land, leads to poverty. This doctrine is unacceptable to George, because its prognosis of inevitable poverty would contradict the benevolence of nature and provide an apologetic for injustice (George 1954, p 185). In order to disprove Malthus, George argues that rising population (with technique constant) will result in increasing efficiency due to greater division of labor (p. 223). Rising population, therefore, need not lead to Malthusian subsistence. Per capita income may remain constant or may rise.

At the same time, George also wishes to show that the share of rent will increase in the process, so as to stress the necessity of public ownership of land. How can the two outcomes be combined? His reasoning is somewhat obscure, as no clear distinction is drawn between rates of return and factor shares. However, his result might be rationalized as follows: The efficiency gain (due to greater division of labor made possible by rising population) might be viewed as raising the efficiency units embodied in an hour of work, thus resulting in an upward shift of the marginal product of labor schedule. At the same time, the rising ratio of labor to capital lowers the marginal product by moving down along the schedule. Combining both changes, the marginal product of labor and the wage rate might remain constant or rise, even though the share of rent increases. His result is thus conceivable, but it implies a rather extreme view regarding the continuing gains from the further division of labor made possible by population growth.[21]

But the picture changes as improvements in the arts are allowed for. Improvements will increase wealth, which will raise the demand for land and bring inferior land into cultivation. As a result, rent will rise. Moreover, it will rise so as to increase its share in national income, with most all income eventually being absorbed by rent and wages tending toward the poverty level. To reach this conclusion, George seems to argue that innovations will be land-using but labor-saving (George 1954, pp. 749 ff.) Resulting changes in the capital share are not allowed for, nor is the possibility that improvement in the arts will raise the productivity of labor and/or of capital at the margin of cultivation. Although deeply concerned with the problem of inequality, George is thus led to neglect inequalities which may arise from the ownership of capital.

The Georgian economic model, as will be apparent from this overview, is driven by single-minded determination to demonstrate that the rental share must rise, and to do so while rejecting the Malthusian argument. If the outcome is unconvincing and the reasoning at times obscure, it should be kept in mind that *Progress and Poverty* was written at a time when the new doctrine of marginal productivity was just beginning to emerge. Moreover, George, as a visionary and a populist, was not given to reading contemporary "professors" and wished to reinvent economic theory in his own image (George 1960, pp. 193, 210).

Having shown that private ownership is both illegitimate and harmful, George unhesitatingly proceeds to the conclusion that the rent of land should be taxed away. He does not worry about how past injustice can be undone. While the return to improvements is carefully excluded, all rent of land should be appropriated forthwith. This should be done even

---

21. I am indebted to Ronald Greason for discussion of this point.

where land was acquired in good faith and paid for by present owners out of justly acquired earnings. George thus rejects Mill's insistence that present owners be compensated if future increments of rents are socialized (George 1954, p. 366; Mill 1921, Book II, Ch. 2, §5).[22] George argues that such a proposal would be better than nothing as rents rise, but it would be insufficient. By the same token, George would have rejected Nozick's base line approach. The drawing of rent, so George notes, "is not merely a robbery in the past; it is a robbery in the present" (George 1954, p. 365). If compensation were paid, both workers and capitalists would continue to lose their just reward. Given the premise of common entitlement, this is correct, but it does not meet the difficulty that the original robbers and the present owners are not one and the same. The question of how to rectify unjust gains which are capitalized remains unresolved, as does that of removing past inequities of taxation.

After rent has been appropriated by common entitlement through land taxation, there remains the question of who is entitled to receive it. George argues that all should share the bounty equally and that by using the land tax to finance the budget, rent would become "equally distributed in public services" (George 1954, p. 440). Of course, the Georgian position need not hold that the entire receipts from the land tax must be used for public services. If some revenue is left over, it might be distributed to the public, presumably on a per capita basis—much as is now done in some oil-rich jurisdictions. But what if revenue from the land tax does not suffice to finance the required level of public services? It is here that the claim of *single* taxers becomes untenable. While it might be conceivable that the prevailing level of property tax revenue could be obtained by including only land in the base, it would be totally impossible to finance all tax revenue from this source.[23] Perhaps this situation was not visualized by George, who saw the rental share increasing rapidly without anticipating a correspondingly large increase in the size of the public sector. But though the term "single tax" has done the Georgian

22. John Stuart Mill, in his discussion of property, distinguishes between property in land and property in other things: "The essential principle of property being to assure to all persons what they have produced by their labor and accumulated by their abstinence, this principle cannot apply to what is not the produce of labor, the raw material of the earth." Property in land is justified only to the extent that the owner improves it. "When private property in land is not expedient, it is unjust." But compensation must be paid if the state decides to take over land. See Mill (1921, Book II, Ch. 2, §C).

23. Taking land values as 40 percent of total real estate value, the high estimate of the share as given by Manvel (1968), it would be necessary to raise the effective rate of property tax by a multiple of 2.5. With a mill rate of close to 4 percent and a yield of, say, 5 percent, 100 percent taxation of land rent would be approximated. Allowing for the fact that property tax revenue provides little over 10 percent of total (federal, state, local) tax revenue, the impossibility of the single tax proposition is evident.

case a disservice, the fact that other taxes are needed as well is no reason not to begin with land as the preferred base.

Economists have been generally favorable towards the taxation of rent, but for different reasons. With land inelastic in supply, the taxation of rent permits public funds to be obtained without the deadweight loss which accompanies other forms of taxation. In fact, economic theory suggests that the same be done with regard to all rents, that is, returns in excess of those needed to solicit the factor supply. Labor on this basis would receive its marginal return for the last hour, while the intra-marginal surplus or rent would be subject to tax. By including the rent to all factors, the available tax base would vastly exceed that offered by land rent only, and even a large budget could be financed without dead-weight loss. This is an appropriate prescription in the context of economic efficiency, but it has nothing to do with the entitlement doctrine which stipulates a common claim to the rent of land but *not* to the economist's rental component of labor.

In all, George must be given credit for carrying the premise of dual entitlement to its logical conclusion. This is more than can be said for the two other authors here examined. The weakness of his doctrine lies in its exaggerated claim that land ownership constitutes *the* dominant cause of inequality, and that land taxation should be viewed as *the* single tax. It is because of these claims that the doctrine lost credibility, except in the inner circle of close followers.

Conclusion

The purpose of this essay has been to examine the internal logic and economic implications of a dual theory of entitlement, not to defend it as an ethical doctrine or to advocate its policy implications. The sense that a person is entitled to the fruits of his or her labor has long antecedents and is still widely reflected in or, indeed, dominates how people feel about property. The further sense that the contribution of land is received in common is also of ancient vintage and, though less fully shared, continues to enter into contemporary mores about property rights.

For economic analysis, the dual entitlement theory enters in two ways. First, if the worker is entitled to the fruits of his or her labor, a theory of factor shares is needed to lend operational meaning to this dictum. The question then is whether the economist's resolution in terms of efficient factor pricing also provides the ethically appropriate principle of imputation. The answer to this determines whether or not justice and efficiency coexist. Secondly, the economist's generalized concept of rent as intra-marginal gain, applicable to all factors, differs from the distinct role of land in the entitlement context. In that context the peculiar characteristic of land does not rest on its inelastic supply, but results because the claim to its factor share is held in common. The economist's case for generalizing the tax on rent as an efficiency device does not follow from the entitlement framework.

There are important differences in the approach to dual entitlement among the authors I have dealt with. A first difference relates to their interpretation of how absolutely the common entitlement is to be viewed. Locke first establishes the common claim to land as a divine and natural right, but then abandons it to the needs of a monetary economy. Nozick takes the basic right to land (and resulting obligation not to leave others worse off) more seriously. But in the end he also bypasses the issue of just acquisition through his base line–amnesty construct. George alone considers the common entitlement to be absolute and draws the inevitable conclusion that society should appropriate the rent of land. A further difference pertains to the consequences of private ownership of land. Locke and Nozick both view such ownership as essential to economic growth and welfare. For Locke this suspends the proviso, while for Nozick the common claim is redefined as derived only. For George, on the contrary, private ownership of land is evil in its economic consequences. Thus justice and expediency coincide in calling for its termination.

The dual entitlement doctrine shows the intricate way in which the economic theory of factor shares has been interwoven with the ethical theory of property rights. Economic analysis, to be sure, may view the theory of factor shares as unrelated to the ethics of distribution, and the spirit of modern economics will do just that. Where concerns with distribution enter, they do not come in via factor pricing. Yet, the theory of factor pricing, as it developed through the marginal productivity doctrine, evolved in a culture in which entitlement to earnings played a central role in just distribution. Like it or not, this relation has remained alive in the public mind, and there is much to be said for thinking it through in rigorous terms, including allowance for imperfect markets, for externalities, and for the special role of land in the entitlement doctrine.

References

Clark, Barry S. 1980. "John Locke and the Origins of the Liberal Theory of Justice." Working Paper No. 30. University of Wisconsin–LaCrosse: Bureau of Business and Economic Research.

Clark, Barry S. Review of Karen Iverson Vaughn, *John Locke: Economist and Social Scientist.* In *Eighteenth Century Studies:* A Bibliography, 1981.

Clark, Barry S., and Herbert Gintis. 1978. "Rawlsian Justice and Economic Systems." *Philosophy and Public Affairs* 7, 4(Summer 1978):307.

Clark, J. B. 1899. *The Distribution of Wealth.* New York: Macmillan.

Collier, Charles. 1979. "Henry George's System of Political Economy." *Hope* 2, 1.

George, Henry. 1954. *Progress and Poverty.* New York: Robert Schalkenbach Foundation.

George, Henry. 1955. *A Perplexed Philosopher.* New York: Robert Schalkenbach Foundation.

George, Henry, Jr. 1960. *The Life of Henry George.* New York: Robert Shalkenbach Foundation.

Locke, John. 1963. *Two Treatises of Government,* ed. P. Laslett. Rev. ed. New York: Mentor Book, New American Library.

McPherson, C. B. 1962. *Possessive Individualism.* New York: Oxford University Press.

Manvel, Allen D. 1968. *Three Land Research Studies.* Research Report No. 12. Washington, D.C.: The National Commission on Urban Problems.

Michelman, F. I. 1966. "Property, Utility and Fairness: Comments on the Ethical Foundations of 'Just Compensation' Law." *Harvard Law Review* 80: 1165–1258.

Mill, John Stuart. 1921. *Principles of Political Economy, Book II,* ed. W. J. Ashley. London: Longmans, Green & Co.

Nagel, T. 1975. "Libertarianism Without Foundations," *The Yale Law Journal* 85.

Nozick, Robert. 1969. "Coercion." In *Philosophy, Science and Method,* ed. S. Morgenbesser, P. Suppes, and M. White. New York: St. Martin's Press.

Nozick, Robert. 1974. *Anarchy, State, and Utopia.* New York: Basic Books.

President's Economic Report. 1974. Washington, D.C.: U.S. Government Printing Office. January 1974.

Stigler, George. 1941. *Production and Distribution Theory.* New York: Macmillan.

Vaughn, Karen Iverson. 1980. *John Locke, Economist and Social Scientist.* Chicago: University of Chicago Press.

Viner, Jacob. 1963. "Possessive Individualism as Original Sin." *Canadian Journal of Economics and Political Science* 29 (November): 548–66.

Weymark, John A. 1980. "Money and Locke's Theory of Property." *History of Political Economy* 12, 2:282–90.

10 *Arthur D. Lynn, Jr.*

The Property Tax in the 1980s: Evolution or Devolution?

> Myself when young did eagerly frequent
> Doctor and Saint, and heard great argument
> About it and about: but evermore
> Came out by the same door where in I went.
> —*Rubaiyat of Omar Khayyam,* Canto XXVI

A forward view of state and local finance in the American polity during the decade of the '80s inevitably raises questions about the role and scope of the property tax during that period. Some forecast of what may be expected from venerable property tax institutions is desired, naturally enough. However, the temptation to brashly pierce the veil of the future is best treated with appropriate caution. This careful approach is especially proper, since institutional forecasting about the property tax has abounded with exaggerated predictions which time has often proved incorrect. In this area, like so many others, *natura non facit saltum* still retains more than a grain or two of wisdom, because both the public policy formation process and institutional change retain much of their familiar incremental character. As in the past so it is likely to be in this decade.

Nonetheless, institutional forecasting, like other forecasting, is not altogether impossible if trends continue as projected. Even so, all forecasting is difficult, *especially about the future.* Given the possible—indeed probable—discontinuities of the decade ahead, the cautious analyst seeks to find the consensus of expert opinion, for there lies safety, reassurance, and, one hopes, the minimization of uncertainty. For that reason, this chapter relies heavily upon the prior work and predictive insights of Roy Bahl, George Break, Dick Netzer, Frederick Stocker, and Ronald Welch, since in many respects their consensus represents, at least in my opinion, much of the best in contemporary American property tax thought. This group, of course, is in no sense particularly responsible for the results—dubious or otherwise—of the crystal-ball gazing herein contained.

Evolution or Devolution

Before moving forward, a caveat about the title of this chapter is necessary and appropriate. What of evolution or devolution indeed? Evolution implies growth, development, and continuous adaptation resulting from various integrating agencies such as selection, inbreeding, and mutation. The concept bespeaks positive change. Devolution, *per contra,* suggests degeneration, retrograde evolution, and/or the transfer of power from a central to a local government. The second meaning, of course, is the relevant one here. For present purposes, the contrast between the two concepts will be considered in terms of three questions. Are property tax institutions in the '80s likely to be characterized by positive development or not? Will property tax policy and administration be further centralized at the state level, or will they devolve further to substate governmental loci? Lastly, will the heterogeneity of the tax increase or decrease?

Patterns of Yesteryear

When one speaks of the property tax in a generic way, the uniform *ad valorem* levy of 19th-century America comes to mind where all property, moveable and immoveable, visible and invisible, or real and personal, is or was taxed at one uniform rate. However, property tax history is a richer and more complex vein than just the general property tax of yesteryear. As Bastable, Seligman, and others have noted, a property tax cycle appears repeatedly in fiscal history. That is, as a particular society and economy develops, property taxation moves from a specific to an *ad valorem* rate: from taxation of land to tax coverage of all or most property. Then, as property becomes more heterogeneous, other taxes are substituted for some property categories and the property tax reverts to a levy essentially on realty. Historically, this cyclical pattern has tended to recur (Lynn 1967, p. 16).

While future repetition of past cyclical change in property tax patterns is an uncertain contingency, it is certain that the property tax of today is no longer, if it ever was, the uniform *ad valorem* levy of the 19th-century American Midwest. It is now a heterogeneous collection of disparate levies. So the general property tax of yesteryear is no longer with us. As my colleague Fritz Stocker (1979, p. 6) put it in a recent Lincoln Institute Tax Policy Roundtable paper:

The property tax has been around a long time. Like an old friend whom we see every day, it changes so slowly over the years that we hardly notice the difference. We tend to assume that it has always existed in essentially its present form and always will. Is it possible that, without our realizing it, the property tax has changed in the past several decades into something bearing very little likeness to the levy we learned about in school, and in the case of some of us, still describe in our classes?

Certainly the property tax is a changing fiscal instrument. Post–World War II property tax developments have included the following significant modifications according to Ronald B. Welch (1980, p. 1f.):

1. proliferation of tax exemptions;
2. wide acceptance and adoption of the property tax "circuit-breaker";
3. frequent availability of use-value assessment, especially for farm realty;
4. various limitations upon full-value assessment and upon the discretion of the assessor:
5. the development of various limitations on the amount and rate of the property tax and, hence, upon the fiscal discretion of local legislative bodies; and
6. the spread of *de jure* classified property taxes in contrast to prior legal uniformity at times accompanied by variable *de facto* classification resulting from the exercise of assessor discretion.

These several well-known developments constitute property tax relief[1] efforts responding to the various impacts of inflation, development, and contemporary frustrations with the public sector. Welch (1980, p. 18) notes that,

[t]he mystery that has long surrounded the property tax but had begun to burn off has deepened as incredibly complicated laws have supplemented or supplanted traditional fiscal institutions. . . . Much more experience needs to be accumulated, recorded, and analyzed before policy makers can be expected to know the past and not be condemned to repeat it.

1. In general, see Gold (1979).

However, past patterns and recent change are but prelude here to speculation about where we are going with property tax evolution and devolution. First, however, what of the environment within which future property tax modification, if any, will develop?

Environmental Constraints

A considerable variety of environmental factors constrain future property tax change. Only a few of this large set are considered here.

Public Attitudes. Public attitudes, like other aspects of mass behavior, apparently have become relatively volatile. For example, the 1979 Advisory Commission on Intergovernmental Relations poll (p. 2 and Table 3) reports a sharp flip-flop—a decrease—in antiproperty tax feeling and a significant increase in antifederal income tax attitudes influenced, no doubt, by inflation, bracket creep, the marriage penalty, and general attitudes about the proper scope of the public sector. The development of limitations upon local tax and spending authority plus proliferating property tax relief measures provide a partial explanation of attitudinal shifts and the perceived decrease in hostility towards the property tax. Such developments may have partially defanged the public. If so, acceptance of continued but moderate application of existing property tax patterns, variably constrained with inevitable jurisdictional variation, may be a reasonable expectation for the decade of the '80s. However, as the tax limitation movement of the '70s suggests, moderation is likely to be the characteristic tone of property tax policy in the '80s.

Revenue alternatives. Local governments may obtain revenue from property taxes, nonproperty taxes, user charges, and grants and transfers. Clearly, future trends in intergovernmental transfer policy will constitute a significant facet of the environment within which property tax change will occur or not occur. As Professor Break (1980a, p. 57) has observed, "Extrapolation of past trends is always a dangerous game; it appears to be especially so at this time." In fact, one may not altogether unreasonably suppose that the near term growth of intergovernmental transfers will be less than in the past, so that such receipts will probably be insufficient to finance the demise of the property tax. They may, however, facilitate moderation in its application. So also with user charges; one simply doubts that augmentation of such charges will really change very much fundamental property tax scenery.

Local income, sales, and perhaps in some cases value added taxes will usefully supplement property tax revenues and intergovernmental transfers as well as providing revenue system balance.[2] Where levied, they will

2. See Break (1980b, pp. 252–55).

merely permit property tax moderation rather than dramatic revenue system redesign. These reflections, in sum, suggest that transfers, user charges, and local nonproperty taxes will probably at best merely alleviate the sting of *ad valorem* property taxes in the decade of the '80. They argue for the probability of moderation in this tax policy area.

Similarly, concentration of fiscal activity at the state level argues for possibly greater use of income and activity-based taxes and a decline in the importance of property taxation. The trend towards centralization, professionalization, and computerization seems likely to continue but hardly at a rate consistent with the property-tax-fading-away hypothesis. Given this preamble, what of the property tax in the '80s?

A Forecast for the '80s

At least one forecast suggests that in the 1980s the property tax—that congeries of disparate elements—will gradually decline in relative importance but that it will remain the most important source of local government tax revenue. For example, Roy Bahl (1979, p. 12) concluded a recent paper as follows:

All indications point to a continuing decline in the importance of the property tax. The growth in its base is slowing as national economic and population growth slows and it is not as stimulated as are other taxes during inflation. Less growth in the state-local sector, more fiscal centralization and fewer school children accentuate this trend. The ongoing regional shifts in economic activity and population are toward the sunbelt states which traditionally make lighter use of the property tax. Finally, there is the taxpayer revolt which has made the property tax a focal point. Indeed, it is difficult to draft a scenario under which the property tax will increase in relative importance in the next few years. Yet, this declining importance not withstanding, the property tax will remain the major local government revenue source and interest in improving its operation will not likely diminish.

Dick Netzer (1979, pp. 18–19) at the 1979 TRED conference arrived at a parallel conclusion:

So the forecast here is that the property tax will remain important enough to engage policy makers and scholars, for a generation to come. However, it will be a property tax that is far from uniform in its treatment of privately owned real property, even within a single taxing jurisdiction. Formal classification by property types with differential effective rates will be common, typically providing lower rates for residential and farm property. Present use-value assessment also will be common, generally favoring the same property classes. These provisions, together with individually negotiated abatements and exemptions, for ''economic development,'' to subsidize specific groups of housing consumers and for other even more bizarre purposes, will result in a good deal of erratic untaxing of buildings. But they will also involve much erratic untaxing of land values as well. The task before researchers of the TRED persuasion is to convince policy makers to maximize the resulting untaxing of buildings and minimize the untaxing of land.

Assuming the correctness of the Bahl/Netzer view—and it is a logically persuasive one—what of the probable form of the property levy during the decade? Several scenarios come to mind—some quite unlikely—that do illustrate the range of potentials and may suggest possible lines of future policy direction.

I. *Nostalgia and Tax Design.* Only with great difficulty can one imagine re-creation and modernization of the 19th-century general property tax. If that were done, significant property categories now untaxed —the automobile and the family television set, for example—would be once more placed upon the tax rolls. After all, the failure to tax net wealth effectively is considered by some as a great lucuna in American fiscal institutions. While a net wealth or worth tax might be a logical fiscal instrument, it would involve significant administrative difficulties, especially at the local level. Moreover, logically, there is the question of how to treat the value of human capital—a problem stout New England tax men faced squarely and walked away from long ago. And, possibly most compelling of all to academics, civil servants, and employed intellectuals, the inclusion of the present value of pension rights in a net worth tax base might be expected to generate at least some disenchantment with this potential tax instrument. Given all this plus recent history and probable near term developments in gratuitous transfer tax policy, this pattern seems a totally unlikely prospect.

II. *LVT, SVT, and Their Progeny.* Land value taxation, site value taxation, and their conceptual progeny might be considered as one possible scenario for the future. However, the problem of "windfalls and wipeouts"—to use Professor Donald Hagman's sturdy phrasing— continues to make adoption of this form of tax unlikely, except possibly as a conceptual element in the design of classified property tax patterns, where land is placed in a higher value class than other property categories (Netzer 1976, p. 233). A review of broader perspectives on this matter is outside the scope of this chapter;[3] quite simply, little action along this line is to be expected in the near-term future.

III. *A Stripped-Down Model.* One can imagine—not without some difficulty—a stripped-down, simplified property tax applicable only to residential real estate with business otherwise taxed and user charges greatly expanded. Such a modified property tax would or could serve as a local benefits levy to fund property-related services. While not without

---

3. In general, see Lindholm and Lynn (1982).

attractive logic, this concept would entail rather drastic revision of local and urban fiscal systems. A decade like the '80s seems overbrief for the gestation and genesis of such a system. If scenarios I through III seem improbable, what is probable? Scenario IV emerges.

IV. *Incremental Complexity Reexamined.* Reality, rather more complex than the models briefly described above, involves an incremental, developmental sequence, varying in time and place, that constitutes a kind of property tax dialectic. This sequence may be generalized as follows:

1. A uniform market-value–based *ad valorem* property tax is established by law with the administrative arrangements and institutional contours so often described in property tax literature.
2. Then, following familiar fiscal sociology, local governments and/ or local assessors conclude that complete assessment or tax burden uniformity would produce undesirable distributional or locational effects.
3. Administrative discretion, sometimes assisted by difficulty in the assessment and tax administrative process, implements the decision to abandon total uniformity and differentiate taxpayers or classes of taxpayers in a *de facto* system of assessment or burden classification.
4. Subsequently some combination of legislative action, judicial mandate, or assessor professionalism leads to renewed administrative emphasis upon assessment and, hence, tax burden uniformity.
5. As a result newly achieved but already customary burden distribution and tax pattern equilibria are disturbed; this may be accentuated by inflation's impact upon residential housing values—in recent times the principal effective inflation hedge of the man in the street—and by considerable uncertainty about the level of near-term tax obligations, which violates Adam Smith's ancient observation that often certainty in taxation is preferable to equity (Break 1979).
6. Then legislative and/or administrative amelioration of the resultant socio-fiscal disequilibrium is effectuated by some combination of
   (a) authorization of use value rather than market value assessment for some property categories;
   (b) adoption of *de jure* classification for property tax purposes with the resultant split-assessment role taking account of differential taxable capacity, mobility, political power, and sometimes sheer vociferousness (Sonstelie 1978):
   (c) limitations upon tax rates, assessment levels, revenues, or expenditures;

(d) eventual legislative/judicial redefinition of the property tax base possibly followed in due course by reassertion of administrative discretion in the tax administrative process,

(e) accompanied by various mixes of other forms of property tax relief, such as circuit breakers and new exemption patterns.

This sequence is simply a generalized view of recent property tax history. I suspect that this pattern, inelegant as it is, used in moderation, lubricated with intergovernmental fiscal transfers and local nonproperty taxation, will characterize the property tax of the 1980s. Further differentiation of property tax burdens by formal classification, exemption proliferation, assessment variation, and rate limitations will in all probability characterize the period. I also suspect that, despite the proliferation of statutory complexity, rule certainty may well give way once again to renewed administrative discretion as administrators seek to reconcile fiscal realities and emergent public attitudes. Achieving a great degree of Smithian certainty will continue to be a challenge to property tax policymakers and administrators.

As to the initial question of evolution or devolution, property tax adaptation has been achieved by selective technique, institutional hybridization, creative inbreeding, and continuous mutation. Like beauty, the question of whether evolution or devolution best describes the process may well lie in the eye of the beholder. My opinion is that the decade will witness positive development, both centralization and some devolution to substate units, and, most significant, a definite increase in the heterogeneity of the property tax. Nonetheless, the property tax will remain both an important fiscal support of local government and a perennial candidate for structural reform.

References

Advisory Commission on Intergovernmental Relations. 1979. *Changing Public Attitudes on Government and Taxes.* Washington, D.C.: U.S. Government Printing Office.

Bahl, Roy. 1979. "Property Taxation in the 1980's." Lincoln Institute of Land Policy Tax Roundtable, Property Tax Papers Series No. TPR-2. Cambridge, Mass.

Break, George F. 1979. "Adam Smith and the Property Tax: Some Neglected Advice." Lincoln Institute of Land Policy Roundtable, Property Tax Papers Series No. TPR-3. Cambridge, Mass.

Break, George F. 1980a. "The Role of Government: Taxes, Transfers and Spending." Conference Paper no. 16 presented to the National Bureau of Economic Research. Cambridge, Mass.

Break, George F. 1980b. *Financing Government in a Federal System.* Washington, D.C.: Brookings Institution.

Gold, Steven. 1979. *Property Tax Relief.* Lexington, Mass: Lexington Books.

Lindholm, Richard W., and Arthur D. Lynn, Jr., Ed. 1982. *Land Value Taxation.* Madison, University of Wisconsin Press.

Lynn, Arthur D., Jr. 1967. "Property Tax Development: Selected Historical Tendencies." In *Property Taxation USA,* ed. Richard W. Lindholm, pp. 7–19. Madison: University of Wisconsin Press.

Netzer, Dick. 1976. "Property Tax Reform and Public Policy Reality." In *Property Taxation, Land Use and Public Policy,* ed. Arthur D. Lynn, Jr., pp. 223–33. Madison: University of Wisconsin Press.

Netzer, Dick. 1979. "The Property Tax a Generation Hence." Paper presented to the 1979 TRED Conference.

Sonstelie, Jon. 1978. "Should Business Pay More Taxes Than Individuals? The Rush to Split Rolls: A Cautionary Note." *Taxing and Spending* 1 (October/November):16–19.

Stocker, Frederick D. 1979. "Farm-Use Assessment Revisited." Lincoln Institute of Land Policy Tax Policy Roundtable, Property Tax Papers Series No. TPR-1. Cambridge, Mass.

Welch, Ronald B. 1980. "The Property Tax Under Pressure: A Policymaker's Guide." Lincoln Institute of Land Policy Tax Policy Roundtable, Property Tax Papers Series No. TPR-4. Cambridge, Mass.

11 *Richard M. Bird and Enid Slack*

Urban Finance and User Charges

The rapid growth period of most older North American metropolitan areas appears to be over; some areas, indeed, are even losing population. Although other cities in the U.S. Sun Belt and in western Canada continue to expand rapidly, one might well think that the pressures on urban finance should have been somewhat alleviated by the slowdown of urban growth. This does not, however, appear to have happened. Indeed, those cities with the most severe financial problems—New York, Cleveland— are among those with low or negative growth rates.

The problems of urban finance seem at least as severe when population growth slows as when it accelerates: growing cities need a capital infrastructure and resources to maintain service levels for a larger population; stagnant and declining cities need to replace old infrastructure; and both must pay relatively higher prices for the resources' required to produce expected service levels. The urban fiscal problem has been considerably exacerbated in recent years by increasing taxpayer resistance to the traditional mainstay of urban public finance in North America—the local property tax. That there is often little logical basis for this resistance does not make it any less politically important.[1] In these circumstances, cities in both the United States and Canada have become increasingly dependent on aid from higher levels of government—in the United States

1. For a critical analysis of the drive for property tax relief, see Bird and Slack (1978).

Table 11.1. Sources of Municipal Revenue, Canada and the United States, Selected Years 1960-1977 (amounts in percentages)

	Canada					Annual Average % Change 1970–77[e]	United States					Annual Average % Change 1970–77[e]
	1960	1965	1970	1975	1977		1960	1965	1970	1975	1977	
Tax Revenues												
Property taxes	64.5	61.2	39.5	32.0	32.5	11.5	42.5	41.2	37.0	31.3	30.7	9.0
Business and other taxes	7.8	3.5	4.2	3.1	3.1	9.8	5.8	5.9	6.4	6.9	7.2	13.9
Special assessments and charges	4.8	4.2	3.4	1.7	1.7	4.1	1.0	.9	.6	.5	.4	6.6
Total taxation[a]	*77.2*	*69.1*	*47.7*	*37.3*	*37.8*	*10.9*	*49.3*	*48.0*	*44.0*	*38.7*	*38.4*	*9.8*
Nontax revenues												
Sales of goods & services[b]	—	1.4	5.0	7.1	7.9	22.3	19.6	19.3	19.1	18.2	19.0	11.9
Licenses, permits, and other	6.6	6.6	3.8	4.0	3.7	14.0	4.3	4.4	3.7	4.3	3.4	10.6
Total nontax revenues	*6.6*	*8.0*	*8.8*	*11.1*	*11.6*	*19.1*	*23.9*	*23.7*	*22.8*	*22.5*	*22.4*	*11.7*
Total revenues from own sources	83.8	77.1	56.5	48.5	49.4	12.4	73.2	71.7	66.9	61.2	60.8	10.4
Intergovernmental transfers[c]	16.2	22.9	43.5	51.5	50.6	17.1	26.8	28.3	33.1	38.8	39.2	14.7
Total gross revenues[d]	*100.0*	*100.0*	*100.0*	*100.0*	*100.0*	*14.6*	*100.0*	*100.0*	*100.0*	*100.0*	*100.0*	*12.0*

Sources: U.S. *Statistical Abstract*, Vol. 100 (1979); Statistics Canada, *Local Government Finance* (selected years).

[a] Includes small "other" taxes in Canadian data.

[b] For the United States, sales of goods and services include utility and liquor store revenue.

[c] For Canada, grants-in-lieu of taxes have been included in intergovernmental revenues in part because these data were not available separately for 1960 and 1965.

[d] May not add to totals owing to rounding.

[e] This period has been chosen because of substantial changes in Canadian statistics in 1970.

mainly from the federal government, but in Canada almost exclusively from the provinces. Indeed, as shown in Table 11.1, in both countries the decline in the relative importance of property tax revenues has been almost exactly offset by the rise in the relative importance of intergovernmental transfers.

Table 11.1 also shows that the responsiveness of higher-level governments to municipal fiscal needs has been more generous in Canada than in the United States. In 1977, half of the resources available to Canadian local governments came from the provinces, compared to only 40 percent from higher-level governments in the United States. Despite the difference in dependence on transfers, property taxes in Canada remained similar to those in the United States in the 1970s and have continued to account for a slightly higher proportion of total municipal revenues. If intergovernmental transfers are substantially more important in Canada than in the United States and property taxes are similar, it of course follows that the third component of local revenues distinguished in Table 11.1, nontax revenues, is more important south of the border.

In neither country, however, have the oft-discussed revenue pressures of recent years resulted in any great effort to exploit nontax revenues, even if broadly defined to include special assessments, more heavily. The combined total of special assessments and nontax revenues rose in Canada from 12.2 percent of revenues in 1970 to only 13.3 percent in 1977, while in the United States it actually fell slightly from 23.4 percent to 22.8 percent over the same period. Were it not for a substantial increase in "sales of goods and services" in Canada (perhaps due in part to an expansion of statistical coverage in the early 1970s), a sharp decline in the total would have occurred there also.[2]

In Canada, as in the United States, there are significant differences among the different provinces in the relative use of property taxation and intergovernmental transfers and in the role of the provincial government in providing local services. For example, some provinces directly provide important public services such as education and welfare, whereas in others these services are provided locally. Local revenues are of course less significant in provinces where major local services are financed at the provincial level. The reliance of local governments on user charges also varies considerably across provinces, ranging in 1978 from less than 3 percent of total municipal revenues in Nova Scotia to 13 percent in neighboring New Brunswick (Bureau of Municipal Research 1980, p. 4). In

2. The detailed pre-1970 figures in Canada are not very comparable with those for later years. It should also be noted that the sales figures for utility and liquor revenues included in the U.S. have no counterpart in Canada, where these are generally provincial, not local, activities.

Table 11.2. User Charges as a Percentage of Government Spending, Ontario, Selected Functions, 1976–1977

General government	2.6%
Protection	
Fire	0.3
Police	2.3
Transportation	
Roads and highways	2.4
Transit	57.5
Environment	
Sewers	24.0
Water	64.2
Solid waste	10.6
Parks and recreation	22.6
Libraries	2.3
Social and family	
Health	3.5
General assistance	0.7
Assistance to aged persons	35.5
Assistance to children	2.6
Planning and development	15.9

Source: Ontario Ministry of Treasury and Economics, *Local Government Finance in Ontario, 1977,* Part II, Table 1-2.

Ontario, for example, user charges accounted for 5 percent of total municipal revenues in 1978. As Table 11.2 shows, among the major expenditure functions for which user charges are important in Ontario are the traditional areas of water, transit, sewers, and parks and recreation. It is more surprising, perhaps, that user charges are also important in some "social" areas, notably assistance for the aged (in the form of charges for room and board in homes for the aged). In the United States, municipal user charges are particularly prominent in such areas as water terminals (127.5 percent of expenditures), airports (96.9 percent), and hospitals (34.0 percent) in which Canadian municipal governments are not heavily involved (U.S. Department of Commerce 1979, Table 8).[3] On the whole, however, it appears that in both countries user charges are most common in financing the traditional "hard" areas of transportation and water and sewers, and, to a lesser extent, a few social services. Where charges are applied, they appear often to finance a much larger

3. For more detailed discussion of urban user charges, see Mushkin (1972) for the United States and Bird (1976, Part III) for Canada.

proportion of expenditure in the United States (sometimes greater than 100 percent) than in Canada.

These crude data appear to offer little support to a proposition commonly heard in the United States, namely, that the nondeductibility of user charges and special assessments for income tax purposes results in greater opposition to their use as compared to such deductible general revenue sources as the property tax. On the contrary, Table 11.1 shows that not only are user charges somewhat more heavily utilized in the United States than in Canada (where neither they nor property taxes are deductible) but also that user charge revenues have grown more rapidly than tax revenues in recent years (in both countries). On the other hand, it seems plausible that reliance on user charges has been less in Canada than in the United States because of the greater readiness to finance urban services through intergovernmental transfers in the former country. Increasing fiscal pressures on higher-level governments in recent years, however, make it appear unlikely that these transfers will be so generous in the future in either country—indeed, a slight decline in their relative importance is already apparent in the data included in Table 11.1. It therefore seems quite likely that more attention may be paid in the near future to the possibility of financing urban public services through "user charges," broadly defined to include various explicit linkages between expenditures and revenues.[4]

User charges are thus most likely to be viewed by hard-pressed urban officials as a potential additional source of revenue. To an economist, however, the real value of user charges is to promote economic efficiency by providing information to consumers and officials, enabling them to make more efficient use of resources. In an interesting article a few years ago, Wilbur Thompson (1968) labelled the city "a distorted price system" and pointed out the need for more rational urban prices to ration the use of existing facilities, to guide the distribution of income, to enlarge the range of choice, and to change tastes and behavior. In a sense, our principal purpose in the present paper is to outline briefly a few ways in which more reliance on user charges might reduce the present level of "distortion." What increased use of user charges, public prices, and benefit taxes accomplishes, if it is done properly, is to reestablish the missing link between government revenues and government expenditures[5] —the link which so much recent discussion shows us is badly needed in today's cities.

4. Bird (1976, pp. 17–18) distinguishes quasi-private prices, public prices, fees, special assessments, and benefit taxes. For present purposes, all of these will be loosely referred to as "user charges."

5. For a more elaborate argument along these lines, see Bird (1978).

The major virtue of pricing urban public services whenever possible is thus to improve efficiency. The major costs of doing so, according to many, are, on the one hand, that it is very costly to price and, on the other, that the distributional consequences of pricing are likely to be undesirable. Any argument in favour of more charging must, therefore, pay attention not only to the potential for pricing with respect to revenue, improved knowledge and information, and improved efficiency, but also to its limitations with respect to administration, politics, and distribution. Since it is difficult to say in general much new about so well-worked a field,[6] the balance of this chapter briefly considers three particular questions concerning expenditure-revenue linkages: special assessments, the relation between pricing and investment decisions, and charges for social services, drawing mainly on Canadian experience. Only in the concluding section do we return briefly to the more general question of why governments seem so reluctant to make more use of user charges in any area.

Special Assessments and Lot Levies

Special assessments and related devices such as subdivision exactments or lot levies are compulsory payments (in cash or kind) intended to defray the cost of certain public sector capital outlays. They are not "user charges" as normally defined, because the amount charged is not related to the use made of any good or service provided by governments. However, the basis upon which individual property owners are assessed is related to the benefits presumed to accrue to them from a particular public investment. Moreover, special levies to finance certain public capital facilities would appear to be a natural complement to user-charge financing of the current operating costs of such facilities—as it were, the first part of a multipart tariff approach to pricing public outputs. For these reasons, some discussion of this particular form of benefit taxation is appropriate in the present context.

The case for special assessments on benefit grounds can also be considered in the broader context of local government as a benefit unit. It has generally been argued by economists that one of the main justifications for the existence of local government, given free mobility of individuals, is that it provides a range of choices among different public service packages to meet the diverse preferences of potential residents. For example, in a metropolitan area composed of small, relatively homogeneous communities, the mix of public services probably varies so that a

6. In addition to the sources cited earlier, see Downing (1974 and 1980), Goetz (1973), Kafoglis (1969), and Institute of Economic Affairs (1967).

choice is presented to potential inhabitants. Other things being equal, they will choose that community whose public service package best satisfies their requirements. In this quasi market for public services, property taxes can be thought of as the price one pays to live in a particular community. The property tax in this model is thus largely a benefit tax or user charge.[7]

An even stronger case can be made for special assessments on benefit grounds, because they are more closely related to the benefits received than are property taxes. Many public works directly increase the value of the properties which they serve, thereby providing a financial benefit to the property owners. Since these owners benefit from the improvements through no efforts of their own, it seems appropriate to charge them for the costs. There are several ways this can be done. One approach is to require developers to provide certain services (such as water, sewers, and parks) to municipal standards before they are permitted by the municipality to develop and sell lots. Another possibility is a subdivision agreement between the developer and the municipality in which the developer pays a "lot levy" to the municipality to provide certain services. A third option is to have the municipality provide the services and then charge the property owners through special assessments. A fourth possibility is to have the developer provide all services internal to the subdivision and have the municipality charge a lot levy for off-site services. Finally, the municipality can provide all or part of the services and finance them from such general revenue sources as the property tax.[8]

Traditionally, special assessments (under such names as local improvement taxes or capital levies) have been employed in a variety of ways in Canadian municipalities. In Ontario, 50–100 percent of the capital cost of such local improvements as sidewalks and sewers have been recovered by special assessments, usually in the form of a front-footage charge on owners whose properties abutted the work in question. Table 11.3 illustrates the nature and diversity of such charges in the province of Ontario a few years ago. In no case have they produced much revenue, however. There is no evidence since this survey was taken either of any convergence in practice or of any improvement in the basis on which these charges are set. The situation in other provinces seems equally complex

7. Some support for this view of the property tax as a benefit tax comes from discussions of property tax relief. It is often argued by groups such as the elderly, farmers, and cottagers, for example, that since the property tax largely finances education at the local level, those who do not directly benefit from the school system should be exempt.

8. Another approach is through so-called "land readjustment" systems; see W. A. Doebele (1979). Although this approach is not further discussed here, largely because there is no relevant North American experience with it, it should perhaps be noted that, conceptually, at its best land readjustment appears to offer certain advantages over special assessments and lot levies. For further discussion, see Ho (1981).

Table 11.3. Special Capital Levies, Ontario Municipalities, 1971

Municipality	Special Capital Levies as Percent of Total Revenue[a]	Amount and Basis of Levy[h]					
		Sidewalks	Pavement[d]	Water main	Sanitary sewer	Storm sewer	Off-street parking
Borough							
Scarborough	1.28	50%; FF[e]	100%; FF	$5/FF (max.)	$10/FF (residential), $24/FF (commercial)	0	0
Cities							
Hamilton	NA	40%	40%cost	0	$8.50/FF	0	0
Sault Ste. Marie	0.33	25%; $2.50-4/FF	25%; $5-6/FF	0	90%; $6.50/FF	30%; $3.00/FF	0
Kingston	3.03	40%	40%	80%	80%	15%	100%
Sarnia	3.62	80%; $4.89/FF	80%; $4.89/FF	50%; $7.77/FF	50%; $7.77/FF	50%; $7.66/FF	0
Peterborough	2.70	60%	60%	100%	100%	100%	0
Cornwall	2.02	60%	60%	100%	100%	100%	0
Waterloo	2.61	40-75%	40-75%	50-75%	50-75%	30-60%	50%
Barrie	1.16[b]	100%; FF	100%/FF	100%; FF	100%; FF	0	0
Towns							
Oakville	1.66	0	0	60%; $7/FF	60%; $7/FF	0	0[f]
Richmond Hill	1.12	0	0	100%	100%	25%	0
Timmins	0.70[c]	50%	0	0	100%	0	0
Kapuskasing	2.65	0	0	66⅔%	66⅔%	0	0
Ajax	0.0	0	0	0	0	0	0
Orangeville	NA	100%	100%	0	0	0	0
Picton	0.0	0	0	0	0	0	0
Vaughan	1.42	FF	FF	FF	FF	FF	0
Townships							
Pickering	NA	[g]	[g]	100%; FF	100%; FF	0	0

Source: Information from municipal authorities as reported in Bird (1976, p. 110).

[a] Six-year average (1965–70) except where otherwise indicated.
[b] Two years only.
[c] Three years only.
[d] Pavements constructed as local improvements.
[e] Front footage basis.
[f] Paid out of parking revenue.
[g] Although streets, sidewalks, etc., are paid for out of general revenues, street lighting is paid for by a special rate on the assessed value of properties within defined street light areas.
[h] Percentages refer to percent of cost to be covered by special levy.

Table 11.4. Ontario: Structure of Lot Levies, 1979[a]

Summary of Lot Levy Structure	Timing of Payments			Differentation of Levy				Size of Levy[c]	
	Signing of Subdivision Agreement	Issuing of Building Permit	Combination of the Two Policies	By Housing Type	By Number of Bedrooms	Uniform	Indexed Levies	Total	Local Share
Durham									
Ajax			x	x	x		x	$4,230	42.6%
Brock			x			x		3,180	23.6
Newcastle		x		x				3,930	38.2
Oshawa		x				x	x	4,969	51.1
Pickering		x				x		3,930	38.2
Scugog		x			x			3,430	29.2
Uxbridge		x		x				3,530	31.2
Whitby			x	x				4,780	49.2
Halton									
Burlington		x		x	x		x	3,495	56.4
Halton Hills		x		x	x		x	3,037	50.0
Oakville		x		x				3,025	49.6
Milton		x		x[b]	x		x	3,870	60.6
Peel									
Brampton		x		x	x		x	4,610	57.5
Mississauga		x		x			x	4,413	55.6
Caledon	x					x		3,959	50.5
York									
Aurora	x					x		3,245	92.3
East Gwillimbury		x				x		3,925	93.6
Georgina	x			x				2,750	90.9
King	x					x		3,750	93.3
Markham			x			x		2,889	91.3
Newmarket	x			x	x			2,750	90.9
Richmond Hill	x					x		2,000	87.5
Whitchurch-Stouffville	x					x		3,750	93.3
Vaughan	x					x		2,663	79.3

Source: Amborski (unpubl.)

[a] Metropolitan Toronto is not included in the table because of the few municipalities that use levies in this jurisdiction.

[b] Milton does not set its levy specifically by housing type but by density, which could be considered to be related to housing type.

[c] Total levies for single-family detached units: in some cases special arrangements have been made for particular areas in the municipality.

219

220 Local Policy Options

and inconsistent, being based more on custom than on reason (Bird 1976, pp. 109–13).

For the most part, special assessments in Canada have been confined to relatively minor public works in existing neighborhoods: perhaps the major exception has been the extension of sewer systems to already built-up fringe areas. The growing need in some older cities to finance the reconstruction of decaying infrastructure provides ample reason for reconsideration and rationalization of these policies in the future. Of more immediate concern, however, has been the continuing need to create new infrastructure to accommodate residential and industrial expansion. For the most part, such capital works have been financed in Ontario through "lot levies," or cash imposts on developers of new subdivisions that are intended to cover the costs of providing water, sewers, roads, street lights, and so on.

Table 11.4 summarizes some of the findings in a recent study of the structure of lot levies in a group of contiguous regional municipalities surrounding Toronto.[9] It is in these areas, rather than Metropolitan Toronto itself, that most new housing in Ontario has been located in recent years. All of the twenty-four local municipalities surveyed charge developers of single-family detached houses levies ranging from $750 to $3,700 per lot. In addition, the four regional municipalities—which are responsible, for example, for providing water service—also charge levies ranging from $250 to $2,430. The total lot levy charged in 1979 ranged from a low of $2,000 in Richmond Hill to a high of $4,969 in Oshawa. The division of this total between the two levels of local government varied sharply among the regions, with York Region collecting a much smaller proportion than the others and Durham somewhat more. Although various other features of these levies also varied across regions, they tended to be more consistent within regions, no doubt in part reflecting intermunicipal competition and in part simple imitation.

With respect to the timing of payments, for example, some municipalities require that the levy be paid at the time the subdivision agreement is signed. The majority of municipalities surveyed, however, do not require payment until just prior to the issuance of the building permit. The third approach, used by municipalities in one region, is to require half of the payment when the subdivision agreement is signed and half when the building permit is issued. (As can be seen in Table 11.4, local municipalities usually adopt the same policy as their regional government). Obviously, the earlier the funds are obtained, the less the financing problem for the municipality—and the greater the problem for the developer.

9. All the factual information on lot levies is taken from the 1980 study by David P. Amborski (unpubl.).

Table 11.5. An Example of Lot Levy Structure

Region of Durham[a]	
Sanitary sewer construction	$1,110
Watermain and plant	710
Regional roads	405
Other regional capital works	205
	$2,430
City of Oshawa[b]	
Local roads	$ 945
Fire station	84
Libraries	168
Recreation and park facilities	1,009
Water course improvements	333
	$2,539
Total levy	*$4,969*

Source: Amborski (unpubl., pp. 56, 59)

[a] Dwellings with two or more bedrooms. The sewer and water components are reduced to $560 and $355 respectively for one bedroom dwellings.

[b] The water course improvement charge is lowered to $246 in certain areas of the city.

The timing of payments also has implictions for the degree of provincial control over municipal expenditure decisions. All capital expenditures by municipalities have to be approved by a provincial agency, the Ontario Municipal Board. The municipality is required to forecast capital needs over a five-year period and include the estimated cost to issue debentures. If the board accepts the forecast, it then sets a quota against which it charges subsequent applications for expenditure. In this way, the board maintains fairly strict control over municipal capital budgets. If the municipality can raise its own capital funding through lot levies in advance of providing the services, it can gain more flexibility with respect to provincial constraints on budgetary decisions.

Some municipalities apply uniform levies to all new residential development, while others differentiate by housing type, and some go so far as to differentiate by the number of bedrooms. In some instances, the levies charged are increased annually or semiannually in accordance with some price index (usually a construction cost index). Again, there is a clear tendency for policy to be relatively consistent within regions.

Table 11.5 illustrates the structure of a typical lot levy in the City of Oshawa in the Region of Durham. In addition to being unusually high, the basis for these charges is unusually well documented. Although all the regional governments surveyed had a formal study—sometimes publicly available—outlining the basis for their levies, it appeared that about one-third of the local municipalities in the sample had no formal basis at all for the levies charged. In the case of the Durham regional levy, however, annual water and sewer rates are set so as to cover all annual operating costs, and lot levies are intended to finance capital expenditures for facilities (based on a 1977 cost study, indexed semiannually). Half the levies are paid at the time the subdivision agreement is signed and the other half within one year (or upon the issuance of building permits, if sooner): the funds thus collected are earmarked for the purpose for which they are collected. The basis for the other components of the regional levy is less clear, but it is perhaps worth noting that the "other" works thus financed are primarily capital costs related to such regional social services as day care facilities.

The Oshawa municipal levy depicted in Table 11.5 is based on a similar mixed bag of careful studies and more arbitrary assumptions. Most components of the lot levy are based on (indexed) average per capita capital costs for the facilities noted, multiplied by the average expected number of persons in each unit. In the case of libraries and parks, for instance, these costs are determined on the basis of such arbitrary standards as 0.5 square feet per person for main branch library expansion plus 0.2 square feet for branch libraries.[10] As Amborski's detailed discussion of the Oshawa case shows, however, very little attention appears to have been paid to the implications of this charging system for economic efficiency. In short, even where the rationale for lot levies is most carefully developed, as in Oshawa, the principal discernible policy objective is simply to obtain revenue—presumably coupled with the general equity aim of charging the inhabitants of new residential units for the capital costs to which they give rise.

Where the pricing mechanism used as the basis of lot levies is explicitly stated, it is usually some form of average-cost pricing, which generally means average per capita costs multiplied by the average number of persons per type of unit. Efforts to use any form of marginal cost pricing have been limited. Those municipalities which differentiate lot levies according to housing type in effect try to recognize the incremental costs of each additional person in a unit, but they still use average costs as the basis for the levy. Some jurisdictions differentiate their levies according to what services are available. This attempt to relate the levy more closely to the benefits received is admirable but, again, average-cost pricing is used. On the whole, none of the extensive Ontario experience with lot levies appears to show any obvious influence of the enormous economics literature on the efficient pricing of public services.

10. In the case of parks, one-fifth of the total requirements is assumed to be satisfied by a separate levy of 5 percent of the developable land or its equivalent in cash imposed under Section 33 of the provincial Planning Act.

In analytical terms, both special assessments and lot levies may be considered to be methods of capturing anticipated "betterment" or increases in property values.[11] Special assessments, for example, are intended to recapture the cost of such special local improvements as sidewalks fairly by allocating the cost among properties in accordance with some (arbitrarily determined) presumed pattern of benefits. In reality, it is clear that, since "other things" are never equal, any increases in property values consequent to an improvement can only very roughly be attributed to that improvement. It was in part for this reason that earlier studies suggested that the greatest potential for special assessments perhaps lay in rapidly expanding communities, where any errors in benefit attribution would tend to be swamped by other factors.[12] The effects of special assessments on property values depend only in part upon their accuracy as benefit taxes, however. Perhaps even more important is the question of whether the earmarked funding they provide is perceived as increasing the quantity and quality of public capital works—as was apparently the case in Bogotá, Colombia, for example.[13]

Any actual formula used to allocate benefits (see Table 11.3 for examples) is likely to result in a complex pattern of horizontal inequities. As has been argued elsewhere, however, in many instances any price paid in terms of increased horizontal inequities as a result of special assessment financing of local improvements seems likely to be more than compensated for by their probable progressive incidence, their apparent political acceptability, their revenue potential, and their nature as a lump-sum tax —which means they are unlikely to give rise to undesirable incentive effects.[14]

Like special assessments, lot levies are imposed on select groups in a particular area. Unlike special assessments, such levies are a very recent phenomenon, having largely been created in response to the pressure on urban resources arising from rapid urbanization. As the description of current Ontario practice suggests, it is difficult to conclude that the formulas currently used to determine such levies are either fair or efficient.[15] This is the result not so much of the deficiencies of municipal administration as of the intractable nature of the problem. In effect,

11. Much of the following discussion follows Ho (1981).
12. See Rhoads and Bird (1969).
13. See Doebele, Grimes, and Linn (1979).
14. See Rhoads and Bird (1969) for more discussion on these aspects of special assessments in the particular case of Colombia.
15. As might be expected, many developers have made the same complaints; see Grayhurst (1981). Another common complaint, however, that such levies should not finance "soft services" such as police, fire, and libraries seems without merit. There is some evi-

every individual subdivision proposal gives rise to different infrastructure costs (and environmental effects) and therefore ideally requires an individually determined formula. To reduce uncertainty—and the influence of interdependent bargaining behavior—many municipalities have developed rules such as those described above instead of deciding each case on its particular merits. Such rules are, of course, generally inappropriate in some respects for each particular case; when they are too obviously inappropriate—or when enough pressure is applied—most municipalities have in fact proved amenable to some negotiation.[16] The result of this combination of essentially arbitrary rules with the possibility of individual adjustment has often been to maximize political conflict in the process and inequity and inefficiency in the results.

The perhaps surprising conclusion of the very quick review in this section is that the ancient instrument of special assessments may have more to be said for it than the new tool of lot levies (or subdivision exactments generally). Both devices have distinct merits in terms of equity and perhaps political acceptability in comparison with the property tax. Both are also inherently somewhat arbitrary and hence give rise to horizontal inequities in the form of windfall gains and losses. Lot levies create more uncertainty, however, and as often applied shift more of the financing costs onto developers. They thus tend to block development and may affect resource allocation adversely while special assessments have little, if any, adverse allocative effect. Moreover, since the era of rapid urban expansion appears to be past, devices such as lot levies, which are only applicable on the urban fringe, will inevitably fade in importance relative to the continual need to improve and replace capital works that can be financed through special assessments.

In view of the strength of the case for more use of special-assessment financing and the resistance to local property taxes, it is surprising that so little attention has been paid to this subject in North American municipalities in recent years. In particular, more explicit consideration seems needed in the case for using special assessments to cover the capital costs and for user charges to cover the current costs of a wide range of urban services.[17]

---

dence (reported by Grayhurst) that the era of lot levies may be passing as a result of the weakening of the housing boom in recent years.

16. This has been particularly obvious in Ontario in the case of industrial developments, on which most municipalities have not imposed levies—though it can easily be shown that such developments may be very costly in terms of the additional facilities required to service them.

17. For a recent interesting attempt to consider this question more analytically, see Vars (unpubl.)

Current Charges and Investment Decisions

When economists consider how public services should be priced, their usual conclusion is that the price charged for each product should equal the marginal cost of producing an extra unit of that product. The rationale is that only marginal cost reflects the value that the resources used could have produced if employed elsewhere. If the price charged is less (or more) than this cost, resources are clearly being diverted from uses deemed more valuable by citizens to uses deemed less valuable. The central rationale for applying marginal-cost pricing in the public sector is thus to secure efficiency in the allocation of resources.

There are many reasons in any real-world situation why precise adherence to the marginal-cost rule may be neither feasible nor desirable. All this means, however, is that some deviations from strict marginal-cost pricing may be justified either in strict efficiency terms or as a "second-best" way of achieving some distributive goal. The main justification for marginal-cost pricing is in no way affected by such qualifications.

More basically, economic efficiency as defined above is only a worthwhile objective of public policy if "consumer sovereignty" prevails. Citizen-consumers are presumed to know what they want in the way of goods and services, and how much they are prepared to give up to get it. What is more important is the presumption in this argument that people *should* get what they want. The free choices made by individuals when faced with prices reflecting the opportunities foregone in producing one set of goods and services—that is, prices equal to marginal costs—will, it is assumed, result in their being better off than they would be in any other situation. Without prices, it is all too easy for the public sector to produce the wrong things, in the wrong quantity—"wrong" in the sense that decisions were not made on the basis of full knowledge of economic costs.

If correct economic prices are not charged, however, and public services are therefore provided free or below cost, a likely result will be political pressure from beneficiaries to *expand* the level of expenditure even further beyond the efficient level. The lower the price facing consumers, the more will be demanded, up to the point at which the value to consumers of an additional unit of service is equal to the price charged—zero, in the case of a service provided for free. Budget-maximizing suppliers may therefore find it in their interests to charge zero (or too low) prices in order to increase the demand for the service they supply and to provide "objective" evidence of the need for such expansion.[18]

18. This point is developed clearly in Vars (1976).

Suppose that by some accident—and, in the absence of correct pricing, it would be only by accident—the efficient quantity of some public service such as day care centers or roads was initially provided. If no price is charged for this service, consumers will obviously press for more and more service—up to the point at which it would be worth to them just what they have to pay for it—nothing. Since no one has to face the real cost of such expansion, no one does. Political pressures are thus likely to be strongest to expand precisely those services which are most underpriced and hence, by definition, socially worth least. Correct pricing thus encourages not only better decisions on the *use* of existing public services but also provides better guidance for *investment* decisions. The relevance of this point to the earlier discussion of financing capital improvements should be clear.

It is, of course, most unlikely that the optimal amount of any public facility is in fact provided at the present time. What is the efficient pricing rule in this case?[19] If the demand for such services exceeds the supply, prices should be raised to ration the existing supply in the short run unless there are strong distributive reasons against such action. An appropriately conducted benefit-cost analysis in such a case would presumably indicate that, taking indivisibilities into account, some expansion of facilities is warranted.

More likely, there may appear to be a shortage under the present set of pricing rules, even though existing capacity would in fact turn out to be greater than its optimal size if full costs were charged, because users would not be willing to pay the necessary prices. In these circumstances the correct price will not cover all the fixed costs of providing such capacity, in effect because there are in fact *no* current economic costs involved in providing capacity that already exists. Instead, the prices charged on facilities already oversupplied should in principle recover only those costs currently incurred in operating and maintaining the facilities.

The most important point to note in this connection, however, is that prices less than "full" economic costs are justified only because there are too many facilities already in place. The fixed charges attributable to providing the excess capacity are paid out of general government revenues not because this is fairer than charging direct users the full costs of the services, but because it is more efficient to use facilities already built, so long as the revenues produced exceed the current costs of doing so. Physical assets wear out and have to be replaced, however, and in cases

19. For a good discussion of the complex interaction between pricing rules and benefit-cost analysis, see Millward (1971, especially pp. 218–42). As shown there, there are no simple solutions in this area, but the basic principles are those stated here.

of excess capacity such as those described here, a correct benefit-cost analysis of the replacement decision should show that some of the capacity which is now being used (because below-full-cost prices are being charged) should *not* be renewed, in effect because the cost of doing so exceeds the amount which potential users are willing to pay for the services provided.

The somewhat paradoxical suggestion emerging from this brief incursion into some fairly complex theoretical waters, then, is that one possible justification for the present low prices charged users of much urban infrastructure is to insure that facilities already in place are used in an efficient fashion. This is particularly true because most such infrastructure is relatively long-lived, so that charging full (long-run) costs may involve sizeable economic losses. If the full cost of providing such facilities were to be charged, however, apparent "shortages" might vanish and the underlying reality of economically excess capacity be revealed.

Past mistaken investment decisions might thus justify what at first glance may seem to be present mistaken pricing decisions. It is crucial, however, not to be misled by the appearance of full (or over-full) utilization of present facilities to conclude that facilities should therefore be replaced or perhaps even expanded. On the contrary, in the circumstances postulated, the excess capacity should be allowed to evaporate over time as facilities wear out and are not replaced. When new facilities are created, their full costs should be charged to users, though perhaps in part through devices such as special assessments rather than full-cost pricing.

User Charges in the Social Services

As noted earlier, user charges provide a surprisingly large part of the funding for some social services, such as assistance to the aged. The role of pricing with respect to such services seems rather paradoxical. Since explicit redistribution is the principal rationale for most state provision of social services, allocating such services by prices would seem to defeat their main purpose.

In the case of old age care on Ontario, for example, extended care in old age homes (that is, where residents require limited but regular medical assistance) was offered to recipients for a basic fee of $8.70 per day in 1977.[20] The actual average per diem cost in municipal homes was $31.46,

20. All information on this subject is taken from Krashinsky (1981). This work appears to be the first major study of this area and has been drawn on heavily here. For an earlier discussion, in a less rigorous analytical framework, of some of these issues, see Bird (1976, Part IV).

with the provincial government covering $20.37 of the difference and the municipal share being only $2.39. In the case of residential care, in contrast, a user charge equal to the full cost of providing the service ($17.80 in municipal homes) is levied on all who can afford it (as defined by rather strict income-asset tests). In total, municipal homes in 1977 received almost 40 percent of their revenue from user charges, with 66 percent of the residents of such homes receiving some subsidy and an average charge of $11.15 per day.

In his interesting recent study, Michael Krashinsky (1981) puts forth several reasons why subsidizing institutional old age care makes sense. Basically, his argument is that older people who are unable to take care of themselves require more resources to achieve some minimum level of well-being than those who can live in the community.[21] Moreover, since it is too costly and difficult to determine *exactly* how many additional resources individual old people need, the most efficient way to redistribute income to them may be through subsidizing such particular public services as care in municipal old age homes. Institutional care is particularly attractive from this point of view precisely because it is *not* attractive to those who do not need it. If a person can stay out of an old peoples' home, he or she usually will! Although the "targeting" efficiency of such subsidies is hardly perfect, it is bound to be better than such generalized cash transfers as old age pensions or similar demogrants.

This argument seems persuasive. It does not, however, imply that the present level and form of subsidy found in Ontario—or its obverse, the user charge—is correct. The maximum user charge of $8.70 for extended care, for example, when compared to the $17.80 charged for residential care, in effect charges less to those who use more costly services. This differentiation between residential and extended care cannot, however, be justified (in an extension of the earlier argument) as an efficient means of reaching those with greater inability, because if one can apply the differential rate one must be able to distinguish adequately the two categories. (Even if user charges were equal in the two cases, the subsidy would of course still be greater to those requiring the more costly extended care.) The only effect of lower user charges to extended care residents in this instance appears to be to enrich their potential heirs, a result which seems unlikely to be an appropriate objective of public policy. The effects of the rate differential on resource allocation seem most unlikely to be serious in this instance, however, since it seems improbable that healthy

21. Krashinsky also develops other arguments (e.g., a "social insurance" rationale) that are not discussed here.

people would be classified as needing extended care simply to save them a few dollars a day.

In other areas of social services, however, the potential inefficiencies introduced by inappropriate pricing policy may be more serious precisely because there is more room for individual choice. In the case of day care centers, for example, different families clearly have very different needs for day care. Moreover, evidence suggests that there is a high price elasticity of demand for institutional day care. For this reason, Krashinsky in an earlier study suggested both that the maximum subsidy to day care that could be justified was equivalent to the marginal tax rate on earnings and that present subsidies to day care centers in Ontario unduly encouraged use of the highest cost (publicly provided) facilities (Krashinsky 1977). Subsidizing services with these characteristics, supposedly to help those most in need, may not be very efficient if cheaper, equally effective substitutes are available elsewhere.[22] In such circumstances, user charges may often be necessary to discourage overuse.

The costs of obtaining information sufficient to distinguish the truly "needy" therefore may sometimes make the provision of in-kind transfers (subsidized services) both an efficient and an equitable policy choice. Except in the most extreme cases, however (e.g., complete incompetence of recipients, that is, a paternalistic approach), completely free provision of any service is seldom warranted. There is thus an important potential role for economic analysis in determining the degree and type of subsidization suitable for each particular service. The other side of the subsidy coin is of course the degree of "unsubsidy" or user charge that should be levied. The significance of social service expenditures, even at the municipal level of government, makes it important that these issues be more clearly recognized than seems generally to have been the case to date.

It should be stressed, however, that in the absence of an adequate general income-support system, little progress towards designing a proper user-charge system can be expected anywhere, let alone in the critically redistributive social field.[23] User charges are indeed often needed to ensure efficient use of publicly provided services; to be effective, however, all consumers, even the poorest, should pay them; and this is clearly not possible without obviating the redistributive intent of providing the services in the first place, unless the poor receive enough income to enable them to do so.

22. In his two studies (1977, 1981) Krashinsky considers in detail all the many qualifications that obviously underlie such sweeping statements as this.

23. For an extended argument along these lines, see Bird (1976, Ch. 15). A partly alternative approach is to design a "credit card" system as sketched in Wilcox and Mushkin (1972).

Problems with Pricing

The pervasiveness of subsidized prices in the urban public sector suggests that many people do not see the issues to be as straightforward as they have been assumed to be in this chapter. Indeed, the argument that users should pay has been the subject of contentious political debate in both Canada and the United States in recent years, even in so clear-cut a case for charging as the transport area.[24] There appear to be two principal reasons for the prevalent confusion on this matter. First, there are indeed some legitimate qualifications to the case for user charges and some difficulties in implementing it. These points are discussed briefly below. In total, however, these qualifications do not upset the presumption that many of that large class of government activities that provide direct benefits to identifiable individuals (or groups) *should* be priced properly, and that the country as a whole (not to mention taxpayers) loses when this is not done.

Secondly, there are a number of common but misconceived arguments about the nature of public-sector activity—arguments which are often used, no doubt sometimes in good faith, to defend the special interests of the beneficiaries of subsidized programs. In the end it is such essentially political considerations as these that are likely to determine the success or failure of any attempt to introduce more rational pricing in any field, whether traditional or novel.[25] The most important arguments turn on the redistributive effects of subsidized public services.

In the first place, it is essential that policymakers recognize the extent and nature of the redistribution to particular groups that invariably results from present subsidization policies. The facts—that such redistribution, if it were done openly, might well be politically indefensible—seem less important in practice in determining the prices charged for public services than the mere fact that the existence of such redistribution creates a powerful lobby against any introduction of correct pricing.

Redistribution through subsidized prices is generally both inefficient and ineffective: it not only negates the efficiency virtues of pricing, but it also provides benefits to users of the subsidized service in proportion to use, not need—unless use is taken as a proxy for need, a proposition which at most holds for a limited range of social services.[26] In the case of water, for example, it is hard to think of any good reason why public

24. For an extensive discussion of the issues in transport pricing, see Bird (1976, Part II).

25. For general discussions of the issues discussed in the present section, see Bird (1976), Seldon (1977), and Krashinsky (unpubl.).

26. The use-need nexus seems strongest when there are in effect two levels of service provision: one provided privately for the well-to-do and one provided publicly for the poor. Only when this "nightmare of the egalitarian" prevails does redistribution through free or subsidized provision seem the most efficient way to proceed.

policy would want to distribute resources in proportion to use (at least beyond some minimal level).

Quite apart from the poor principle of using below-cost prices of services for redistributive purposes, the *results* in practice are unlikely to be very satisfactory either. Indeed, there is very little evidence, despite the number of times such arguments are heard, that most subsidies extended through the public price system benefit the poor: Do the poor own yachts? If not, how do they benefit from subsidized public marinas? The presumption that harbor users, for example, should face the full costs that their activities impose on society does not appear likely to be outweighed by any reasonable distributional argument.

To continue with the marina example, it is nevertheless common to encounter such arguments as the following: "lower income groups benefit from lower moorage prices and launch fees," with the implication being that such pricing policies are therefore socially justified. But if the purpose of policy is to benefit lower income groups, why should the extent of benefit they receive be made conditional on their use of boating facilities? Why give the same low prices to all boaters regardless of their income? In the absence of some stronger argument, no weight should be given to such views—particularly since what little evidence there is suggests that most recreational boaters are from higher-income groups anyway. Subsidizing prices to a large group of well-off people in order to provide miniscule benefits to the few poor people who use public boating facilities is not likely to make sense from any perspective.

Once people become "entitled" to any public-sector benefit, however, they do not readily give up their "right" to their accustomed subsidy. Unless those now benefiting from the subsidy can be compensated in some way (or else a very good argument can be made to them as to why they should not be compensated), no radically new pricing policy is likely to be easy to implement in any political system, no matter how rational it might be in principle. An obvious corollary is that new pricing policies are more likely to be implemented if they embody limited and incremental changes from existing practices rather than radically different policies (and if some sort of offset is provided to previously favored groups).

Such vague concepts as "regional development" are also often invoked to justify below-cost pricing of publicly provided services, particularly with respect to industrial plants. The case for subsidizing out of general revenues facilities providing direct (separable) services to identifiable private individuals or firms requires more justification than ritualistic invocations of "regional development," however. Some efforts must be made to estimate concretely the size of the expected benefits, particularly when, as is often the case, those who put forth such arguments are themselves gainers from industrial development (e.g., owners of real estate firms or related industrial facilities). Being human, such proponents of subsidization are all too likely to confuse the general benefits of such policies with the undeniable private benefits accruing to them. Indeed, the pressures to overestimate external benefits are great, both on direct users (who can obviously increase their private gains if they pay below-cost prices) *and* on suppliers of services (who may thus justify their existence and expand the scale of their operations.[27] There are no obvious countervailing forces to such pressures except perhaps better public information on who benefits and how much.

These issues are, at root, political and do not in the end affect the general "efficiency" case for correctly pricing urban services. Nevertheless, there are several necessary qualifications to this efficiency case as well as some technical questions on the practicality of "correct" (marginal cost) pricing. The balance of this section reviews some of these matters briefly.

In the first place, so long as some markets in the economy do not function properly (in the sense of setting prices equal to costs), the case for correct pricing in any one sector is, even in theory, weaker than indicated above. This point is most relevant, however, when a directly competing service is subsidized. In the case of public marinas mentioned above, for example, the competition of subsidized public facilities both keeps down the prices charged by existing private facilities and, since private operators require expectations of at least a normal rate of profit to expand operations, also discourages new private investment in such facilities. More adequate pricing in public marinas might therefore result in a rise in private prices and private investment, thus reducing the "need" for public investment by both lowering demand and raising supply.

Although other forms of outdoor recreation may also be subsidized (e.g., parks and campgrounds), the level of such subsidization is generally unknown, and at least in the short run, the substitution possibilities are probably limited. In the long run, a full study of this area would obviously need to consider more explicitly the pricing of recreational substitutes for boating; but it seems likely that the conclusion of such a study would be that recreational subsidies elsewhere should also be reduced rather than that the prevalent level of subsidization in public marinas is justified.[28]

On the whole, then, it seems a fair conclusion that the undoubted existence of imperfections and distortions that result in prices being less than marginal costs elsewhere offers little support for charging less than full

27. For some consideration of the political and bureaucratic motives behind such expansion, see Bird (1980, especially pp. 28–32).

28. For a preliminary look at the pricing of recreational services in Canada, see Bird (1976, Ch. 14).

economic prices in the case of public marinas. Similar conclusions could no doubt be drawn in many other areas.

A second qualification is the argument that the provision of such services benefits other than direct users. The inference usually drawn from this assertion is that prices should therefore be set below costs in order to ensure that the direct users of the service do not underconsume it. In theory, this argument is of course correct.

The relevance of this analysis clearly depends on the existence of external benefits, and its practical applicability in any particular case depends upon the extent to which information on external benefits is available. Partly because such information is in reality almost never available in the detail needed to determine the optimal degree of subsidization, the best practical approach to public pricing would appear to be to assume that there remains a presumption in favor of correct pricing *unless* it is offset by clearly demonstrable external benefits. Where the burden of proof is placed may be an important determinant of policy outcomes. Moreover, once externalities are taken into account, it must be remembered that they can be negative as well as positive. In particular, direct users of facilities such as roads (and marinas) may impose indirect costs on others through, for example, pollution and congestion.

A final consideration to be borne in mind in determining whether and how to charge for public services concerns the "price of pricing," or how much it costs to run a charging system. The fact that some sort of pricing system now exists in many areas suggests that this question may already have been answered satisfactorily. Nevertheless, it is important to remember that if prices cannot be enforced and collected at a reasonable cost (that is, if the efficiency gains from pricing are less than the resource costs of implementing a pricing system), then pricing makes no sense. In the end, this purely administrative consideration may well prove to be a more serious constraint on the applicability of pricing rules in many areas than the other qualifications mentioned here.

Other practical problems of designing and administering a pricing system include the "stickiness" of public sector prices (i.e., the difficulty of changing such prices once established) and the difficulty of determining what prices should be in the first instance. The first of these problems reflects in part the "entitlement" problem discussed above. To the extent this problem is considered serious, the case for charging "full-cost" prices (long-run marginal cost) rather than the economically more correct short-run marginal cost price, even at the expense of underutilizing existing capacity, is strong.[29] If prices can be changed only with great difficulty, it is probably better to set them at a level which is "correct"

29. Arguments to this effect have been made by such prominent exponents of marginal-cost pricing as Turvey and Boiteux, for example (see Millward [1971, p. 241]).

when viewed over a long time period. What this means is that correct
user charges should include some allowance for capital as well as for
operating costs.[30] If a two-part approach of charging for capital costs
through special capital levies is adopted, the "stickiness" problem can be
alleviated by some form of indexing, as is now practiced in some Ontario
municipalities. There appear to be no comparable examples of indexing
current user charges, however.

In some ways, the problem of determining what the prices should be in
the first instance is the heart of the matter. Even if one accepts all the
arguments up to this point on the general merits of pricing public services, little specific guidance has been provided here as to what these
prices should be in any particular instance. The *principle* to be followed
is clear: services should be priced to reflect the costs of the resources used
up in providing them. Only two theoretical qualifications to this rule
appear to apply generally. First, past investment may have resulted in
excess capacity, which will be fully utilized only if no effort is made to
recover capital costs. This possibility, however, was in part counterbal-
anced by the later argument on "sticky" prices. Secondly, pricing should
perhaps also be used to ration congested facilities, if congestion still
exists when full-cost pricing is applied.[31]

How to implement correct prices in *practice,* however, is a more
complex question. In the case of "congested" facilities, for example,
estimated full-cost prices should in principle be applied in those cases
where the total revenue produced would be sufficient to warrant the cost
of collecting it. In the case of underutilized facilities, charging such
prices would reduce usage even further, so prices should just cover current running costs—again only when the volume of business warrants it
(and, of course, such facilities should not be replaced when they wear
out).

Once it is established what prices *should* be charged, the next problem
is how best to collect them. As noted above, a full-fledged pricing system
may be administratively practicable only in a relatively few large, and
perhaps congested, facilities.[32] Some form of multipart pricing may be

30. It is important not to confuse this matter by confounding the economic costs of
capital with financial accounting costs. With some adjustments, the latter can be manip-
ulated to calculate the former, but they are not identical; for a more detailed discussion of
this relationship, see Haritos (1972).

31. For a recent example of the case for congestion pricing of harbor facilities, for
example, see Bennathan and Walters (1979). Congestion charges improve efficiency only if
demand is elastic, of course.

32. Whether any seasonal price variation should be introduced to deal with peak-load
problems is a second-order problem. First, levy full-cost prices; then, if congestion persists,
consider the use of time-variable prices as a possible rationing device. (The main alternative
is nonprice rationing through queuing.)

more widely applicable, perhaps including a variant of lot levies with a periodic "connection" charge and a charge more directly related to use.

Exactly what should be done for any specific service in any particular area is a matter for much closer investigation than can be carried out here.[33] What seems beyond question, however, it that many users of urban public services are at present being significantly subsidized by general taxpayers for no apparent economic or social reason. If it is decided to rectify this situation—and ample reason for doing so has been suggested here—what seems required is the collection of some "engineering" information, the application of some simple economic principles, and a good deal of political courage. Since the first two parts of this triumvirate of requirements do not, it would appear, present any particular problems, the future of user-charge financing in North American cities appears to be very much a matter that will be decided in the political sphere.

References

Amborski, David P. Unpubl. "Lot Levies: Service Pricing to Financing Urban Growth." Paper prepared for the Lincoln Institute of Land Policy, Cambridge, Mass. January 1980. Mimeo, 100 pp.

Bennathan, E., and A. A. Walters. 1979. *Port Pricing and Investment Policy for Developing Countries.* New York: Oxford University Press.

Bird, Richard M. 1976. *Charging for Public Services.* Toronto: Canadian Tax Foundation.

Bird, Richard M. 1978. "A New Look at Benefit Taxation." In *Secular Trends in the Public Sector,* ed. H. C. Recktenwald, pp. 241-52. Paris: Editorial Cujas.

Bird, Richard M. 1980. *Central-Local Fiscal Relations and the Provision of Urban Public Services.* Research Monograph no. 30, Centre for Research on Federal Financial Relations. Canberra: The Australian National University.

Bird, Richard M., and Enid Slack. 1978. *Residential Property Tax Relief in Ontario.* Toronto: University of Toronto Press.

Bureau of Municipal Research. 1980. "Municipal Services: Who Should Pay?" Topic no. 13. Toronto: The bureau. Mimeo, 51 pp.

Doebele, W. A. 1979. " 'Land Readjustment' as an Alternative to Taxation for the Recovery of Betterment: The Case of South Korea." In *The Taxation of Urban Property in Less Developed Countries,* ed. R. W. Bahl, pp. 163-89. Madison: University of Wisconsin Press.

Doebele, W. A., O. F. Grimes, Jr., and J. F. Linn. 1979. "Participation of Beneficiaries in Financing Urban Services: Valorization Charges in Bogota, Colombia." *Land Economics* 55, 1(February): 73-92.

33. For more detailed analyses, see Krashinsky (1977; 1981; and unpubl.) and Downing (1974; 1980).

Downing, Paul B., Ed. 1974. *Local Service Pricing Policies and Their Effect on Urban Spatial Structure.* Vancouver: University of British Columbia Press.

Downing, Paul B. 1980. "User Charges and Services Fees." An Information Bulletin for the Management, Finance, and Personnel Taskforce of the Urban Consortium.

Grayhurst, Denis. 1981. "Lot Levy Can Add $5,000 to Price of a New Home." *Toronto Star,* 7 February: E1.

Goetz, Charles J. 1973. "The Revenue Potential of User-Related Charges in State and Local Governments." In *Broad-based Taxes—New Options and Sources,* ed. R. A. Musgrave, pp. 113–29. Baltimore: Johns Hopkins Press.

Haritos, Z. 1972. *Rational Road Pricing Policies in Canada.* Ottawa: Canadian Transport Commission.

Ho, Lok Sang. 1981. "Value Capture: An Analysis of Policy Alternatives." Unpublished Ph.D. thesis, University of Toronto.

Institute of Economic Affairs. 1967. *Essays in the Theory and Practice of Pricing.* London: The institute.

Kafoglis, Milton A. 1969. "Local Service Charges: Theory and Practice." In *State and Local Tax Problems,* ed. Harry J. Johnson, pp. 164–86. Knoxville: University of Tennessee Press.

Krashinsky, Michael. 1977. *Day Care and Public Policy in Ontario.* Toronto: University of Toronto Press.

Krashinsky, Michael. 1981. *User Charges in the Social Services.* Toronto: University of Toronto Press.

Krashinsky, Michael. Unpub. "User Charges and Government Restraint." Paper prepared for the Conference on the Politics and Management of Government Expenditure Restraint, sponsored by The Institute for Research on Public Policy. Toronto. September 1979. Xerox, 27 pp.

Millward, Robert. 1971. *Public Expenditure Economics.* London: McGraw-Hill.

Mushkin, Selma, Ed. 1972. *Public Prices for Public Products.* Washington, D.C.: The Urban Institute.

Rhoads, W. G., and R. M. Bird. 1969. "The Valorization Tax in Colombia: An Example for Other Developing Countries?" In *Land and Building Taxes,* ed. Arthur P. Becker, pp. 201–37. Madison: University of Wisconsin Press.

Seldon, A. 1977. *Charge.* London: Temple Smith.

Thompson, Wilbur. 1968. "The City as a Distorted Price System." *Psychology Today* 2 (August): 30–33; reprinted in part in Oldman, O., and F. P. Schoettle, Eds. 1974. *State and Local Taxes and Finance,* pp. 127–35. Mineola, New York: The Foundation Press.

U.S. Department of Commerce. 1979. *City Government Finances in 1976–77.* Washington, D.C.: The Bureau of the Census.

Vars, R. Charles, Jr. 1976. "The Consequences of Non-Clearing Public Service Prices." In *Proceedings of the 68th Annual Conference on Taxation,* pp. 104–14. Columbus, Ohio: National Tax Association–Tax Institute of America.

Vars, R. Charles, Jr. Unpubl. "Forward-Looking Charges for Sewer and Water Services." Undated mimeo.

Wilcox, Marjorie C., and Selma Mushkin. 1972. "Public Pricing and Family Income." In *Public Prices for Public Products,* ed. Selma Mushkin, pp. 395–408. Washington, D.C.: The Urban Institute.

Index

Ability-to-pay, 58

Accounting: balance sheet, 7–8, 11–12, 24–27; separate, 32, 33–34, 37, 38, 39, 41, 42, 44, 45, 48–49

Advisory Commission on Intergovernmental Relations, 5

Airports, 214

Alaska, 135, 136

Alberta, 56, 61, 66, 67, 68, 72, 135, 136, 137

Alberta Heritage Savings Trust Fund, 135, 137, 146, 156

Allocation: of capital, 139, 141, 143, 147, 148, 149, 154–55; of dividends, 33, 35, 47; of labor, 139, 141, 143, 147, 148, 149, 154–55; specific, 32, 33, 35, 38, 41, 44, 47

Antipoverty programs, 75–78

Apportionment: formula, 32–33, 34, 35, 37, 38, 39, 42, 44, 45, 47, 49, 66–67; full, 33, 35, 44

Assessments, special, 213, 214, 216–24; and benefits, 216–17; in Canada, 217–22, 223; efficiency of, 222, 223; and property values, 223; resistance to, 224; when paid, 220–21, 222

Belgium, 37

Benefit: and special assessment, 216–17; taxation, 6, 58, 134, 216 (*see also* User charge). *See also* Cost/benefit analysis

Birthright, 154, 155–56

Boomtowns, 139, 151–53

British Columbia, 61, 72

British North America Act (1867), 5, 59, 60, 156

Brookings Institution, 93, 94

Budget, 11–12, 13

Business. *See* Unitary business; Unitary combination, worldwide

California: corporate income tax in, 30, 33, 36, 43; education financing in, 161–62

Canada: birthright issue in, 156; corporate income tax in, 60, 61, 62, 64, 66–67, 71; direct taxes in, 62, 63, 68, 71; double taxation in, 61–62, 68, 69; economic rents in, 135, 136, 146; estate taxes in, 5–6, 61, 62, 67–68; federal v. subfederal taxes in, 55–56, 57, 58, 59, 62–64, 69, 71, 73; federalism in, 53, 59–60; formula apportionment in, 66–67; gift taxes in, 5–6, 67–68; nexus v. allocation in, 66; nontax revenue in, 213; personal income tax in, 60, 61, 64–66, 71; property taxes in, 213; reciprocal tax agreement in, 69; revenue sharing in, 5, 56–57, 62, 63, 65, 69, 70, 71, 215; sales taxes in, 60, 62, 66, 68, 69, 71, 72; special assessments in, 217–22, 223; tax burden in, 70; tax credits in, 54, 55, 64–65; tax distribution in, 63, 64; tax harmonization in, 5–6, 64, 70, 136; tax incentives in, 72; tax reform in, 71; trade barriers in, 71–72; urban revenue sources in, 211, 213; user charges in, 213–14, 215, 227–28, 229, 230; World War II in, 63. *See also* British North America Act

Capital: allocation, 139, 141, 143, 147, 148, 149, 154–55; as factor of production, 189; return on, 189, 190, 194, 195

CETA, 93, 100–101

Clark, J. B., 186, 190

Clean Air Act, 109

Coal, 135, 136, 157, 158

Committee on Taxation, Resources and Economic Development (TRED), 3

Commonwealth Edison et al. v. Montana, 136, 157

Community Development Block Grant program, 76, 88

Community development block grants, 93, 95, 97, 100

Contribution and dependency, 46

COMPOSED BY THE COMPOSING ROOM
KIMBERLY, WISCONSIN
MANUFACTURED BY CUSHING-MALLOY, INC.
ANN ARBOR, MICHIGAN
TEXT AND DISPLAY LINES ARE SET IN TIMES ROMAN

Library of Congress Cataloging in Publication Data
Main entry under title:
State and local finance.
(Publications of the Committee on Taxation, Resources,
and Economic Development; 12)
"Proceedings of a symposium sponsored by the Committee
on Taxation, Resources and Economic Development (TRED)
at the Lincoln Institute of Land Policy, Cambridge,
Massachusetts, 1980."
Includes bibliographies and index.
1. Finance, Public—United States—States—Congresses.
2. Finance, Public—Canada—Congresses. 3. Local
finance—United States—Congresses. 4. Local finance—
Canada—Congresses. I. Break, George F. II. Committee
on Taxation, Resources and Economic Development.
III. Series.
HJ275.S675   1983   336.73   83-47757
ISBN 0-299-09340-9